The **music**socket.com

Music Industry Directory 2020

The **music**socket.com

Music Industry Directory 2020

EDITOR

J. PAUL DYSON

Published in 2019 by JP&A Dyson
27 Old Gloucester Street, London WC1N 3AX, United Kingdom

https://www.jpandadyson.com
https://www.musicsocket.com

ISBN 978-1-909935-30-3

Foreword

This directory includes hundreds of listings of **record labels** and **managers**, updated in **MusicSocket**'s online databases between 2017 and 2019.

It also provides free access to the entire current databases, including over 2,000 record labels, and over 1,300 managers, with dozens of new and updated listings every month.

For details on how to claim your free access please see the back of this book.

Included in the subscription

A subscription to the full website is not only free with this book, but comes packed with all the following features:

Advanced search features

- Save searches and save time – set up to 15 search parameters specific to your work, save them, and then access the search results with a single click whenever you log in. You can even save multiple different searches if you have different types of work you are looking to place.
- Add personal notes to listings, visible only to you and fully searchable – helping you to organise your actions.
- Set reminders on listings to notify you when to submit your work, when to follow up, when to expect a reply, or any other custom action.
- Track which listings you've viewed and when, to help you organise your search – any listings which have changed since you last viewed them will be highlighted for your attention!

Daily email updates

As a subscriber you will be able to take advantage of our email alert service, meaning you can specify your particular interests and we'll send you automatic email updates when we change or add a listing that matches them. So if you're interested in labels dealing in hard rock in the United States you can have us send you emails with the latest updates about them – keeping you up to date without even having to log in.

User feedback

Our databases include a user feedback feature that allows our subscribers to leave feedback on each listing – giving you not only the chance to have your say about the markets you contact, but giving a unique artist's perspective on the listings.

Save on copyright protection fees

If you're sending your work away to record labels and managers you should first consider protecting your copyright. As a subscriber to **MusicSocket** you can do this through our site and save 10% on the copyright registration fees normally payable for protecting your work internationally through the Intellectual Property Rights Office (https://www.CopyrightRegistrationService.com).

For details on how to claim your free access please see the back of this book.

Contents

Foreword v

Contents vii

Protecting Your Copyright 1

Record Labels

US Record Labels 3

UK Record Labels 39

Canadian Record Labels 77

Australian Record Labels 81

Record Labels Index 83

Managers

US Managers 103

UK Managers 135

Canadian Managers 173

Managers Index 175

Free Access

Get Free Access to the MusicSocket Website 191

Protecting Your Copyright

Protecting your copyright is by no means a requirement before submitting your work, but you may feel that it is a prudent step that you would like to take before allowing strangers to hear your material.

These days, you can register your work for copyright protection quickly and easily online. The Intellectual Property Rights Office operates a website called the "Copyright Registration Service" which allows you to do this:

- *https://www.CopyrightRegistrationService.com*

This website can be used for material created in any nation signed up to the Berne Convention. This includes the United States, United Kingdom, Canada, Australia, Ireland, New Zealand, and most other countries. There are around 180 countries in the world, and over 160 of them are part of the Berne Convention.

Provided you created your work in one of the Berne Convention nations, your work should be protected by copyright in all other Berne Convention nations. You can therefore protect your copyright around most of the world with a single registration, and because the process is entirely online you can have your work protected in a matter of minutes.

US Record Labels

For the most up-to-date listings of these and hundreds of other record labels, visit https://www.musicsocket.com/recordlabels

*To claim your **free** access to the site, please see the back of this book.*

4AD

2035 Hyperion Ave
Los Angeles, CA 90027
Email: 4AD@4AD.com
Website: http://www.4ad.com
Website: http://facebook.com/fourad

Genres: Indie; Rock

Record label with offices in New York, Los Angeles, and London.

6/8 Records

41 W 46th St
New York, NY
Email: management@68records.com
Website: https://www.68records.com
Website: https://www.facebook.com/68recordsnyc

Genres: Indie

Independent record label, dedicated to the development of indie female artists with a unique sound.

A&M Records

2220 Colorado Avenue, 5th Floor
Santa Monica, CA 90404
Website: https://www.interscope.com

Genres: Indie; Pop; Rock; Singer-Songwriter; Alternative; R&B

Part of a record label based in Santa Monica, California.

A-Blake Records

3710 Center Street, Ste. 101
Deer Park, TX 77536
Website: http://www.ablakerecords.com

Genres: All types of music

Contact: Dave Darus; Daniel Sanders; Ami Blackwell

Describes itself as a new kind of label for an ever-changing music industry. Offers everything from developmental deals, licensing, and traditional to full-blown 360 recording deals. Diverse roster spanning many genres.

A-F Records

PO Box 71266
Pittsburg, PA 15213
Email: press@a-frecords.com
Website: http://www.a-frecords.com
Website: https://www.facebook.com/AFrecordsPGH/

Genres: Punk Rock

Independent punk rock record label based in Pittsburgh, Pennsylvania. Send demos, press kits, etc. by post or send email with links to music online. No attachments.

Acoustic Disc

PO BOX 4143
San Rafael, CA, 94913

Email: business@acousticdisc.com
Email: sales@acousticdisc.com
Website: http://www.acousticdisc.com

Genres: Acoustic Jazz; Acoustic Latin; Acoustic Folk; Classical; Acoustic Blues; Roots; World

Contact: David Grisman

Handles acoustic music only. Query by phone in first instance.

Activate Entertainment

11054 Ventura Boulevard, Suite 333
Studio City, CA 91604
Email: info@activate1.com
Website: http://www.activate1.com

Genres: Hip-Hop; Rock

Contact: Jay Warsinske (A&R President)

Full service label based in Studio City, California.

Affluent Records

201 Varrick Street
New York, NY 10014-4811
Fax: +1 (509) 351-7217
Email: oscarsanchez@affluentrecords.com
Website: http://affluentrecords.com
Website: http://www.facebook.com/affluent
Website: http://www.myspace.com/affluentrecords

Genres: Urban

Contact: Oscar Sanchez

Urban record label based in New York.

Alias Records

838 EAST HIGH STREET # 290
Lexington, KY 40502
Email: accounts@aliasrecords.com
Website: http://www.aliasrecords.com
Website: https://www.facebook.com/Alias-Records-186847657059/

Genres: Indie Rock; Electronic; Singer-Songwriter

Record label based in Lexington, Kentucky.

Alive Naturalsound

919 Isabel – Unit G
Burbank, CA 91506
Email: label@alive-records.com
Website: http://www.alive-totalenergy.com
Website: https://soundcloud.com/alivenaturalsound/

Genres: All types of music

Small indie label based in Burbank, California. Accepts demos and listens to everything received, but responds only if interested.

Alligator Records

P.O. Box 60234
Chicago, IL 60660
Fax: +1 (773) 973-2088
Email: info@allig.com
Website: http://www.alligator.com
Website: https://www.facebook.com/AlligatorRecords
Website: https://myspace.com/alligatorrecords

Genres: Blues; Americana; Roots

Contact: New Material

Handles blues and blues-based music only. Send a maximum of four songs by post. Response by post only, so ensure legible postal address included. No email submissions or requests to visit artist's website. Response time of around three months.

Alternative Tentacles Records

PO Box 419092
San Francisco, CA 94141
attn. Jello Biafra
Fax: +1 (510) 596-8982
Email: jb@alternativetentacles.com
Website: http://www.alternativetentacles.com

Genres: Country; Hardcore; Indie; Metal; Pop; Punk; R&B; Rock

Contact: Jello Biafra

Accepts demos on CD, tape, or vinyl. No MP3s. Will not listen to music online. Most demos get listened to, but response not guaranteed. No way to "check status" of your submission so don't ask for updates after you've submitted.

Amathus Music

Att: A&R
PO Box 95
Hewlett, NY 11557
Email: demo@amathusmusic.com
Email: info@amathusmusic.com
Website: http://www.amathusmusic.com
Website: http://www.soundcloud.com/amathusmusic
Website: http://www.myspace.com/amathusmusic

Genres: Electronic Dance; Underground House; Trance; Commercial

Send query by email with Soundcloud links only. No MP3 attachments, or hard copy submissions. Response not guaranteed.

American Eagle Recordings

13001 Dieterle Lane
St. Louis, MO 63127
Fax: +1 (314) 984-0828
Email: info@americaneaglerecordings.com
Email: americaneaglerecordings@earthlink.net
Website: http://www.americaneaglerecordings.com

Genres: All types of music

Contact: Dr. Charles Max E. Million

Record label based in St Louis, Missouri. Send demos by CD only, accompanied by completed Questionnaire (available for download from website). Extensive submission guidelines on website. Any submissions not adhering to the submission guidelines will be ignored. No MP3s or links by email.

American Laundromat Records

P.O. Box 85
Mystic, CT 06355-0085
Fax: +1 (860) 245-3669
Email: americanlaundromat@hotmail.com
Website: http://www.americanlaundromat.com
Website: https://www.facebook.com/americanlaundromatrecords

Genres: Alternative; Folk; Indie; Pop; Rock; Singer-Songwriter

Contact: Joseph H. Spadaro

Record label based in Mystic, Connecticut. Not accepting new submissions as at May 2017.

Anti

2798 Sunset Boulevard
Los Angeles, CA 90026
Email: publicity@anti.com
Website: http://www.anti.com
Website: https://www.facebook.com/antirecords

Genres: Indie Rock

Contact: Brett Gurewitz

Record label based in Los Angeles, California.

Aphagia Recordings

6 Rivas Ave.
San Francisco, CA
Email: aphagia@outlook.com
Email: soundtweaker@outlook.com
Website: http://www.aphagiarecordings.com/
Website: https://aphagiarecordings.bandcamp.com/

Genres: Experimental Electronic Industrial Progressive Glitch Instrumental Rock Soundtracks

Contact: Dan Menapace

A San Francisco based Independent Record Label focusing on odd forms of electronic and rock music.

API Records

PO Box 7041
Watchung, NJ 07069
Email: apirecords@verizon.net
Website: http://www.apirecords.com

Genres: Classical; Pop Rock

Contact: Meg

Record label based in Watchung, New Jersey. Accepts solicited demo submissions only. Unsolicited submissions will be discarded without being listened to.

Appleseed Recordings

Music Submissions Department
PO Box 2593
West Chester, PA 19380
Email: jim@appleseedmusic.com
Email: alan@appleseedmusic.com
Website: http://www.appleseedmusic.com

Genres: Contemporary; Folk; Roots

Contact: Jim Musselman

An independent, idealistic and internationally distributed record label devoted to releasing socially conscious contemporary, folk and roots music by both established and lesser-known musicians. Send demo on CD or CD/R (no MP3s or cassettes) with bio and other relevant info. Listens to everything but response not guaranteed if not interested. See website for full guidelines.

Arabesque Recordings

5 International Drive, Suite 112
Rye Brook, NY 10573
Email: info@arabesquerecords.com
Website: http://www.arabesquerecords.com

Genres: Classical; Jazz

Record label based in Rye Brook, New York, specialising in elegant classical and jazz music. Send query via form on website with info about you and your project and links to the music online.

Ardent Records

Open Door
2000 Madison Avenue
Memphis, TN 38104
Fax: +1 (901) 725-7011
Email: info@ardentmusic.com
Website: http://www.ardentrecords.com
Website: http://www.ardentstudios.com

Genres: Christian; Rock

Label based in Memphis dealing in Christian/Rock. Send demos on CD by post, or email links to your music online. Do not send MP3s.

Asthmatic Kitty Records

Post Office Box 1282
Lander, WY 82520
Email: info@asthmatickitty.com
Website: http://asthmatickitty.com
Website: http://www.facebook.com/asthmatickitty

Genres: Alternative Pop

Record label based in Lander, Wyoming. Not accepting submissions as at July 2017. Check website for current status.

Astralwerks Records

A+R Department
150 5th Avenue
New York, NY 10011
Email: astralwerks.astralwerks@gmail.com
Website: http://www.astralwerks.com
Website: https://www.facebook.com/astralwerks

Genres: Alternative; Electronic; Dance; Techno

Record label based in New York.

Asylum Arts

Emeryville, CA
Email: kalib@asylumarts.com
Website: http://www.asylumarts.com

Genres: Electronic; Metal

Independent record label based in Emeryville, California.

Atlantic Records

New York, 10019
Website: http://www.atlanticrecords.com
Website: https://www.facebook.com/atlanticrecords

Genres: All types of music

Record label with offices in New York and Burbank, California.

ATO Records

10 East 40th Street, 22nd Floor
New York NY 10016
Fax: +1 (212) 422-6814
Email: info@atorecords.com
Website: http://www.atorecords.com

Genres: Alternative; Rock; Acoustic; Indie; Pop

Independent record label committed to artists and building their careers. Send demos and queries by email.

Average Joes Entertainment

3728 Keystone Avenue
Nashville, TN 37211
Email: info@averagejoesent.com
Website: http://averagejoesent.com

Genres: Country

Independent record label specialising in film, television, technology and country music.

Aware Records

800 18th Avenue South, Suite C
Nashville, TN 37203
Email: info@awaremusic.com
Email: gregg@awaremusic.com
Website: http://www.awarerecords.com

Genres: Contemporary; Indie; Pop; Rock

Contact: Gregg Latterman

Not currently accepting submissions as at August 2017, but website states that this does change from time to time, so check website for current situation.

Ba Da Bing Records & Management

181 Clermont Avenue, Suite 403
Brooklyn, NY 11205
Email: hello@badabingrecords.com
Website: http://www.badabingrecords.com
Website: http://soundcloud.com/badabingrecords
Website: http://www.myspace.com/badabingrecords

Genres: All types of music

Record label based in New York, operated by film and TV comedian.

Babygrande Records, Inc.

101 West 23rd Street Suite 296
New York, New York 10011
Email: inquiries@babygrande.com
Website: http://babygrande.com
Website: https://soundcloud.com/babygrande

Genres: Hip-Hop; Rock; Indie Rock; Electronic; Instrumental

Record label based in New York. Describes itself as "one of the premier independent record labels operating today". Send query by email with relevant info and streaming links only.

Bad Boy Entertainment

1710 Broadway, 6th Floor
New York, NY 10019
Email: hpierre@badboyworldwide.com
Website: http://www.badboyonline.com

Genres: Hip-Hop; Pop; Rap; Urban

Contact: Sean Combs, CEO; Harve Pierre, President

New York rap, hip-hop, urban and pop record label.

Bar/None Records

PO Box 1704
Hoboken, NJ 07030
Email: glenn@bar-none.com
Email: info@bar-none.com
Website: http://www.bar-none.com
Website: http://soundcloud.com/barnonerecords
Website: http://www.myspace.com/barnonerecords

Genres: Alternative; Indie; Rock

Record label based in Hoboken, New Jersey. Those looking to approach are asked to check out the website and artists currently worked with, then if you still think it's appropriate send a CD or query by email with a link to music online. No large music file attachments by email.

Barbarian Productions

Email: talent@barbarianproductions.com
Website: http://www.barbarianproductions.com

Genres: Pop; R&B; Hip-Hop; Singer-Songwriter; Soundtracks

Send submissions by email.

Barsuk Records

PO Box 22546
Seattle, WA 98122
Fax: +1 (206) 762-0152
Email: questions@barsuk.com
Website: http://www.barsuk.com
Website: https://soundcloud.com/barsuk-records

Genres: Indie; Rock

Contact: Josh Rosenfeld

Record label based in Seattle. Send links to demos or electronic press kits online via form on website. Do not send audio files or physical CDs. Response not guaranteed.

Beggars Group (US)

134 Grand Street
New York, NY 10013
Email: banquet@beggars.com
Website: http://beggarsgroupusa.com

Genres: Alternative; Dance; Electronic; Indie; Punk; Rock; Singer-Songwriter; World

International group with offices in the UK, US, and Canada. The group is not accepting demos itself, but individual labels are – see website for links.

Beluga Heights

845 Highland Avenue
Los Angeles, CA 90038
Email: info@belugaheights.com
Website: http://www.belugaheights.com
Website: https://www.facebook.com/The-Official-Beluga-Heights-178638752184552/

Genres: All types of music

Record label based in Los Angeles, California.

Bieler Bros. Records

Pompano Beach, FL
Email: info@bielerbros.com
Website: http://bielerbros.com
Website: http://soundcloud.com/bielerbros/sets/bieler-bros/
Website: http://www.myspace.com/bielerbros

Genres: Hard Rock; Metal

Contact: Jason and Aaron Bieler

Record label based in Florida. Always looking for new music and new artists. Sign bands they feel passionate about and not for any other reason. Send EPK by email with links to music online. No physical submissions.

Big Beat

1633 Broadway
New York, NY 10019
Email: info@wearebigbeat.com
Website: http://www.wearebigbeat.com
Website: https://soundcloud.com/wearebigbeat

Genres: House; Hip-Hop; Dance; Electronic

Originally a record label founder in 1987, imprint was re-launched in 2010.

Big Crown Records

117 Dobbin St. Suite 115
Brooklyn, NY 11222
Email: demos@bigcrownrecords.com
Email: info@bigcrownrecords.com
Website: https://bigcrownrecords.com
Website: https://soundcloud.com/bigcrownrecords

Genres: Soul

Brooklyn based independent record label started in 2016.

Big Deal Records

15503 Ventura Blvd, Suite #300
Encino, CA 91436

NEW YORK
15 West 26th St., 12th Floor
New York, NY 10010

NASHVILLE
115 29th Ave. South
Nashville, TN 37212
Email: info@bigdealmusic.com
Website: http://www.bigdealmusic.com
Website: https://www.facebook.com/BigDealPublishing
Website: https://myspace.com/bdrecords

Genres: Pop; Rock

Record label based in Encino, California. Not accepting submissions as at September 2017.

Big Loud Records

Email: Clay@bigloudrecords.com
Email: Stacy@bigloudrecords.com
Website: http://bigloudrecords.com
Website: https://www.facebook.com/thisisbigloud/

Genres: Country

Contact: Clay Hunnicutt; Stacy Blythe

Record label dealing in country music.

Big Machine Records

1219 16th Avenue South
Nashville, TN 37212
Email: chris.stacey@bmlg.net
Website: http://www.bigmachinerecords.com
Website: http://www.facebook.com/bigmachinerecords

Genres: Country

Contact: Chris Stacey

Country music label based in Nashville Tennessee.

Big Noise

11 South Angell Street, Suite 336
Providence, RI 02906
Email: al@bignoisenow.com
Email: algomes@bignoisenow.com
Website: http://www.bignoisenow.com

Genres: All types of music

Contact: Al Gomes; A. Michelle

Seeking artists who are unique, talented, professional, and ready to launch. Please call or email for demo submission instructions. All genres considered.

The Birdman Recording Group, Inc.

2636 Judah St. #190
San Francisco, CA 94122
Email: info@birdmanrecords.com
Website: http://www.birdmanrecords.com

Genres: Underground Garage; Blues; Jazz; Country; Modern Classical

Record label based in San Francisco, dedicated to quality music of all genres, attempting to win over new fans by "grassroots marketing and making the best records around".

Black River Entertainment

Email: info@blackriverent.com
Website: http://www.blackriverent.com

Genres: Country; Christian

Entertainment company based in Nashville, involved in music publishing and operating a number of labels.

Blackberry Records

PO Box 16469
Jackson, MS 39236
Fax: +1 (601) 206-1777
Email: blackberry@blackberryrecords.com
Website: http://www.blackberryrecords.com

Genres: Gospel

Contact: Doug Williams

Record label based in Jackson, Mississippi.

Blackheart Records Group

636 Broadway
New York, NY 10012
Fax: +1 (212) 353-8300
Email: blackheart@blackheart.com
Website: http://www.blackheart.com

Genres: All types of music

Contact: Zander Wolff

Record label based in New York. Contact by email in first instance.

Blind Pig Records

P.O. Box 2344
San Francisco, CA 94126
Email: info@blindpigrecords.com
Website: http://www.blindpigrecords.com
Website: https://www.facebook.com/Blindpigrecord/

Genres: Blues; Roots

Record label based in San Francisco. Send a 3-5 song CDr with one-page bio. Currently seeking talent with a booking agent or at least a touring schedule playing outside of regional clubs. If you have a management company or booking agency, include their information along with your demo.

Bloodshot Records

3039 W. Irving Park Rd
Chicago IL 60618
Fax: +1 (773) 604-5019
Email: demo@bloodshotrecords.com
Email: bshq@bloodshotrecords.com
Website: http://www.bloodshotrecords.com

Genres: Alternative; Blues; Country; Indie; Latin; Punk; R&B; Rock; Roots; Singer-Songwriter; Soul

Send demo by post after consulting website and familiarising yourself with the label's roster. MP3s accepted to demo email address only. No demos via third parties, such as lawyers or promotion companies. Unlikely to work with part-time artists who have a day job, and does not work with bands based overseas.

Blue Note Label Group

1750 North Vine Street
Hollywood, CA 90028-5274
Website: http://www.bluenote.com
Website: https://www.facebook.com/bluenote

Genres: Jazz; Pop; R&B

Record label based in New York, specialising in Jazz.

BMG

1745 Broadway, 19th Floor
New York, NY 10019

LOS ANGELES:
6100 Wilshire Boulevard, Suite #1600
Los Angeles, CA 90048

NASHVILLE:
29 Music Square East
Nashville, TN 37203
Email: info.us@bmg.com
Website: https://www.bmg.com

Genres: All types of music

International record label with US offices in New York, LA, and Nashville.

Bolero Records

18653 Ventura Boulevard, Suite 314
Tarzana, CA 91356
Email: info@bolero-records.com
Website: https://www.bolero-records.com

Genres: World; Jazz; Latin; New Age

Independent record label based in Tarzana, California, specialising in Nuevo Flamenco, Traditional Flamenco, World, Jazz, Latin and New Age.

Bomp Records

Fax: +1 (818) 729-9235
Email: MAILORDER@BOMPRECORDS.com
Website: http://www.bomp.com
Website: https://www.facebook.com/bomprecords

Genres: Indie; Punk; Power Pop; Pop; Garage Rock; New Wave; Traditional Rock

Contact: Suzy Shaw

Label based in Burbank, California. Back catalogue only, so no submissions.

Brash Music

c/o New Music
888 3rd Street NW, Suite A
Atlanta, GA 30318
Email: info@brashmusic.com
Website: http://www.brashmusic.com
Website: https://www.facebook.com/Brash-Music-168206919862613/

Genres: All types of music

Record label based in Atlanta, Georgia. Not accepting new music as at January 2018.

Bridge Nine Records

119R Foster Street, Building 4 Suite 3
Peabody, MA 01960
Fax: +1 (978) 532-3806
Email: chris@bridge9.com
Email: rushton@bridge9.com
Website: http://www.bridge9.com
Website: https://www.facebook.com/bridge9

Genres: Hardcore

Contact: Chris Wrenn; Bryan Rushton

Record label based in Peabody, Massachusetts.

Bright Antenna Records

146 East Blithedale Avenue
Mill Valley, CA 94941
Email: info@brightantenna.com
Website: http://www.brightantenna.com
Website: https://soundcloud.com/brightantenna

Genres: Rock

Accepts submissions via Soundcloud only. No physical submissions.

Brushfire Records

424 North Larchmont Avenue
Los Angeles, CA 90004-3014
Fax: +1 (323) 957-9931
Website: http://brushfirerecords.com
Website: https://www.facebook.com/brushfirerecords

Genres: All types of music

Record label founded in Hawaii in 2002, and now based in Los Angeles. Strives to make music and films that are positive and works to connect like-minded musicians and artists in the surf community and beyond.

Bullet Tooth

ATTENTION A&R
23 Farm Edge Lane
Tinton Falls, NJ 07724
Fax: +1 (732) 542-7957
Email: demo@bullettooth.com
Email: info@bullettooth.com
Website: http://bullettooth.com

Genres: Rock; Hardcore; Metal; Emo; Punk

Contact: Josh Grabelle

Handles rock and all sub-genres. Send demo on CD by post, or send email with info, Myspace links, Bio, etc. Do not email MP3s! Include band name, contact name, phone number, email address, Myspace, and street address either on the CD itself, or on the packaging. Considers bands from overseas. Only interested in hard working bands. See website for full submission guidelines.

Burnt Toast Vinyl

PO Box 42188
Philadelphia, PA 19101
Email: btv@burnttoastvinyl.com
Website: http://www.burnttoastvinyl.com
Website: https://www.facebook.com/burnttoastvinyl

Genres: Alternative; Singer-Songwriter

Record label based in Philadelphia.

Cantaloupe Music

80 Hanson Place, Suite 702
Brooklyn, NY 11217
Fax: +1 (718) 852-7732
Email: info@cantaloupemusic.com
Website: http://www.cantaloupemusic.com

Genres: Classical; Electronic; Jazz; New Age; Punk; Rock; World

Contact: Cantaloupe A&R

Send demos by email or by US mail. All submissions listened to, but response not guaranteed. Include details of past and upcoming performances.

Cantora

New York
Email: hello@cantora.com
Website: http://cantora.com
Website: https://www.facebook.com/WeAreCantora

Genres: Progressive Pop

Record label based in New York, releasing artists who make forward-thinking pop music.

Canvasback Music

1633 Broadway 10th Floor
New York, NY 10019-6708
Fax: +1 (212) 405-5427
Email: steve@canvasbackmusic.com
Website: http://www.canvasbackmusic.com
Website: https://www.facebook.com/canvasbackmusic/

Genres: All types of music

Contact: Steve Ralbovsky

Record label based in New York.

Canyon

1761 West University Drive, Suite 145
Tempe, Arizona 85281
Email: canyon@canyonrecords.com
Website: https://www.canyonrecords.com
Website: https://www.facebook.com/canyonrecords

Genres: Regional; World

Native American record label.

Capitol Christian Music Group

PO Box 74008453
Chicago, IL 60674-8453
Website: http://www.capitolchristianmusicgroup.com
Website: https://www.facebook.com/capitolchristiandistribution

Genres: Christian; Gospel

Christian record label based in Chicago, Illinois. Unsolicited demos will not be responded to.

Capitol Music Group

1750 Vine Street
Los Angeles, CA 90028
Website: http://www.capitolrecords.com
Website: https://www.facebook.com/capitolrecords

Genres: Dance; Indie; Pop; Rock; Urban

Accepts submissions through established sources (managers, etc.) only. All other material returned without being listened to.

Capitol Records Nashville

3322 West End Avenue, 11th Floor
Nashville, TN 37203
Website: http://www.capitolnashville.com
Website: http://www.emimusic.com

Genres: Country

Contact: Autumn House, A&R

Country record label based in Nashville, Tennessee. No unsolicited demos direct from artists – must be through talent scouts or established figure in music industry.

Carnival Music

24 Music Square West #200
Nashville, TN 37203-3204
Email: info@carnivalmusic.net
Email: fliddell@carnivalmusic.net
Website: http://www.carnivalmusic.net
Website: https://soundcloud.com/carnivalmusic

Genres: Americana; Country; Indie; Pop; Rock

Contact: Frank Liddell; Travis Hill

Describes itself as neither a record label or publishing company, but doing the work of both.

Carpark Records

PO Box 42374
Washington, DC 20015
Email: carparkrecords@gmail.com
Website: http://carparkrecords.com
Website: https://soundcloud.com/carparkrecords

Genres: Alternative; Rock

Independent record label based in Washington DC.

Carved Records

Email: info@carvedrecords.com
Website: http://www.carvedrecords.com

Website: https://www.facebook.com/carvedrecords

Genres: All types of music

Record label describing itself as being "powered by a family of music industry professionals, musicians and entrepreneurs who offer unparalleled expertise in A&R, Digital and Physical Sales, Promotion, Press, and Brand Marketing, as well as New Media and Social Network Marketing."

Cascine

New York, NY
Email: demos@cascine.us
Email: info@cascine.us
Website: http://www.cascine.us
Website: https://soundcloud.com/cascine

Genres: Alternative Pop; Electronic

Independent record label based in New York. Known for its consistently stylish brand of alternative pop and electronic music. Send demos by email.

Cash Money Records

Miami, FL
Website: http://www.cashmoney-records.com
Website: https://www.facebook.com/cashmoneyrecords

Genres: Hip-Hop; Urban; Pop

Record label based in Miami, Florida.

Castle Records

Attn: Dave Sullivan
106 Shirley Drive
Hendersonville, TN 37075
Email: DaveSullivan@CastleRecords.com
Email: CastleRecords@CastleRecords.com
Website: http://www.castlerecords.com

Genres: Traditional Country; Modern Country; Blues; R&B; Pop; Rock; Gospel; Alternative Country

Contact: Dave Sullivan; Ed Russell

Send tape/CD, bio, photo, and VHS video if available by post. See website for current code to place on front of package.

Century Media Records (US)

12706 W Washington Blvd
Los Angeles, CA 90066
Attn: A&R
Fax: +1 (323) 418-0118
Email: mail@centurymedia.com
Website: http://www.centurymedia.com
Website: https://soundcloud.com/centurymedia

Genres: Metal; Rock; Traditional Metal; Gothic Metal; Black Metal; Hard Rock; Hardcore

Send demos by post on CD, vinyl, or cassette only. No Video Cassettes, Mini-Discs, DATs, MP3s, etc. Include all contact details. Response only if interested.

Cheap Lullaby Records

5115 Excelsior Boulevard #242
Minneapolis, MN 55416-2906
Fax: +1 (310) 622-4189
Email: joe@cheaplullaby.com
Website: http://www.cheaplullaby.com

Genres: All types of music

Record label based in Minneapolis, Minnesota.

Cherrytree Records

1418 4th Street
Santa Monica, CA 90401
Email: info@cherrytreemusiccompany.com
Website: http://www.cherrytreerecords.com
Website: https://www.facebook.com/CherrytreeMusicCompany

Genres: All types of music

Pop Alternative Record label based in Santa Monica, California.

Chesky Records

1650 Broadway, Suite 900
New York, NY 10019
Email: info@chesky.com
Website: http://www.chesky.com

Genres: Classical; Jazz; World

Record label based in New York, specialising in classical, jazz, and world music.

Chicago Kid Records

2420 N. Catalina Street
Los Angeles, CA 90027
Email: Chicagokid1@earthlink.net
Website: http://www.chicagokidrecords.com

Genres: All types of music

Record label based in Los Angeles. Send query by post with CD, Tape, or DAT of your best material, bio, photo, and contact info.

Cleopatra Records

11041 Santa Monica Blvd PMB #703
Los Angeles, CA 90025
Fax: +1 (310) 312-5653
Email: cleoinfo@cleorecs.com
Website: http://www.cleorecs.com
Website: https://www.facebook.com/CleopatraRecords
Website: https://myspace.com/cleorecs

Genres: Metal; Punk; Pop; Electronic; Rap; Hip-Hop; Jazz; Gothic; Reggaeton; Industrial

Record label based in Los Angeles.

Clickpop Records

PO Box 5765
Bellingham, WA 98227-5765
Email: clickpop@gmail.com
Email: demos@clickpoprecords.com
Website: http://www.clickpoprecords.com

Genres: Ambient; Electronic; Folk; Metal; Pop; Punk

Contact: Dave Richards

Record label based in Bellingham, Washington. For best chance of consideration, send demos as hard copy by post. Otherwise, send MP3s, AACs, or links by email.

CMH Records

2898 Rowena Avenue, Suite 201
Los Angeles, CA 90039
Email: info@cmhrecords.com
Website: http://www.cmhrecords.com
Website: http://www.crosscheckrecords.com

Genres: Blues; Country; Gospel; Instrumental; Rock; Pop

Contact: Greg Sanford (A&R / Promo)

Record label based in Los Angeles. Send submissions by post.

Collect Records

67 West Street, Suite 401-04
Brooklyn, NY 11222
Website: http://collectrecords.org
Website: https://soundcloud.com/collectrecords

Genres: All types of music

An independent record company based in Brooklyn, New York.

Columbia Records

550 Madison Avenue
New York, NY 10022-3211

WEST COAST OFFICE:
9830 Wilshire Boulevard
Beverly Hills, CA 90212
Website: http://www.columbiarecords.com
Website: https://www.facebook.com/columbiarecords/

Genres: All types of music

Record label with offices in New York and LA, dealing in all genres.

Communion Records US

Brooklyn, NY
Email: info@communionmusic.com
Website: https://www.facebook.com/CommunionMusic

Genres: All types of music

Artist-led organisation combining elements of live promotion, publishing and recording to create a hub for artists to develop and flourish. Founded in London in 2006.

Compass Records

916 19th Avenue South
Nashville, TN 37212
Fax: +1 (615) 320-7378
Email: submissions@compassrecords.com

Email: info@compassrecords.com
Website: http://compassrecords.com
Website: https://www.facebook.com/CompassRecordsGroup

Genres: Blues; Folk; Americana; Jazz; Pop; Alternative; Roots; World; Celtic

Record label based in Nashville, Tennessee. No hip hop, rap, hard rock, or commercial country. Send query by email with link to music online. Explain why you think this label is right for you and vice versa, and provide details of last two years of touring history.

Compound Entertainment

1755 Broadway
New York, NY 10019
Email: info@compoundent.com
Website: http://compoundent.com

Genres: Pop; Urban

Record label based in New York.

Concord Music Group

100 North Crescent Drive
Garden Level
Beverly Hills, CA 90210
Fax: +1 (310) 385-4134
Email: submissions@concordmusicgroup.com
Website: http://www.concordmusicgroup.com
Website: https://twitter.com/ConcordRecords

Genres: Jazz; Pop; Rock; R&B; Blues; Soul; Classical; World; Latin

Record label based in Beverly Hills, California. Describes itself as "one of the largest independent record and music publishing companies in the world".

Crush Music

New York
Email: info@crushmusic.com
Website: https://www.crushmusic.com

Genres: Pop; Rock; Punk; Singer-Songwriter

Record label based in New York.

Curb Records

48 Music Square East
Nashville, TN 37203
Email: curb@curb.com
Website: http://www.curb.com

Genres: Christian; Country; Pop Rock; Classical; Dance; Instrumental; Jazz; Soundtracks; Urban; R&B

Contact: Mike Curb

Christian and Country label based in Nashville, Tennessee.

Dangerbird Records

3801 Sunset Boulevard
Los Angeles, CA 90026
Email: info@dangerbird.com
Website: http://www.dangerbirdrecords.com
Website: https://www.facebook.com/dangerbirdrecords

Genres: Alternative; Indie; Rock

Record label based in Los Angeles, California. Not accepting unsolicited demos as at June 2018.

Daptone Records

115 Troutman
Brooklyn, NY 11206
Fax: +1 (718) 366-3783
Email: info@daptonerecords.com
Website: http://daptonerecords.com
Website: https://www.facebook.com/daptonehouseofsoul

Genres: All types of music

Record label based in Brooklyn, New York.

Dauman Music

137 North Larchmont
Los Angeles, CA 90004-3704
Email: jason@daumanmusic.com
Website: http://www.daumanmusic.com

Genres: Dance

Contact: Jason Dauman

Record label based in Los Angeles. Founder has procured songs for artists including U2, Bruce Springsteen, Garth Brooks, Billy

Steinberg and Tom Kelly, Burt Bacharach and Carole Bayer Sager.

DCD2 Records

Email: info@dcd2records.com
Website: http://dcd2records.com
Website: https://www.facebook.com/DCD2Records

Genres: All types of music

US record label.

Deep Elm Records

Maui, HI
Email: info@deepelm.com
Email: media@deepelm.com
Website: http://www.deepelm.com

Genres: Indie; Punk; Rock; Emo; Post Rock

Independent label based in Maui, Hawaii. Send submissions via online form on website, including links to music online. No submissions accepted by other means. No submissions by email.

Deep South Records

PO Box 17737
Raleigh, NC 27619

NASHVILLE
PO Box 121975
Nashville, TN 37212
Email: Info@DeepSouthEntertainment.com
Website: http://deepsouthentertainment.com
Website: https://www.facebook.com/deepsouthent

Genres: Rock

A record label, artist management firm, talent agency, and concert production company with offices in Raleigh, NC and Nashville, TN.

Delmark Records

4121 N. Rockwell
Chicago, IL 60618
Fax: +1 (773) 887-0329
Email: online@delmark.com
Website: http://www.delmark.com

Genres: Blues; Jazz

Blues and jazz record label based in Chicago, Illinois.

Delos

PO Box 343
Sonoma, CA 95476
Fax: +1 (415) 358-5959
Email: delosmusicproductions@gmail.com
Website: https://delosmusic.com
Website: https://soundcloud.com/delos-radio

Genres: Classical

Classical music label based in Sonoma, California.

Delta Groove Music

16555 Sherman Way, Suite B2
Van Nuys, CA 91406
Fax: +1 (818) 907-1620
Email: info@deltagroovemusic.com
Website: http://deltagroovemusic.com

Genres: Blues; Roots

Describes itself as the West Coast leader in roots and blues music.

Delved in Dreams, inc.

PO Box 11653
South Bend,IN 46634
Email: delvedindreamsplus@gmail.com
Website: https://www.delvedindreamsmusic.com

Genres: Christian Classic Electronic Industrial Mainstream Progressive Soulful Regional Traditional Tribal Ambient Classical Country Cuban Dance Ethnic Folk Fusion Gospel Indie Instrumental Jazz Pop Nostalgia New Age Techno Swing Soul Roots Rhythm and Blues Singer-Songwriter Reggae

Contact: Pamela Carl

An independent label who handles digital distribution. We get our artists on all major sites such as itunes, Amazon, CDbaby, Spotify and others. We market all of our artists' music, this includes radio, reviews, and social media.

Derrty Entertainment

9648 Olive Blvd # 230
St Louis, MO 63132-3002
Email: BluBolden@DerrtyEnt.com
Email: Taj@DerrtyEnt.com
Website: http://www.derrtyent.com
Website: http://www.facebook.com/pages/DERRTY-ENT/89589703772

Genres: Urban; Hip-Hop

Contact: Blu Bolden; Taj McDade

Record labal based in St Louis, Missouri.

Dewey Dog Records

263 West 21st Street, 1st Floor, Front
Erie, PA 16502
Email: joe@deweydogrecords.com
Website: http://www.deweydogrecords.com

Genres: Alternative Avant-Garde Electronic Funky Progressive Soulful Tribal Urban Blues Dance Deep Funk Ethnic Folk Funk Hip-Hop Indie Jazz Latin R&B Punk Rap Remix Singer-Songwriter Soul Techno

Contact: Joe Kotyuk

An independent, developmental record label that specializes in artist / band development for new and some ignored older talent.

Excited to be the first record label headquartered in the Erie, Pa., with a major branch office in Terra Haute, In., to initiate an all digital strategic marketing, publicity, and distribution plan for all Single, EP and LP releases.

We have been producing top quality commercial releases for some of the most talented artists, producers, and independent record labels around.

Takes a hybrid approach to making records, working with a huge collection of the best software and plugins, as well as splitting out key tracks, groups, or even the whole mix to analog mixers, compressors, delays and other processors to find that perfect sound for each track of an album.

Our "Old School" techniques, combined with today's technology is what sets us apart from other Independent Labels.

Encourages artists to be as creative as they can be and that's the key to the Label's fast growth in such a competitive market.

DFA Records

225 West 13th Street
New York, NY 10011
Email: hold.on@dfarecords.com
Website: http://www.dfarecords.com
Website: https://www.facebook.com/dfarecords
Website: http://www.myspace.com/dfarecords

Genres: Indie; Disco House; Electronic

Contact: Jonathan Galkin; James Murphy; Tim Goldsworthy

Record label based in New York. Not accepting demos as at July 2018.

DigSin

Nashville, TN
Email: jay@digsin.com
Website: http://digsin.com
Website: http://www.musicxray.com/profiles/2512?afid=ef81d670cce8012eea2b1231381bf5de

Genres: All types of music

Contact: Jay Frank

A new model record label based in Nashville, Tennessee. Distributes music for free to those who subscribe to the label. Submit online (see website).

Dirty Canvas Music

New York
Email: shep.goodman@gmail.com
Website: https://www.facebook.com/DirtyCanvasProductions/

Genres: Alternative Rock; Pop

Contact: Shep Goodman

Full scale music production company based in NY.

Disney Music Group

500 South Buena Vista Street
Burbank, CA 91521

Fax: +1 (818) 560-3230
Website: https://www.waltdisneystudios.com/disney-music-group/

Genres: All types of music

Record label arm of children's entertainment multimedia giant based in Burbank, California.

Disruptor Records

25 Madison Avenue
New York, NY 10016
Email: info@disruptorrecords.com
Website: http://disruptorrecords.com
Website: https://soundcloud.com/disruptorrecs

Genres: Dance; Pop

Record label based in New York. Joint venture with Sony Music Entertainment.

Disturbing Tha Peace Records (DTP)

1451 Woodmont Lane NW Suite A 29th floor
Atlanta, GA 30318
Email: alamodtp@gmail.com
Website: http://dtprecords.com
Website: http://facebook.com/dtprecords

Genres: Urban

Contact: Ken Bailey; Sean Taylor; Erica Novich

Record label based in Atlanta, Georgia.

DM Music Group

265 South Federal Highway, #352
Deerfield Beach, FL 33441
Email: mark@dmrecords.com
Email: david@dmrecords.com
Website: http://www.dmrecords.com

Genres: Dance; Pop; R&B; Country Rap

Contact: Mark Watson; David Watson

Independent music content company based in South Florida. Aims to exploit the full spectrum of revenue opportunities within the industry. Seeks talented, unique, new, and authentic country rap artists and songwriters for upcoming compilations and album projects.

DO IT Records

80 Cabrillo Highway, Suite Q429
Half Moon Bay, CA
Email: doitmanagement@xtra.co.nz
Website: http://www.doitmanagement.com
Website: http://www.myspace.com/doitmanagement

Genres: All types of music

Contact: Paul Marshall

I offer services such as; International artist management, concert promoter and record label. I am originally from London, England.

We strive to enhance the lives and careers of the music artists we represent, to be approachable and amicable in all business dealings and to provide the best possible value for money. Our goal is to build a lasting trust and partnership with our artists. We will connect our artists with publishers, tour promoters, sponsors and marketing opportunities to further their careers. In addition, we will seek to develop new products for the mutual benefit of the company and its artists. Last but not least, we are committed to assisting our artists to effortlessly export their music internationally.

Doghouse Records

118 16th Avenue S, Suite 4-144
Nashville, TN 37203-3100
Email: info@doghouserecords.com
Website: http://doghouserecords.com
Website: http://www.facebook.com/doghouserecords
Website: http://www.myspace.com/doghouserecords

Genres: Alternative; Rock; Punk; Hardcore

Record label based in New York.

Domino Record Co. Ltd

Website: http://www.dominorecordco.us

Genres: Electronic; Indie; Punk; Rock

Record label with offices in the US and UK.

DOMO Records, Inc.

11022 Santa Monica Blvd. #300
Los Angeles, CA 90025
Fax: +1 (310) 966-4420
Email: newtalent@domomusicgroup.com
Website: http://www.domomusicgroup.com
Website: https://soundcloud.com/domo-records

Genres: Contemporary; Classical; Electronic; Folk; Indie; New Age; Pop; Rock; Singer-Songwriter; World; Ambient; Soundtracks

Contact: A&R

Record company based in Los Angeles, California. Prefers to receive links to music online (FaceBook / MySpace, etc.) by email or via online submission form, but will not download music files or accept files attached to emails. Also accepts CDs – ensure your contact details are written on the CD itself. Response only if interested.

Don Giovanni Records

PO Box 628
Kingston, NJ 08528
Email: info@dongiovannirecords.com
Email: dongiovannirecords@gmail.com
Website: http://www.dongiovannirecords.com
Website: https://www.facebook.com/dongiovannirecords/

Genres: Punk

Punk label based in Kingston, New Jersey. Happy to listen to tracks by post or by email (no MP3s), though has never previously signed a band from a demo submission alone.

Don Rubin Productions

250 West 57th
New York, NY 10001
Email: drubin6573@aol.com

Genres: Pop; Rock

Record label based in New York.

Dovecote Records

231 Norman Ave # 102
Brooklyn, NY 11222
Email: info@dovecoterecords.com
Website: http://www.dovecoterecords.com
Website: https://soundcloud.com/dovecote-records/

Genres: Indie; Rock

Independent record label and artist management company based in New York City.

Downtown Records

New York, NY
Email: hello@downtownrecords.com
Website: http://downtownrecords.com
Website: https://www.facebook.com/DowntownRecords

Genres: All types of music

Independent record label based in New York.

Drag City

P.O. Box 476867
Chicago, IL 60647

UK OFFICE:
Drag City Inc.
Unit 409
Bon Marche Centre
241-251 Ferndale Rd
London, SW9 8BJ
Fax: +1 (312) 455-1057
Email: press@dragcity.com
Email: webmaster@dragcity.com
Website: http://www.dragcity.com

Genres: Pop; Rock; Alternative; Hard Rock; Experimental

Record label with offices in Chicago and London. No longer accepts demos "unless they're amazing".

DRG Records Incorporated

22 Harbor Park Drive
Port Washington, NY 11050
Fax: +1 (516) 484-2365
Email: info@drgrecords.com
Website: https://www.drgrecords.com

Genres: Soundtracks

Focuses on Broadway, vocal artists, cabaret and soundtracks.

Dualtone Records

3 Mcferrin Ave
Nashville, TN 37206
Fax: +1 (615) 320-0692
Email: info@dualtone.com
Website: http://www.dualtone.com
Website: http://www.facebook.com/dualtonemusic

Genres: Americana; Folk; Indie Rock; Singer-Songwriter

American-based independent record label specializing in folk, singer/songwriter, Americana and indie rock.

Duck Down Music

Email: demos@duckdown.com
Email: info@duckdown.com
Website: http://www.duckdown.com
Website: https://soundcloud.com/duckdown

Genres: Urban; Hip-Hop

Urban record label based in New York. For beats and demos, send query by email with:

1) Artist Name
2) Hometown
3) Age
4) SoundCloud page
5) YouTube channel
6) Twitter, Facebook, Instagram pages
7) Phone number

Earache Records Inc.

4402 11th Street, #400A
Long Island City, NY 11101
Email: al@earache.com
Website: http://www.earache.com
Website: https://www.facebook.com/earacherecords/
Website: http://www.myspace.com/earacherecords

Genres: Metal; Rock; Blues Rock; Extreme Metal

Contact: Al Dawson

American office of a UK label. Submit demos via form on website.

Earwig Music Company, Inc.

2054 W. Farwell Avenue, Suite G
Chicago, IL 60645
Email: info@earwigmusic.com
Website: https://www.earwigmusic.com
Website: https://www.facebook.com/earwigmusicpage/

Genres: Blues; Jazz

Founded in 1978 as a record label and artist management company. Also offeres music career consulting and music marketing services.

ECR Music Group

511 Avenue of the Americas, Suite #K144
New York, NY 10011
Email: contact@ecrmusicgroup.com
Website: http://www.ecrmusicgroup.com
Website: https://www.facebook.com/ecrmusicgroup

Genres: Pop; Rock

Record label based in New York. Describes itself as one of the world's leading independent music companies.

Elektra Music Group

3400 West Olive Avenue, 2nd Floor
Burbank, CA 91505
Website: http://www.elektramusicgroup.com

Genres: All types of music

Music group with offices in Burbank, California, New York, and Nashville, Tennessee.

Elm City Music

New Haven, CT
Website: http://elmcitymusic.net
Website: https://www.facebook.com/ElmCityMusicRecords/

Genres: All types of music

Contact: Michael Caplan

Full service music and entertainment company based in New Haven, Connecticut.

Emblem Music Group

23679 Calabasas Rd #739
Calabasas CA 91302
Email: info@emblem-music.com
Website: http://www.emblem-music.com

Genres: All types of music

Record label based in Calabasas, California.

The End Records

PO Box 20529
New York, NY 10023
Email: all@theendrecords.com
Website: http://www.theendrecords.com
Website: https://www.facebook.com/theendrecords/
Website: http://www.myspace.com/theendrecords

Genres: Rock; Metal; Indie; Alternative

Indepdent record label based in New York, specialising in rock and alternative music.

Entertainment One (eOne)

10 Harbor Park Drive
Port Washington, New York 11050
Website: https://www.entertainmentone.com
Website: https://www.facebook.com/EntertainmentOneGroup/

Genres: All types of music

Entertainment company with interests in film, television, and music, and offices in multiple locations in North America and around the world.

Epic Records Group

25 Madison Avenue, 10th Floor
New York, NY 10022-3211

CALIFORNIA OFFICE:
9830 Wilshire Boulevard,
Beverly Hills, CA 90212
Website: http://www.epicrecords.com

Genres: All types of music

Contact: Farra Matthews, VP A&R; Michael Klein, A&R Operations

Label with offices in New York and Beverly Hills, California. Handles all genres, but in particular pop, hip-hop, rock, alternative, and electronica. Accepts approaches via known managers/agents only.

Epitaph

2798 Sunset Boulevard
Los Angeles, CA 90026
Website: http://www.epitaph.com
Website: https://www.facebook.com/epitaphrecords

Genres: Punk; Indie; Hardcore; Emo; Garage; Alternative Rock; Post Hardcore; Punk Rock; Hip-Hop

Contact: Brett Gurewitz

Record label based in Los Angeles, California. Submit links to music online via demo submission form on website.

Equal Vision Records

P.O. Box 38202
Albany, NY 12203-8202
Fax: +1 (518) 458-1312
Email: music@equalvision.com
Email: info@equalvision.com
Website: http://www.equalvision.com
Website: https://soundcloud.com/equalvision

Genres: Alternative; Indie; Metal; Punk; Rock

Label based in Albany, New York. No physical demos. Send email with links to your music online (no downloads), plus bio.

Ernest Jenning Record Co.

Brooklyn, NY
Email: info@ernestjenning.com
Website: http://www.ernestjenning.com
Website: https://www.facebook.com/ErnestJenning

Genres: Modern Pop; Rock

Independent record label based in Brooklyn, New York. Send demos by email.

Everloving

2658 Griffith Park Boulevard #115
Los Angeles, CA 90039
Email: andy@everloving.com
Email: jp@everloving.com

Website: http://www.everloving.com
Website: http://soundcloud.com/everloving

Genres: All types of music

Contact: Andy Factor (Partner); JP Plunier (Partner)

Record label based in Los Angeles, California. No longer accepts demos by post. All submissions must be made via Soundcloud dropbox.

Fade To Silence

Email: info@fadetosilencerecords.com
Website: http://www.fadetosilencerecords.com
Website: https://www.facebook.com/fadetosilencerecords

Genres: All types of music

Independent label / digital services/ music publishing.

Fair Trade

Website: http://www.fairtradeservices.com

Genres: Christian

Christian record label that aims to foster relationships with artists in a spirit of partnership and fairness.

Famous Records

4577 N. Nob Hill Road, Suite 201
Sunrise, FL 33351
Fax: +1 (954) 368-2740
Email: famousfontana1@gmail.com
Email: jeffrey@famousmusicgroup.com
Website: http://www.famousmusicgroup.com
Website: https://soundcloud.com/famousfontana

Genres: All types of music

Record label based in Sunrise, Florida. Considers all genres of music. Send query by email with MP3s or links to music online.

Fat Possum Records

PO Box 1923
Oxford, MS 38655
Fax: +1 (662) 234-2899
Email: matthew@fatpossum.com
Email: bruce_w@fatpossum.com
Website: http://www.fatpossum.com
Website: https://soundcloud.com/fatpossum

Genres: Blues; Indie

Contact: Matthew Johnson; Bruce Watson

Record label based in Oxford, Mississippi.

Fearless Records

5870 W Jefferson Blvd, Suite E
Los Angeles, CA 90016
Email: demos@fearlessrecords.com
Email: info@fearlessrecords.com
Website: http://www.fearlessrecords.com
Website: https://www.facebook.com/fearlessrecords

Genres: Indie; Punk; Rock; Hardcore; Pop; Alternative

Contact: Bob B (President/A&R)

Record label based in Los Angeles, California. Send demos by email with links to music online, or by post. Include contact information, 3-4 of your best songs, band bio and band photo.

Ferret Music

1290 Ave of the Americas, 24th Floor
New York, NY 10104
Email: ferretstyle@ferretstyle.com
Website: http://ferretstyle.com
Website: https://www.youtube.com/profile?user=FERRETMUSICNJ
Website: http://www.myspace.com/ferretmusic

Genres: Alternative Rock; Hard Rock; Metal

Record label based in New York. Send query by email with links to online community pages only. No links to MP3s, EPKs, etc. Do not chase for response.

Fervor Records

Email: info@fervor-records.com
Website: http://www.fervor-records.com

Genres: Indie; Contemporary; Traditional; Rock

A boutique indie label representing emerging artists and an extensive catalogue of vintage recordings from 1921 to 1995.

Fool's Gold

147 Grand St
11249 Brooklyn, New York
Email: demos@foolsgoldrecs.com
Website: https://foolsgoldrecs.com
Website: https://www.facebook.com/foolsgoldrecords

Genres: All types of music

Record label based in Brooklyn. Send query by email with links to music online. MP3 attachments will be deleted.

Frenchkiss Records

New York
Email: info@frenchkissrecords.com
Website: http://www.frenchkissrecords.com
Website: https://www.facebook.com/frenchkissrecords

Genres: All types of music

Record label based in New York.

Friendly Fire Recordings

3727 25th Street
San Francisco, CA 94110
Email: info@friendlyfirerecordings.com
Website: http://www.friendlyfirerecordings.com
Website: https://soundcloud.com/friendlyfirerecordings

Genres: All types of music

Record label based in San Francisco. Prefers queries by email with links to music online (no MP3 attachments), but will also consider CDs by post.

Frontier Records

PO Box 22
Sun Valley, CA 91353
Email: info@frontierrecords.com
Website: http://www.frontierrecords.com
Website: https://www.facebook.com/thefrontierrecords?ref=ts

Genres: Punk Rock; Classic Punk; Alternative Rock

Punk label based in Sun Valley, California. Not accepting demos as at May 2018, but is interested in re-releasing vintage punk or alternative rock. Contact by email.

Fueled By Ramen

1633 Broadway 10th floor
New York, NY 10019
Email: erick@fueledbyramen.com
Website: http://www.fueledbyramen.com
Website: http://www.facebook.com/fueledbyramen

Genres: All types of music

Record label based in New York. Send demo by post with bio, contact information, touring information, and more. Do not send emails about demo submissions.

Funzalo Records

PO Box 571567
Tarzana, CA 91357
Email: dan@mikesmanagement.com
Website: http://funzalorecords.com
Website: https://www.facebook.com/funzalorecords/

Genres: Americana; Folk; Indie; Rock

Contact: Mike Lembo; Dan Agnew

Send submissions via online submission form. Submissions without music links will be deleted. No rap music.

G1 Muzic

Email: G1muzic@gmail.com
Website: http://www.g1muzic.com

Genres: All types of music

Indie record label and digital distributor. We are a label that provides services to other labels our indie artists.

Get Hip Recordings

R.J. Casey Industrial Park
1800 Columbus Avenue
Pittsburgh, PA 15233
Email: gregg@gethip.com

Email: barbara@gethip.com
Website: http://www.gethip.com
Website: https://www.facebook.com/GetHipRecordings

Genres: Folk; Punk; Rock; Indie

Contact: Gregg Kostelich; Barbara Garcia-Bernado

Record label based in Pittsburgh. Also acts as a distributor.

Ghostly International

PO Box 220395
Brooklyn, NY 11222
Email: booking@ghostly.com
Website: https://ghostly.com

Genres: Electronic; Indie; Hip-Hop; Pop; Rap; Rock

Label based in Brooklyn, New York.

Glassnote

NEW YORK
770 Lexington Avenue, 16th Floor
New York, NY 10065

LOS ANGELES
2220 Colorado Avenue, Suite 200
Santa Monica, CA 90404
Fax: +1 (646) 237-2711
Email: demos@glassnotemusic.com
Website: http://glassnotemusic.com
Website: https://soundcloud.com/glassnotemusic

Genres: All types of music

Contact: Attn: Demo Submissions

Record label with offices in New York, Los Angeles, London, and Toronto. Send demos by post to the New York address or send queries by email with MP3 attachments or links to music online.

Gotee Records

Email: music@gotee.com
Website: https://www.gotee.com

Genres: R&B; Reggae; Rap; Rock

Submit music by email.

Green Linnet

Compass Records
916 19th Avenue South
Nashville, TN 37212
Fax: +1 (615) 320-7378
Email: submissions@compassrecords.com
Email: info@compassrecords.com
Website: http://www.greenlinnet.com
Website: http://www.myspace.com/greenlinnetrecords

Genres: Folk; World; Celtic

Record label based in Nashville, Tennessee. Describes itself as "the best-known brand in Celtic music". Send query by email with links to website with your music, bio, photos, and upcoming tour dates. Include details of why your think your music is right for this label, and the last 2 years of touring history. If you send in a CD and printed material, this will significantly slow down the review process.

Hacienda Records

1236 South Staples Street
Corpus Christi, TX 78404
Fax: +1 (361) 882-3943
Email: sales@haciendarecords.com
Email: hacienda@haciendarecords.com
Website: http://hacienda-records.myshopify.com
Website: https://www.facebook.com/haciendarecords

Genres: Latin; Gospel

Record label based in Corpus Christi, Texas, producing Latin, Tejano, Traditional Tex-Mex, Conjunto and Norteño music, as well as Banda, Merengue, Duranguense, Rock En Español, Gospel and Christmas music.

Harbour Records

Email: info@harbourrecordings.com
Website: http://harbourrecordings.com

Genres: Electronic; Pop; Rock

Independent boutique record label founded in 2012.

Headliner Records / George Tobin Music

102 NE 2nd Street
Boca Raton, FL 33432
Email: georgetobinmusic@aol.com
Website: http://www.headlinerrecords.com

Genres: Alternative; Pop; R&B

Contact: George Tobin

Record label based in Boca Raton, Florida. Claims to be responsible for the sale of over 25 million records worldwide. Accepts demos and promotion packages.

As at June 2018 this label is conducting a professional talent search for young unsigned male pop singers and vocal groups between the ages of 14-22. No rap. See website for details.

Hidden Beach Recordings

Email: admin@hiddenbeach.com
Website: http://www.hiddenbeach.com

Genres: Gospel; Jazz; R&B; Hip-Hop; Rap

California-based record label. See website for more details.

Highwheel Records

Email: info@highwheelrecords.com
Website: http://highwheelrecords.com

Genres: Alternative; Rock

Boutique label offering high quality, independently spirited records.

Hit City USA

Los Angeles, CA
Website: http://www.hitcityusa.com
Website: http://www.facebook.com/hitcityusa

Genres: Alternative; Pop; R&B

Describes itself as a record label and cultural hub, based in LA.

Hit World Records

Los Angeles, CA / Houston, TX
Email: hitworldrecords@gmail.com
Website: http://www.hitworldrecords.com

Genres: Pop; Urban

Record label with offices in Los Angelse, California, and Houston, Texas.

Hollywood Records

Website: http://www.hollywoodrecords.com
Website: https://www.facebook.com/HollywoodRecords

Genres: All types of music

Record label with a roster that spans genres.

Hopeless Records

Email: ar@hopelessrecords.com
Email: info@hopelessrecords.com
Website: http://hopelessrecords.com
Website: https://www.facebook.com/hopelessrecords

Genres: Hardcore; Indie; Metal; Punk; Rock; Ska

Record label based in Van Nuys, California. Contact by email only, including bio, links to MySpace and Youtube videos, etc. electric press kit if you have one, and/or 2-4 MP3 tracks (maximum). No physical submissions.

Hydra Head Records

Los Angelese, CA
Website: http://hydrahead.com
Website: https://www.facebook.com/hydrahead

Genres: Heavy Metal; Experimental; Hardcore

Independent record label based in LA, specialising in heavy and experimental music.

Iamsound

Los Angeles, CA
Email: hello@iamsound.com
Website: https://iamsound.com
Website: https://www.facebook.com/iamsoundrecords

Genres: All types of music

Record label, agency and visual art studio based in Los Angeles.

Idol Records

Attn: A & R
PO Box 140344
Dallas, TX 75214
Email: info@idolrecords.com
Website: http://www.idolrecords.com
Website: http://www.facebook.com/idolrecordsgroup
Website: http://www.myspace.com/idolrecords

Genres: Indie; Pop; Punk; Rap; Hip-Hop; Rock;; Americana; Instrumental

Contact: Erv Karwelis

Send demo with contact information along with a bio, recent photo, web address, press kit and upcoming show dates. No material returned. Response not guaranteed unless interested.

In the Red Records

PO Box 50777
Los Angeles, CA 90050
Email: info@intheredrecords.com
Website: https://intheredrecords.com

Genres: Garage; Punk; Rock and Roll

Record label based in Los Angeles, California.

Infidel Records

931 Madison Street
Hoboken, NJ 07030
Website: http://infidelrecords.com

Genres: All types of music

Record label based in New Jersey.

Innovative Leisure

2658 Griffith Park Boulevard #324
Los Angeles, CA 90039
Email: info@innovativeleisure.net
Website: https://www.innovativeleisure.net

Genres: All types of music

Independent record label based in Los Angeles, California.

Inspired Studios Inc.

8854 Via Brilliante
Wellington, FL 33411
Fax: +1 (561) 333-9143
Email: dkasen@inspired-studios.com
Website: http://www.inspired-studios.com

Genres: All types of music

Music company based in Wellington, Florida.

Intelligent Noise

Los Angeles, CA
Email: shannon@intelligentnoise.com
Website: http://intelligentnoise.com
Website: https://www.facebook.com/intelligentnoise

Genres: All types of music

Indie label based in LA.

Interscope Geffen A&M

2220 Colorado Avenue
Santa Monica, CA 90404
Website: https://www.interscope.com
Website: https://www.facebook.com/interscope

Genres: Hip-Hop; Indie; Pop; Rap; Rock

Record label based in Santa Monica, California.

Ipecac Recordings

Email: info@ipecac.com
Website: http://www.ipecac.com
Website: https://www.facebook.com/ipecac

Genres: Rock

Aims to be an honest, artist friendly label run on a shoe string with no outrageous promotional or production costs.

Jaggo Records, LLC

Email: jaggo@jaggo.com
Website: http://www.jaggo.com

Genres: Jazz; Hip-Hop; Pop; R&B; Rock; Soul; World

Record label based in California, boasting 120 years of collective experience in the industry. Aims to build lasting careers for artists.

Jagjaguwar

213 S. Rogers Street
Bloomington, IN 47404
Email: info@jagjaguwar.com
Website: http://jagjaguwar.com
Website: https://www.facebook.com/Jagjaguwar/

Genres: Alternative; Folk; Indie

Record label based in Bloomington, Indiana.

Javotti Media

Email: info@javottimedia.com
Website: http://www.javottimedia.com
Website: https://www.facebook.com/javottimedia/

Genres: Urban

No audio files by email.

K Records

PO Box 7154
Olympia, WA 98507
Email: info@krecs.com
Email: promo@krecs.com
Website: https://www.krecs.com
Website: https://www.facebook.com/box7154/

Genres: All types of music

Contact: Calvin Johnson

Record label based in Olympia, Washington. Not accepting demos as at March 2019. Check website for current status.

Kanine Records

Email: info@KanineRecords.com
Website: http://kaninerecords.com
Website: https://www.facebook.com/kaninerecords

Genres: Indie; Pop; Punk; Rock

Record label based in Brooklyn, New York. Not accepting demos as at March 2019.

Keyframe Music

Email: keyframe@yahoo.com
Website: http://keyframe-entertainment.com
Website: https://www.facebook.com/keyframe.entertainment/

Genres: Electronic; Trance

Produces, finances, and distributes cutting-edge projects in a variety of media.

Kill Rock Stars

107 SE Washington Street, Suite 155
Portland, OR 97214
Fax: +1 (360) 357-6408
Email: krs@killrockstars.com
Email: portia@killrockstars.com
Website: https://www.killrockstars.com
Website: http://www.myspace.com/killrockstars5rc

Genres: Indie; Punk

Contact: Portia Sabin, President

Only willing to consider bands who are touring and who will be playing in Portland. Send email with links to music online and details of tour dates, and date playing in Portland. No demos by post.

Killroom Records

Seattle, WA
Email: killroomrecords@gmail.com
Website: http://www.killroomrecords.com
Website: https://www.facebook.com/killroomrecords/

Genres: All types of music

Contact: Troy Nelson; Ben Jenkins

Record label based in Seattle, Washington.

Kirtland Records

Dallas, TX 75226
Fax: +1 (214) 849-9807
Email: music@kirtlandrecords.com
Website: http://kirtlandrecords.com
Website: https://www.facebook.com/KirtlandRecords/

Genres: Alternative; Pop; Rock

Contact: John Kirtland

Record label based in Dallas, Texas.

Lakeshore Entertainment

9268 West Third Street
Beverly Hills, CA 90210
Email: MusicDept@lakeshoreentertainment.com
Website: http://www.lakeshorerecords.com

Genres: Soundtracks

Independent music division of film production company.

Lamon Records

PO Box 1907
Mt Juliet, TN 37121
Email: dave@lamonrecords.com
Website: http://www.lamonrecords.com

Genres: Blues; Christian; Country; Folk; Gospel; Latin; Roots

Label with offices in Nashville, Hollywood, and Charlotte. Submit via online submission form.

Landslide Records

PO Box 15117
Fernandina Beach, FL 32035
Email: mrland@mindspring.com
Website: http://www.landsliderecords.com
Website: https://myspace.com/landsliderecordsoriginal

Genres: Americana; Blues; Folk; Jazz; Rock

Contact: Landslide Records

Record label based in Fernandina Beach, Florida.

Lava Records

1755 Broadway
New York, NY 10019
Website: http://www.lavarecords.com
Website: https://www.facebook.com/LavaRecordsUS

Genres: All types of music

Record label based in New York. Discovered and championed artists who went on to sell in excess of 100 million records around the world in the label's first nine years of existence.

Le Grand Magistery, LLC

PO Box 611
Bloomfield Hills, MI 48303
Email: magistery@aol.com
Website: http://www.magistery.com

Genres: Alternative; Rock

Record label based in Bloomfield Hills, Michigan.

Lightning Rod Records

718 Thompson Lane
Suite 108 – PMB 181
Nashville, TN 37204
Email: info@lightningrodrecords.com
Website: https://www.lightningrodrecords.com
Website: https://www.facebook.com/lightningrodrecords

Genres: Americana; Rock; Roots

Record label based in Nashville, Tennessee.

Lightyear Entertainment

Website: http://www.lightyear.com
Website: https://www.facebook.com/lightyearent

Genres: All types of music

Los Angeles and New York based entertainment company. Describes itself as "a multi-layered entertainment company that creates and acquires a mix of music and video product with two key common elements: high quality and strong niche appeal."

Little Fish Records

PO Box 19164
Cleveland, OH 44119
Email: littlefishrecords@gmail.com
Website: http://www.littlefishrecords.com
Website: https://www.facebook.com/LittleFishRecords

Genres: Regional; Reggae; World; Americana; Blues; Folk; Jazz; Rock

Cleveland-based record label, "committed to presenting the finest local and regional sounds within a wide variety of musical genres".

LML Music

Post Office Box 48081
Los Angeles, CA 90048
Fax: +1 (323) 856-9204
Email: lee@lmlmusic.com
Website: http://www.lmlmusic.com

Genres: Contemporary; Pop; Traditional

Record label based in Los Angeles. Send demo with press kit by post. Include SASE if return of material required.

Loma Vista

Website: https://www.lomavistarecordings.com
Website: https://twitter.com/LomaVistaRC

Genres: All types of music

Record label based in California.

Lost Highway Records

Website: https://www.umgnashville.com
Website: https://www.facebook.com/UMGNashville

Genres: Country; Roots; Rock; Americana; Folk

Label based in Nashville, Tennessee.

LoveCat Music

Email: lovecatmusic@gmail.com
Website: http://www.lovecatmusic.com
Website: https://www.facebook.com/LoveCatMusic

Genres: Pop; Rock; Dance; Latin; World; R&B; Jazz; Reggaeton; Latin Hip-Hop; Rap; Hip-Hop

Independent record label and music publisher, founded in 1999. License original songs for use in films, TV, advertisement, trailers and games. Particularly interested in songs with the themes of freedom, moving / action. happiness / joy, and friends / family. Cannot use cover versions or songs that include samples from other songs.

Lovelane Music Group

Sherman Oaks, CA 91423
Email: lovelanemusic@gmail.com

Genres: Blues; Funk; R&B

Record label based in Sherman Oaks, California.

Loyalty Over Royalty Records

Email: loyaltyoverroyaltyrecs@gmail.com
Website: https://www.facebook.com/LoyaltyOverRoyaltyRecords

Genres: All types of music

Contact: Warren Wells

An independent record label and concert promotion company founded in 2019 in Toronto, Canada. As an indie label and booking company, we are dedicated to promoting shows and artists we love in North America and beyond.

Machin Entertainment

11135 Weddington St. #424
N Hollywood, CA 91601
Fax: +1 (270) 717-8862
Email: info@machinentertainment.com
Website: http://machinentertainment.com

Genres: All types of music

Provides fast and easy digital distribution to independent labels and artists.

Mad Decent

Website: https://maddecent.com
Website: https://www.facebook.com/maddecent

Genres: Black Metal; Glam; House; Underground

Record label based in Los Angeles, California. On a mission is to highlight underground, genre-blurring sounds.

Mad Dragon Music Group

3501 Market St
19104 Philadelphia, PA
Email: mdmg@drexel.edu
Website: http://www.maddragonmusic.com
Website: https://www.facebook.com/MADDragonMusicGroup/

Genres: Alternative; Rock

Record label based in Philadelphia, Pennsylvania. Send query through online web form with links to music online.

Maggie's Music

PO Box 490
Shady Side, MD 20764
Email: mail@maggiesmusic.com
Website: https://www.maggiesmusic.com

Genres: Celtic; Acoustic

Celtic record label based in Shady Side, Maryland.

Magna Carta Records

East Rochester, NY
Email: info@magnacarta.net
Website: https://magnacartarecords.bandcamp.com

Genres: Progressive Metal; Rock

Independent record label based in East Rochester, New York. Best known for progressive rock / metal.

Mandala Records

Website: http://mandalarecords.com

Genres: All types of music

See website for details.

Maranatha Music

Email: info@maranathamusic.com
Email: jakob@maranathamusic.com
Website: https://www.maranathamusic.com
Website: https://www.facebook.com/maranathamusicofficial/

Genres: Christian; Gospel

Christian music label founded in 1971.

Marsalis Music

323 Broadway
Cambridge, MA 02139
Fax: +1 (617) 354-2396
Email: info@marsalismusic.com
Website: https://www.marsalismusic.com

Genres: Jazz

Contact: Branford Marsalis

Jazz label based in Cambridge, Massachusetts. Currently closed to new artists as at September 2019.

Mascot Label Group

118 East 28th Street, Suite 701
New York, NY 10016
Email: questions@mlgmerch.com
Website: https://usa.mascotlabelgroup.com
Website: http://www.facebook.com/mascotlabelgroup

Genres: All types of music

Record label with offices in New York and the Netherlands.

Matador Records

304 Hudson Street, 7th Floor
New York, NY 10013
Fax: +1 (212) 995-5883
Email: info@matadorrecords.com
Website: https://www.matadorrecords.com

Genres: Indie

Indie label based in New York. Not accepting unsolicited demo submissions as at June 2019.

Merge Records

Fax: +1 (919) 688-9970
Email: merge@mergerecords.com
Website: https://www.mergerecords.com
Website: https://soundcloud.com/mergerecords

Genres: Indie; Rock; Singer-Songwriter

Record label founded in Chapel Hill, North Carolina, in 1989. No unsolicited demos.

Metal Blade Records, Inc.

5160 Van Nuys, Blvd #301
Sherman Oaks, CA 91403
Email: metalblade@metalblade.com
Website: https://www.metalblade.com

Genres: Hardcore; Metal; Rock

Closed to unsolicited demos as at July 2019. Check website for current status.

Metropolis Records

PO Box 974
Media, PA 19063
Email: demo@metropolis-records.com
Email: info@metropolis-records.com
Website: http://www.metropolis-records.com
Website: https://www.facebook.com/MetropolisRecords

Genres: Alternative; Indie

Contact: Attn: Demos

Send submissions on CD or CD-R by post, with brief bio and contact information (marked for the attention of "Demos"), or send email with soundcloud links. Do not send email attachments (these will be deleted without being opened). Response only if interested.

Middle West

Email: info@middlewestmgmt.com
Website: http://www.middlewestmgmt.com
Website: https://www.facebook.com/middlewestmgmt

Genres: All types of music

Artist management company founded in 2010 in the Midwest.

Milan Records

Burbank, CA 91505
Email: jc.chamboredon@milanrecords.com
Website: https://www.milanrecords.com

Genres: Electronic; Soundtracks; World

Label based in Burbank, California.

Morphius Records

Morphius-A&R/Demo Submissions
100 East 23rd Street,
Baltimore, MD 21218
Fax: +1 (410) 662-0116
Email: info@morphius.com
Website: http://morphius.com

Genres: Experimental; Hip-Hop; Punk; Rock

Record label based in Baltimore, Maryland. Send demo package by post. Wait two weeks before following up. See website for more details.

Moth Man Records

Email: joe@mothmanrecords.com
Website: https://mothmanrecords.com

Genres: Alternative Thrash Psychedelic Acoustic Hard Heavy Funky Melodic Modern Post Progressive Americana Emo Funk Garage Guitar based Hardcore Indie Lo-fi Melodicore Pop Punk Rock Rock and Roll Rockabilly Shoegaze

Contact: Joe

A recording studio located in a Milwaukee basement specializing in indie rock and related genres. When I have time, I record music projects that I enjoy for free. Feel free to message me or send your demos.

1-2-3-4 Go! Records

420 40th Street #5
Oakland, CA 94609
Email: store@1234gorecords.com
Website: http://1234gorecords.com
Website: https://www.facebook.com/1234gorecords

Genres: Rock; Punk; Indie; Hardcore; Garage; Classic Rock; R&B; Soul; Jazz; Hip-Hop; Reggae; Ska; Funk; Country

An Independent record store and label based in Oakland, California.

Rampage Records

195 Gray Fox Dr
Sedona, AZ 86351
Email: officialrampagerecords@gmail.com
Website: https://www.facebook.com/RampageRecords/
Website: https://www.reverbnation.com/label/officialrampagerecords

Genres: All types of music

Contact: Chandler Culler

An independent record label located in Sedona, Arizona.

Sick House Entertainment

Tulsa, Oklahoma
Email: sickhouseentertainment@gmail.com
Website: http://www.facebook.com/sickhouseentertainment

Genres: All types of music

Contact: Nathan Sappington

An independent record label located in Tulsa, Oklahoma.

Skate Mountain Records

PO Box 1607
Point Clear, AL 36564
Website: http://www.skatemountain.com

Genres: Alternative; Americana; Blues; Country; Hip-Hop; Pop; R&B; Rap; Rock; Rock and Roll; Roots Rock; Singer-Songwriter; Soul; Soundtracks; Classic; Commercial; Mainstream; Soulful Rock; Alternative Soul; Alternative Country; Garage; Punk

Bringing Alabama to the forefront of the music industry. With a history of success in film production, we are uniting Alabama's rich music scene with the global film business while concurrently developing and nurturing local and national talent.

This label is a family. With an ear to the street and an eye on quality, we are a close-knit group of artists, musicians, filmmakers and producers collaborating to create a truly unique one-stop shop for music and film production.

Currently creating a catalog of original music that's specifically for the filmmaker. Music from a variety of genres is available for licensing. With our vast resources in the entertainment industry from music and film experience, we uniquely provide the ability to connect artist with artist, filmmaker with musician. We produce custom music for film allowing the filmmaker to have a creative say as well as providing our traditional catalog of bad ass music.

Founded by music lovers with the artist in mind. The structure is not designed to just sell records; but to create damn good records. The rest will speak for itself.

Stryker Records, Inc.

PO Box 10491
Green Bay, WI 54154
Email: cdobry@strykerrecords.com
Email: chesyck@strykerrecords.com
Website: https://www.strykerrecords.com/

Genres: Funky Hard Melodic Progressive; Blues Country Hip-Hop Indie Pop Rap Rock Rock and Roll

Contact: Chris Dobry

What: Managed and recorded Artists, booked and promoted events, press releases, tv appearances, news paper/magazine articles, air play, radio/tv interviews, photo shoots, cd releases, promo cds, Event Coordinator, A&R, Performance rights Agreements ASCAP/BMI, auditions.

Sunset Music Supervision

1928 The Woods II
Cherry Hill, NJ 08003
Email: submissions@sunsetmusicsupervision.com
Email: sunsetcorporate@sunsetcorporationamerica.com
Website: http://sunsetmusicsupervision.com
Website: http://sunset-usa.com

Genres: All types of music

Contact: Don Lichterman

World-Renowned Music Licensing Placements and Global Distribution for Creative and Commercial Uses. Available Tracks by Award-Winning Artists, Composers, Bands, and Orchestras. High-Quality Music for Major Films, TV Shows, Commercials, and Branding -- Fun, Creative, User-Friendly.

Sunset Recordings

1928 The Woods II
Cherry Hill, NJ 08003
Email: artistdevelopment@sunsetrecordings.com
Email: sunsetcorporate@sunsetcorporationamerica.com
Website: http://sunsetrecordings.com
Website: http://sunset-usa.com

Genres: All types of music

Contact: Don Lichterman

An American based record label that operates its business worldwide. It was founded in 2009 as his rock, alternative and pop label.

Sunset Special Markets (SSM)

1928 The Woods II
Cherry Hill, NJ 08003
Email: artistdevelopment@sunsetspecialmarkets.com
Email: sunsetcorporate@sunsetcorporationamerica.com
Website: http://sunsetspecialmarkets.com
Website: http://sunset-usa.com

Genres: All types of music

Contact: Don Lichterman

Opened its door's 2008/2009 when the founder started to put together a new label with licensed product.

Produces, develops and releases special market products, boxed sets, greatest hits titles, stand up comedy LP's, live recordings, collectible releases and exclusive special markets products in the world entertainment.

T&R Recordings

7699 Brams Hill Drive
Dayton, Ohio 45459-4123
Fax: +1 (937) 360-3679
Email: info@tandr.us
Email: justin@tandr.us
Website: https://www.tandrrecordings.com/
Website: https://www.tandr.us/
Website: https://www.facebook.com/tandrddp

Genres: Heavy Metal; Hard Rock; Noise Core; Punk; Hardcore; Pop; Experimental

Contact: Justin Rissmiller

A small independent record label founded in 2015 and operated out of Dayton, Ohio.

Tama Industries

Email: https://www.hypesong.com/demobox/tamaindustries
Website: http://www.tamarecordlabel.com

Genres: All types of music

Contact: Dynasty Holland

More than just a label. Winning the hearts of many musicians we hold no fear in our explanation of what makes our company the best. Our contract is simple, sweet and to the point. We hold one of the highest payout to signed talents. And more team building with outside companies than many other labels.

This label prides itself in the support of supporting its hometown San Antonio, TX, and its local police department "SAPD". Connecting all of San Antonio's start-up companies and musicians in one area of promotion has been the greatest achievement for this label.

This label has since put together many programs for up rising talents such as a housing program and a tv network for uprising actors, actress and musicians. We are more than just a label we are connected to "Straight Defined Community" Born in Austin but raised within San Antonio, city limits.

Since the high calling for our services we have connected a future for many.

Tama Industries Record Label

Email: info@tamaindustriesrecordlabel.com
Website: https://www.tamaindustrieslabel.com

Genres: Acoustic Christian Classic Commercial Hard Modern New Wave Non-Commercial Underground Urban Soulful Club Country Blues Dance Dubstep Gospel Gothic Hardcore Hip-Hop Indie Instrumental

Jazz Latin Metal New Age Pop R&B Punk Ragga Rap Reggae Reggaeton Relaxation Rock Rock and Roll Rhythm and Blues Singer-Songwriter Spoken Word Techno Trip Hop World

Delivers innovative, customization, complete record deals, and music distribution packages to musicians around the world. For 5 years, we've worked closely with our artists and producers to provide an easy and effective all-in-one Record Deal portfolio. Our music goes to one million sites in 250 countries and territories, and the largest global music distribution network of retailers, broadcasters, licencors and channels.

More than just a label. Winning the hearts of many musicians we hold no fear in our explanation of what makes our company the best. Our contract is simple, sweet and to the point. Holding the highest payouts to signed talents. Prides itself in supporting its hometown of San Antonio Texas and its local police department "SAPD". Connecting San Antonio's start-up companies and musicians in promotion are the greatest achievement for us.

What we do!
We put together many programs for uprising talents such as a housing program and TV networks for actors, actress, and musicians. Since the high calling for our services, we have connected a future for many. Getting a record deal should be simple for any artist trying to thrive. You should be able to sign a contract with any label without being asked for money or to prove yourself. Partnering with our label is simple; sign our e-agreement and receive an email on next steps and how to get started.

Each Artist will receive a login to their accounting software to revive monthly and quarterly payments. Payroll link to fill out there 1099's and more. Don't wait we work around the clock so you can do what you love. We provide instant results and proof of placement and income.

37 Records & Management

3617 East Broadway Avenue #19PH
Long Beach, CA 90803
Email: info@37records.com
Website: http://www.37records.com

Genres: All types of music

Contact: Steven McClintock

Record label and management company based in Long Beach, California.

300 Entertainment

New York, NY
Website: http://www.300ent.com
Website: https://soundcloud.com/300-entertainment

Genres: All types of music

Music company based in New York.

Tonally Records

Email: contact@tonallyrecords.com
Website: https://www.facebook.com/tonallyrecords

Genres: All types of music

Contact: Christian Tobon

Independent record label and owns a publishing subsidiary.

00:02:59 LLC

PO Box 1251
Culver City, CA 90232
Email: info@259records.com
Website: http://www.259records.com
Website: https://www.facebook.com/259Records

Genres: Alternative; Americana; Blues; Country; Folk; Gospel; Indie; Pop; Punk; Reggae; Rock; Roots; Singer-Songwriter; World

Contact: Abe Bradshaw; Nicole Mensinger; Ben Bradshaw

Record label based in Culver City, California.

Velour Music Group

26 Dobbin Street, 3rd Floor
Brooklyn, NY 11222
Email: info@velourmusic.com
Email: jeff@velourmusic.com
Website: http://velourmusic.com
Website: https://www.facebook.com/velourmusic

Genres: All types of music

Contact: Jeff Krasno; Sean Hoess

Record label and management company based in Brooklyn, New York.

The Verve Music Group

Universal Music Group
2220 Colorado Ave
Santa Monica, CA 90404
Fax: +1 (212) 331-2064
Website: http://www.vervemusicgroup.com

Genres: Jazz; Contemporary; Pop; R&B

Record label based in Santa Monica, California.

Victory Records

346 N. Justine Street, 5th Floor
Chicago IL, 60607
Fax: +1 (312) 666-8665
Email: contact@victoryrecords.com
Website: http://victoryrecords.com
Website: http://www.facebook.com/VictoryRecords

Genres: Metal; Rock; Indie; Hardcore; Punk

Record label based in Chicago, with UK offices in London. Approach via online demo form, which includes space for providing links to your music online.

Vineyard Worship

Email: info@vineyardmusic.com
Website: http://www.vineyardworship.com
Website: https://www.facebook.com/VineyardWorship

Genres: Christian

Record label releasing Christian music.

Viper Records

PO Box 197
New York, NY 10024
Email: info@viperrecords.com
Email: toure@viperrecords.com
Website: https://www.viperrecords.com

Genres: Hip-Hop; Rap

Currently accepting producer submissions only as at January 2017. No MC submissions. Vocal performers should check website for current status. Submit links to your music online using demo form on website. Response not guaranteed.

Visionary Music Group

Website: http://www.teamvisionary.com
Website: https://soundcloud.com/teamvisionary

Genres: Urban

Not accepting submissions as at January 2017. Check website for current status.

VP Records

89-05 138th Street,
Jamaica, NY 11435

FLORIDA:
6022 S.W. 21st Street
Miramar, FL 33023

LONDON:
3rd Floor, Master House
107 Hammersmith Road
London
W14 0XN
UK

JAMAICA:
1 Upper Sandringham Ave,
Kingston 10, Jamaica
Fax: +1 (718) 658-3573
Email: information@vprecords.com
Website: http://www.vprecords.com
Website: https://soundcloud.com/vp_records

Genres: Reggae

Record label based in Jamaica, New York, with offices in Florida, London, and Jamaica.

VSR Music Group

3520 E Brown Rd
Mesa, AZ 85213
Email: vsrmusicgroup@gmail.com
Website: http://vsrmusic.com
Website: https://www.facebook.com/VSRMusicGroup

Genres: Christian Rock

Contact: Ken Mary

Looking for Christ-centered artists who are willing to share the Word of God through music.

Warm Electronic Recordings

Post Box 1423
Athens, GA 30603
Fax: +1 (706) 369-1650
Email: getwarm@gmail.com
Website: http://www.thewarmsupercomputer.com
Website: http://www.last.fm/label/Warm/
Website: http://www.myspace.com/warmelectronicrecordings

Genres: Alternative Rock

Record label based in Athens, Georgia.

Warner Bros. Records Nashville

20 Music Square East, 3rd Floor
Nashville, TN 37203-4344
Fax: +1 (615) 214-1567
Website: http://www.warnermusicnashville.com
Website: https://www.facebook.com/WarnerMusicNashville

Genres: Country

Country label based in Nashville Tennessee.

Warner Bros. Records

3300 Warner Boulevard
Burbank, CA 91505
Email: fansupport@wbr.com
Website: http://www.warnerbrosrecords.com

Genres: All types of music

Accepts submissions via established agents and managers only. Music sent direct will be returned without being reviewed.

Warner Music Group (WMG)

1633 Broadway
New York, NY 10019
Website: http://www.wmg.com
Website: https://www.facebook.com/warnermusicgroup

Genres: All types of music

No direct submissions. Demos should be submitted to specific label via an established industry professional, such as a manager, agent, lawyer, journalist, or existing artist, etc.

Washington Square Music

Email: info@washingtonsquaremusic.com
Website: http://washingtonsquaremusic.com
Website: https://www.facebook.com/washingtonsquaremusic

Genres: All types of music

Independent record label based in New York.

Watertower Music

4000 Warner Boulevard, Building 76
Burbank, CA 91522
Email: wtmsupport@Warnerbros.com
Website: http://www.watertower-music.com
Website: https://soundcloud.com/watertowermusic

Genres: Soundtracks

Record label based in Los Angeles, California, specialising in movie soundtracks.

Waveform Records

Email: webguest@waveformhq.com
Website: http://www.waveformrecords.com
Website: https://www.facebook.com/Waveform-Records-31654761963/

Genres: Downtempo Electronic; Chill; Ambient

Handles mid to downtempo chill and ambient music they call "exotic electronica".

Send query by email with links to music online.

Wax Records Inc.

Email: info@waxrecords.com
Website: http://www.waxrecords.com

Genres: Pop; Rock

Always looking to expand their roster with new and exciting talent. Send query by email with links to music online. No large file attachments.

Waxploitation Records

Los Angeles
Email: artists@waxploitation.com
Website: http://waxploitation.com
Website: https://soundcloud.com/waxploitation

Genres: Hip-Hop

Record label based in Los Angeles, California.

We Are Free

61 Greenpoint Ave. #508
Brooklyn, NY 11222
Fax: +1 (917) 720-9905
Email: info@wearefree.com
Website: http://www.nowwearefree.com

Genres: Pop

Record label based in Brooklyn, New York.

Wicked Cool Records

New York
Website: http://wickedcoolrecords.com
Website: https://www.facebook.com/WickedCoolRecords/

Genres: Rock and Roll

Label based in New York, created in 2007 to support new Rock and Roll.

Wild Records

Los Angeles, CA
Website: https://wildrecordsusa.com
Website: https://twitter.com/wildrecords

Genres: Blues; Garage; Rockabilly; Soul; Surf

Contact: Reb Kennedy

Record label based in Los Angeles, California.

Word Records

25 Music Square West
Nashville, TN 37203
Fax: +1 (615) 726-7886
Website: http://www.wordrecords.com

Genres: Contemporary; Christian; Country; Hip-Hop; Rap; Rock

Faith-based record label based in Nashville, Tennessee.

Yamaha Entertainment Group of America

Franklin, TN
Website: http://www.yamahaentertainmentgroup.com
Website: https://www.facebook.com/YamahaEntertainmentGroup

Genres: All types of music

Entertainment group based in Franklin, Tennessee, responsible for the growth and support of the parent company brand through artist relations, endorsements, concert and film production, media operations, and product placements in film, television and major publications.

Yep Roc Records

449-A Trollingwood Road
Haw River, NC 27258
Email: info@yeprocmusicgroup.com
Email: billy@yeprocmusicgroup.com
Website: http://www.yeproc.com
Website: https://www.facebook.com/yeproc

Genres: Blues; Country; Folk; Pop; Rock; Roots

Contact: Glenn Dicker; Billy Maupin; Charlie Painter

Record label based in Haw River, North Carolina. Send demo with press kit etc. by post. Everything received will be listened to, but a response is not guaranteed.

UK Record Labels

For the most up-to-date listings of these and hundreds of other record labels, visit https://www.musicsocket.com/recordlabels

To claim your ***free*** *access to the site, please see the back of this book.*

!K7 Records

217 Chester House
Kennington Park
1-3 Brixton Road
London
SW9 6DE
Website: http://www.k7.com
Website: https://soundcloud.com/k7-records

Genres: Electronic

Record label with offices in Berlin, New York, and London. Send query via online form, with details about yourself, how you can be contacted, and why you think your music is special. Response not guaranteed.

0114 Records

Email: 0114records.submissions@gmail.com
Website: https://0114records.com

Genres: Alternative; Rock; Folk; Garage; Hard Rock; Indie; Punk; Reggae; Singer-Songwriter; Ska

Independent record label based in Sheffield. Accepts soundcloud and youtube links by email from UK residents over 18 with original music.

Abattoir Blues

Email: abattoirbluesrecords@hotmail.com
Website: http://www.abattoirbluesrecords.com
Website: https://soundcloud.com/abattoir-blues-records

Genres: Blues; Rock; Alternative; Garage; Guitar based; Psychedelic; Punk; Punk Rock

Record Label based in Manchester – promoters of scuzz, blues, psych, rock. Send query by email with links to music online.

Acorn Records

Email: acornrecords@hotmail.com
Website: https://twitter.com/acornrecordsuk

Genres: All types of music

Send query by email with MP3 attachments.

The Adult Teeth Recording Company

Email: hello@adultteeth.co.uk
Website: http://www.adultteeth.co.uk
Website: https://www.facebook.com/adultteeth/

Genres: Alternative Rock; Experimental Pop; Indie; Electronic; Ambient

Record label founded in 2012, dealing in alternate rock, experimental pop, indie, electronic, ambient and spoken word. Formats: vinyl, CD, cassette and digital.

Akira

Email: stevie@akirarecords.com
Email: info@akirarecords.com
Website: http://akirarecords.com
Website: https://soundcloud.com/akira-records

Genres: Folk; Rock; Indie; Electronic

Label and Production House intent on exposing the best new talents and the most exciting music. Send query by email with links to music online. No MP3 attachments.

Alex King Records

Website: https://sites.google.com/view/akingrecords/contact-us

Genres: Electronic Experimental Psychedelic Uptempo Urban; Club Dance Disco Drum and Bass Dub Dubstep Garage Glitch Grime Hardcore IDM House Melodicore Pop R&B Remix Trance Techno

Artists receive at least 75% of royalties, although most of the time it will be higher. We do not charge for distribution.

We are semi-open. Send demos via form on website.

ALM Records

Email: alm-records@outlook.com
Website: https://alm-records.co.uk
Website: https://www.facebook.com/ALMRecords

Genres: Metal; Rock

Record label based in North East England, looking to sign local rock and metal bands.

Alya Records

Room 16
The John Banner Centre
620 Attercliffe Road
Sheffield
S9 3QS
Email: autumn@dmfdigital.com
Email: hello@alyarecords.com
Website: http://www.alyarecords.co.uk
Website: https://www.facebook.com/AlyaRecords/

Genres: All types of music

Record label based in Sheffield. Send demos via upload page on website.

AnalogueTrash Ltd

83 Ducie Street
Manchester
M1 2JQ
Email: hello@analoguetrash.com
Website: http://www.analoguetrash.com
Website: https://soundcloud.com/analoguetrash

Genres: Alternative

Record label based in Manchester. Send demos by email.

Anchorage Records

Glasgow
Email: anchoragerecords@gmail.com
Website: https://anchoragerecords.wordpress.com

Genres: All types of music

Record label based in Glasgow. Prefers rock music, but will consider all genres. Send query by email with MP3s or links to music online.

Associated Music International (AMI) Media

Red Bus House
34 Salisbury Street
London
NW8 8QE
Fax: +44 (0) 20 7723 3064
Email: eliot@amimedia.co.uk
Website: http://www.amimedia.co.uk

Genres: All types of music

Send query by email with bio and links to streamable music online.

At the Helm Records

Brighton
East Sussex
BN1
Email: jeremy@atthehelmrecords.com
Website: http://www.atthehelmrecords.com
Website: https://soundcloud.com/at-the-helm-records

Genres: Americana

Independent record label based in Brighton, specialising in "un-scrubbed" Americana.

Atlantic Records

27 Wright's Lane
London
W8 5SW
Website: http://atlanticrecords.co.uk

Genres: All types of music

UK branch of international record label. Send demos by post on CD.

Audio Vendor

Email: contact@audiovendor.com
Website: http://www.audiovendor.com
Website: https://soundcloud.com/audiovendor

Genres: Experimental; Folk; Indie; Rock

Independent record label made up of independent artists, songwriters and producers. Send query by email with MP3 attachments or links to music online.

Aveline Records

London
Email: info@avelinerecords.com
Website: http://www.avelinerecords.com
Website: https://twitter.com/avelinerecords

Genres: Americana; Country; Folk; Singer-Songwriter

London-based independent record label.

Avenoir Records

40 Hawkes Way
Kent
ME15 9ZL
Email: enquiries@avenoirrecords.com
Website: https://avenoirrecords.com
Website: https://twitter.com/AvenoirOfficial

Genres: All types of music

Music company based in London, offering artist management, music production, and record label. Send demos by post.

Axtone

Email: contact@axtone.com
Website: https://www.axtone.com

Genres: Dance; House; Disco; Dubstep; Electronic; Techno; Trance

Send demos via online submission system. See website for details.

Bad Bat Records

Chester
Email: badbatrecords@gmail.com
Website: https://badbatrecords.bandcamp.com
Website: https://soundcloud.com/badbatrecords

Genres: Alternative; Electronic; Ambient; Experimental; Dance

Independent record label specialising in alternative, electronic, ambient, dance and experimental music. Looking for artists to support and release.

Battle Worldwide

Brighton
Email: hello@battleworldwiderecordings.com
Website: http://battleworldwiderecordings.com
Website: https://soundcloud.com/battle

Genres: All types of music

Independent record label and publishing (music and literature) company based in Brighton. Send query by email with links to streaming music online. Response only if interested.

Bear Love Records

Email: bearloverecords@hotmail.co.uk
Website: http://bearloverecords.bigcartel.com

Genres: Alternative; Americana; Folk

Accepts approaches from bands and artists who play regular gigs. Send query by email with links to music online.

Beatphreak

Manchester
Email: hello@beatphreak.co.uk
Website: http://beatphreak.co.uk
Website: https://soundcloud.com/beatphreak

Genres: Dance

Dance label based in Manchester. Send query by email with MP3 demos.

Bespoke Records

20B Preston Park Avenue
Brighton
BN1 6HL
Email: info@bespokerecords.com
Website: http://www.bespokerecords.com
Website: https://www.facebook.com/bespokerecords

Genres: All types of music

Indie label on a crusade to change the music industry. Aims to value creatives above their creative products. No unsolicited submissions.

BFS Records

Blackfrog Studios Ltd
Unit 9 Jefferson Way
Thame, Oxfordshire
OX9 3SZ
Email: zoe@bfsrecords.co.uk
Email: info@bfsrecords.co.uk
Website: https://www.bfsrecords.co.uk
Website: https://www.facebook.com/BFSrecordsuk

Genres: All types of music

Contact: Zoe Bourke

Record label based in Thame, Oxfordshire. Send query by email with links to your social media and music online.

Big Bear Records

PO Box 944
Edgbaston
Birmingham
West Midlands
B16 8UT
Email: admin@bigbearmusic.com
Website: http://www.bigbearmusic.com
Website: http://www.birminghamjazzfestival.com

Genres: Jazz; Swing; Blues

Possibly the UK's longest-established independent record label, has recorded jazz, swing and blues [and a little bit of rock] for more than 40 years. It is now available on iTunes world-wide as well as being conventionally distributed.

Birdland Records

Email: hq@birdlandrecords.com
Website: https://birdlandrecords.com
Website: https://soundcloud.com/birdlandrecords

Genres: Singer-Songwriter

Independent record label. Send query by email with links to music online.

Black Bleach Records

Manchester
Email: blackbleachrecords@gmail.com
Website: http://blackbleachrecords.com
Website: https://www.facebook.com/blackbleachrecords

Genres: Alternative; Electronic; Garage; Indie; Post Punk; Punk; Punk Rock; Shoegaze

Indie label based in Manchester.

Blak Hand Records

Email: blakhandrecords@gmail.com
Website: https://blakhandrecords.bandcamp.com
Website: https://www.facebook.com/blakhandrecords

Genres: Garage; Rock; Alternative; Guitar based; Psychedelic Rock; Punk

Independent cassette label based in the UK, specialising in psych, garage, rock and fuzz.

Bluesky Pie Records

Folkestone
Kent
Email: spies@blueskypierecords.com
Email: press@blueskypierecords.com

Website: https://www.facebook.com/blueskypierecords/

Genres: All types of music

Not-for-profit, ethical record label. Send query by email with MP3s or links to music online.

Box Records

Newcastle Upon Tyne
Email: matt@box-records.com
Website: http://box-records.com

Genres: Experimental; Folk; Psychedelic Rock; Underground; Punk; Doom; Alternative Folk

Record label based in Newcastle. Send query by email with links to music online.

Breakfast Records LLP

Bristol
Email: dan@breakfastrecords.co.uk
Email: josh@breakfastrecords.co.uk
Website: http://breakfastrecords.co.uk
Website: https://www.facebook.com/breakfastlabel

Genres: Folk; Garage; Guitar based; Indie; Punk; Punk Rock

Contact: Dan Anthony; Josh Jarman

Record label based in Bristol. Send demos by email.

Brightonsfinest

Brighton
Email: theteam@brightonsfinest.com
Website: https://www.brightonsfinest.com
Website: https://soundcloud.com/BrightonsFinest

Genres: Alternative; Dance; Electronic; Folk; Indie; Pop; Rock

An online music magazine and record label. Send query by email with MP3s or links to music online.

Brock Wild

London
Email: brockwildrec@gmail.com
Website: http://www.brockwildrec.com
Website: https://soundcloud.com/brockwildrec

Genres: House; Acid

Management company based in London. Send query by email with links to music online.

Bubblewrap Collective

The Laundry
Rear of 35 Romilly Cres
Canton
Cardiff
CF11 9NP
Email: rich@bubblewrapcollective.co.uk
Website: http://www.bubblewrapcollective.co.uk
Website: https://soundcloud.com/bubblewrapcollective

Genres: Folk; Indie; Electronic; Alternative

A collective of Cardiff creatives, aiming to create the perfect balance between a design studio and record label. Send demos on CD by post.

Canigou Records

Email: canigourecords@gmail.com
Website: http://canigourecords.co.uk
Website: https://soundcloud.com/canigourecords

Genres: Ambient; Electronic; Folk; Lo-fi; Shoegaze

Record label and community of musicians and visual artists. Send query by email with MP3s or links to music online.

CCT Records

45 Staple Lodge Road
Northfield
Birmingham
B31 3BZ
Website: http://milwaukie2003.wixsite.com/cctrecords

Genres: Alternative; Electronic; Ambient; Dubstep; Hip-Hop; Techno

Record label based in Birmingham. Send query via online form with links to music online, or submit files via website dropbox.

Chalkpit Records Ltd

Email: chalkpitrecords@gmail.com
Website: https://www.chalkpitrecords.com

Genres: Alternative; Funk; Indie; Pop; Soul

Contact: Silas Gregory

Record label based on the Isle of Wight. Send query by email with MP3 attachments or links to music online.

ChillnBass

Email: Patrick@chillnbass.com
Email: Clement@chillnbass.com
Website: http://www.chillnbass.com/
Website: https://twitter.com/Patitude1

Genres: Commercial; Dance

Contact: Patrick Ruane; Clement Ignace

Label with studios in Paris and London.

Circus Recordings

Website: http://www.circusrecordings.com
Website: https://www.facebook.com/CircusRecordings

Genres: House; Techno

Send query via Facebook or contact page of website, with links to music online.

Cold Spring

62 Victoria Street
Glossop
Derbyshire
SK13 8HY
Email: demos@coldspring.co.uk
Email: info@coldspring.co.uk
Website: http://coldspring.co.uk

Genres: Ambient; Industrial; Noise Core; Power Electronic; Doom; Experimental; Soundtracks

Record label / mailorder store / distributor based in Derbyshire. Send demos by post or send links to music online by email, but do not send attachments by email. Replies to all demos, but do not expect an immediate reply.

Coloursounds

Leeds
Website: https://soundcloud.com/coloursoundsuk
Website: https://www.facebook.com/coloursoundsuk

Genres: Electronic; House; Disco; Indie; Pop

Works closely with emerging artists that represent the best of Electronic music; House, Nu Disco, Indie, Pop.

Columbia Records

9 Derry Street
London
W8 5HY
Website: http://www.columbia.co.uk
Website: https://www.facebook.com/ColumbiaRecordsUK/

Genres: All types of music

UK office of the oldest surviving brand name in pre-recorded sound.

Come Play With Me

Leeds
Email: tony@cpwm.co
Email: sam@cpwm.co
Website: http://cpwm.co
Website: https://www.facebook.com/ComePlayWith

Genres: All types of music

Record label based in Leeds. Accepts submissions from artists in the Leeds area (including Bradford, Calderdale, Kirklees, Barnsley, Wakefield, Selby, York, Harrogate, and Craven). Submit via online submission form on website.

Copro Productions

P.O. Box 4429
Henley-on-Thames
Oxfordshire
RG9 1GH
Fax: +44 (0) 1491 412571
Website: http://www.coprorecords.co.uk
Website: http://www.myspace.com/coprorecords

Genres: Heavy Metal; Punk; Rock; Indie; Guitar based

Contact: A&R Department

Send demos by post on audio CD with contact name, band name, email address and phone number written clearly on the CD itself, not just the packaging. Include band bio and photo. No submissions by email, and will not listen to music online / check out your website. Do not query or follow-up by phone. Will contact if interested.

Dance To The Radio

Munro House
Duke St
Leeds
LS9 8AG
Email: sally@futuresoundgroup.com
Email: sam@futuresoundgroup.com
Website: http://www.dancetotheradio.com
Website: https://www.facebook.com/dancetotheradio

Genres: Experimental; Indie

Music group including label, publishing, and artist management. Send demos by email.

Decca Records

364–366 Kensington High Street
London
W14 8NS
Website: http://decca.com
Website: https://www.facebook.com/deccarecords

Genres: All types of music

Describes itself as a legendary British record label, which has been home to "some of the greatest recording artists ever".

Deek Recordings

Website: http://www.deekrecordings.co.uk
Website: https://soundcloud.com/deekrecordings

Genres: All types of music

Contact: Nathan Jenkins

Send query by email with links to music online.

Defenders Ent

Industrial Estate
3A Juno Way
London
SE14 5RW
Email: music@defendersent.com
Email: info@defendersent.com
Website: https://defendersent.com
Website: https://www.facebook.com/DefendersEnt

Genres: Dance; Reggae; R&B; Rap

Record label based in London. Send query by email with links to music online. No MP3 attachments.

Demon Music Group

BBC Worldwide Ltd
Television Centre
101 Wood Lane
London
W12 7FA
Email: info@demonmusicgroup.co.uk
Website: http://www.demonmusicgroup.co.uk
Website: https://www.facebook.com/DemonMusicGroup

Genres: Alternative; Indie

Describes itself as the UK's largest independent record company. Specialises in the reissues of catalogue titles so does not sign new acts.

Dirty Bingo Records

Flat 254 Hardy House
Poynders Garden
Clapham
London
SW4 8PQ
Email: dirtybingorecords@greedbag.com
Website: https://dirtybingorecords.greedbag.com

Genres: Alternative; Electronic; Indie; Indie Pop

Record label based in London. Send query by email with MP3 or links to music online.

Disconnect Disconnect Records

Email: disconnectdisconnect@hotmail.co.uk
Website: https://disconnectdisconnectrecords.bigcartel.com
Website: https://www.facebook.com/disconnectdisconnectrecords

Genres: Emo; Pop Punk; Post Punk; Punk; Punk Rock; Hardcore

Will accept soundcloud links by email, but prefers physical submissions by post. Send email or facebook message requesting postal address.

Discovering Arts Music Group (DAMG)

Email: discovering@damg.co.uk
Website: http://discoveringartsmusicgroup.com
Website: https://soundcloud.com/damg-records

Genres: All types of music

Media company offering management, publishing, record company, and more. Always on the lookout for new talent: use demo submission form on website.

DJD Music Ltd

2A Fairfield Road
Heysham
Email: djd@gmx.com
Website: https://www.djdmusicltd.com
Website: https://www.facebook.com/ukglobal.uk/

Genres: Acoustic Alternative Avant-Garde Electronic Hard Heavy Ambient Dance Hip-Hop Indie Instrumental Metal Pop Punk R&B Rap Reggae New Wave Industrial Experimental Progressive Folk Guitar based Lounge Roots Singer-Songwriter Soul Spoken Word Synthpop

Contact: David John Duckworth

An artist product promotion and online digital distribution company integrated into an Independent UK and International record label. The company caters specifically for unsigned artists, focusing on the traditional ideals of a standard record label but working more closely with the increasingly popular and fast-growing online marketplace. Alongside their distribution aspects, the company offers other services. For further information and details. Visit our website and other locations on the internet by searching through Google.

Doing Life Records

Liverpool
Email: doinglifeltd@gmail.com
Website: https://doingliferecords.bandcamp.com
Website: https://www.facebook.com/doingliferecords/

Genres: Alternative; Emo; Indie; Rock; Singer-Songwriter

Not-for-profit label focused on community and developing the next generation of alternative Liverpool musicians. Send query by email with links to music / EPK online. No attachments.

Don't Try

Suffolk
Email: ben@donttryrecords.com
Website: https://www.donttryrecords.com
Website: https://www.facebook.com/donttryuk

Genres: Alternative; Indie; Pop

An independent record label, music PR agency and management service based in Suffolk. Send query by email with links to music online.

Donut Records

Bristol
Email: donutrecords@hotmail.com
Website: https://donutrecords.bandcamp.com
Website: https://soundcloud.com/donut-records

Genres: Indie; Psychedelic Rock; Rock and Roll

Independent record label based in Bristol, releasing quarterly compilations of unsigned artists. Send query by email with links to music online. No MP3 attachments.

Dose Entertainment
Keys Court
82-84 Moseley St
Birmingham
B12 0RT
Email: info@doseentertainments.com
Website: https://www.doseentertainments.com/doseent-the-label

Genres: Hip-Hop; R&B; Rap

Independent record label founded in 2017 in Birmingham. Send query by email. Prefers links to music online, but will accept MP3s.

Double Denim Records
Email: new@doubledenimrecords.com
Website: http://doubledenimrecords.com
Website: https://www.facebook.com/doubledenimrecords

Genres: Electronic; Pop

Record label founded in 2010. Send query by email with links to music online.

Dove Records
Email: vjartistmanagement@yahoo.com
Website: https://www.facebook.com/vjmediadoverecords

Genres: Contemporary Christian; Gospel; Rap; Reggae

Send query by email with links to music and videos online.

Dreamscope Media Group (DMG)
71-75 Shelton Street
Covent Garden
London
WC2H 9JQ
Email: info@dreamscopemediagroup.co.uk
Website: https://www.dreamscopemediagroup.co.uk
Website: https://www.facebook.com/DreamscopeMG

Genres: Country; Folk; Pop; R&B; Rock; Soul

Record label based in London. No unsolicited post. Accepts queries by email only.

Droma Records
Email: dromarecords@gmail.com
Website: https://dromarecords.bandcamp.com

Genres: All types of music

Record label based in the West Midlands. Always interested in a chat about a potential new project. Send query by email or via website.

Easy Life Records
Email: info@easyliferecords.com
Website: http://easyliferecords.com
Website: https://www.facebook.com/easyliferecords/

Genres: Alternative

Independent label formed in 2014. Send query via online submission form with links to social media and your music online.

Electric Honey Music
Email: electrichoney1992@gmail.com
Website: https://www.facebook.com/electrichoneymusic
Website: https://www.twitter.com/ElectricHoney25

Genres: All types of music

College record label based in Glasgow, Scotland. Run by Music Business students. Send query by email with band name, short bio, your location, and links to your music online.

Elevate Records
Website: https://www.elevaterecords.co.uk
Website: https://soundcloud.com/elevaterecordsuk

Genres: Drum and Bass

Submit demos via online submission system. See website for details.

Endearment Records
Email: endearmentrecords@gmail.com
Website: https://www.facebook.com/endearmentrecords

Genres: Indie

Record label releasing mainly indie music, but willing to consider all genres. Send query by email with links to music online.

Eromeda Records

Email: eromedarecords@gmail.com
Website: https://eromedaentertainment.com
Website: https://www.facebook.com/EromedaEntertainment

Genres: All types of music, except: R&B; Pop

Diverse media company which operates as a music label and as a film and music video production company.

Eton Messy Records

Bristol / London
Email: etonmessysubmissions@gmail.com
Email: info@etonmessy.com
Website: https://www.etonmessy.com
Website: https://www.facebook.com/Etonmessy

Genres: Dance; Electronic

Record label based in Bristol and London. All submissions must be streaming links and photos on flickr or similar. Submit details by email.

Everyday Records

Email: info@everydayrecords.com
Email: media@everydayrecords.com
Website: https://www.everydayrecords.com
Website: https://www.facebook.com/EverydayRecords

Genres: Acoustic Alternative Classic Contemporary Mainstream Melodic Progressive Soulful Blues Classical World Swing Soundtracks Soul Singer-Songwriter Rhythm and Blues Roots Rockabilly Rock and Roll Pop R&B New Age MOR Jazz Instrumental Indie Guitar based Folk

An independent record company, run by in-house composers and songwriters and based in the North of England.

Evil Genius Records

68a Kingston Road
Leatherhead
KT22 7BW
Email: info@egrltd.com
Website: https://www.egrltd.com

Genres: All types of music

Send demos by post or by email as links to music online.

Explosive Beatz Records

Birmingham
Email: djpariswwalker@gmail.com
Website: https://explosivebeatz.com
Website: https://www.facebook.com/ExplosiveBeatzMusic/

Genres: Dance; Hip-Hop; R&B

Record label based in Birmingham. Send query by email with bio and MP3 attachment.

Fame Throwa Records

Fax: +44 (0)
Email: famethrowauk@gmail.com
Website: https://www.famethrowa.com
Website: https://www.facebook.com/famethrowarecords

Genres: All types of music

A collective that seeks to support and promote South-East London's wealth of independent music. Send query by email.

Fire Records

Email: james@firerecords.com
Website: http://www.firerecords.com
Website: https://soundcloud.com/firerecords

Genres: Experimental; New Wave; Post Punk; Psychedelic Rock

Contact: James Nicholls

Send query by email with links to music online. No physical submissions.

Flowers in the Dustbin

Glasgow
Email: info@flowersinthedustbin.org
Website: http://flowersinthedustbin.org
Website: https://soundcloud.com/flowersinthedustbin

Genres: All types of music

Contact: Stephen McKee

Record label based in Glasgow. Send query by email with links to music online.

Focused Silence

Email: hello@focusedsilence.com
Website: https://www.focusedsilence.com
Website: https://soundcloud.com/focused-silence

Genres: Experimental; Electronic; Jazz; Avant-Garde

Contact: Andy Backhouse

Independent record label, publisher and music supervisor, releasing and licensing various electronic, folio and jazz music. Submit demo via we transfer. See website for details.

Forward Motion Records (UK)

Email: fwdmotionrecs@yahoo.com
Website: https://fwdmotionrecs.wixsite.com/forwardmotionuk
Website: https://www.facebook.com/Forward-Motion-Records-UK-409609599823223/

Genres: House; Break Beat; Funky House; Electronic; Hard House; Tribal House

House Music record label based in the North of England. Submit demo via link on website.

Fox Records

Email: jd@foxrecords.net
Website: http://www.foxrecords.limitedrun.com
Website: https://www.facebook.com/foxrecordings/

Genres: Alternative

Alternative label accepting queries with SoundCloud links by email.

Freaks R Us

Email: tim@freaksrus.net
Website: http://www.freaksrus.net
Website: https://www.facebook.com/freakartists

Genres: Alternative; Electronic; Experimental; Post Punk

Record label and artist management. Send query by email with MP3 attachments or links to music online.

Futurist Recordings

Email: shawndavis22@hotmail.com
Website: https://milwaukie2003.wixsite.com/futuristrecordings
Website: https://www.facebook.com/Futuristrecordings/

Genres: Experimental; Acid House; Techno; Underground

Deep cutting edge experimental techno and acid house label. Submit demo via online submission form on website.

Gameplan Records

Email: hello@gameplanrecords.com
Website: https://www.gameplanrecords.com
Website: https://soundcloud.com/user-575401443

Genres: All types of music

Record label, also offering artist development services.

Ganbei Records

Shelton Street
London
Email: info@ganbeirecords.com
Email: paul@ganbeirecords.com
Website: http://www.ganbeirecords.com
Website: https://ganbeirecords.bandcamp.com

Genres: Alternative; Folk; Post Punk; Psychedelic Rock; Rock

Record label that aims to help musicians release and promote their music. Send query by email with links to music online.

Geilston Records

Email: geilstonrecords@gmail.com
Website: https://www.facebook.com/

GeilstonRecords/
Website: https://twitter.com/GeilstonRecords

Genres: Emo; Indie; Punk

Independent record label from the West of Scotland.

God Unknown Records

Email: godunknownrecs@gmail.com
Website: http://www.godunknownrecs.com
Website: https://www.facebook.com/godunknownrecords

Genres: Experimental; Psychedelic Rock; Garage

Describes itself as "a label bringing you the best heavy and far out sounds around".Send query by email with links to music online.

Graphite Records

c/o Northern Music Co.
1st & 2nd Floor
5 Victoria Road
Saltaire
Shipley
West Yorkshire
BD18 3LA
Fax: +44 (0) 1274 730097
Email: andy@northernmusic.co.uk
Email: george@northernmusic.co.uk
Website: http://www.graphiterecords.net
Website: https://soundcloud.com/graphiterecordsltd

Genres: Alternative; Rock; Metal

Independent record label based in Shipley. Send demos by email.

Harbourtown Records

36 The Gill
Ulverston
Cumbria
LA12 7BP
Email: info@harbourtownrecords.com
Website: http://www.harbourtownrecords.com

Genres: Acoustic; Folk; Roots; Traditional

Record label based in Cumbria. Send demo with bio by post.

Haystack Records

Manchester
Email: enquiries@haystackrecords.co.uk
Website: https://www.haystackrecords.co.uk
Website: https://soundcloud.com/haystack-records

Genres: Folk; Acoustic

Independent record label specialising in British Folk and Acoustic music. Send query by email with links to music online.

Heist or Hit Records

12 Hilton Street
Manchester
M1 1JF
Email: team@heistorhitrecords.com
Website: http://www.heistorhitrecords.com
Website: https://www.facebook.com/heistorhitrecords

Genres: Acoustic; Alternative; Indie

Independent record label based in Manchester. Send postcard with email address and links to your music online. Everything sent this way will receive a response. No guarantee of response to any links sent by email.

HQ Familia

38 Charles Street
Leicester
LE1 1FB
Email: yasin@hqrecording.co.uk
Email: yasinelashrafi1980@live.co.uk
Website: http://www.hqrecording.co.uk
Website: https://soundcloud.com/hqrecording

Genres: Electronic; Urban

Contact: Yasin El-Ashrafi

A record label and collective of like minded artists, producers and creatives with the focus on pushing the boundaries of art and music.

Hudson Records

Sheffield
Email: hudson@hudsonrecords.co.uk
Website: https://www.hudsonrecords.co.uk

Website: https://soundcloud.com/hudsonpodcast/sets

Genres: Folk

Independent record label based in Sheffield, dealing mainly in folk. Send query by email with links to music online.

Hyperdub Records

Email: info@hyperdub.net
Email: Marcus@hyperdub.net
Website: https://hyperdub.net
Website: https://www.facebook.com/Hyperdub.Records

Genres: Electronic; Leftfield

Record label based in London. Send query by email with links to music online (private soundcloud link preferred).

i/o Recordings

Website: https://sites.google.com/view/iorecordings/home

Genres: Hip-Hop Grime R&B Rap; Urban

We are looking for artists and producers to join our team.

We would be able to offer:
Promotion, Album Cover Design, Studio Arrangement, Producing and more along with benefits.

Please give us an email so we can further explain and put you in the right section :)

Thank you!

Incessant Records

2 Angel Square
London
EC1V 1NY
Email: contact@incessantrecords.co.uk
Website: http://incessantrecords.co.uk
Website: https://www.facebook.com/incessantrecords

Genres: Dance; Pop; R&B; Rock

Record label with offices in London and LA. Send query via online form with links to music online and social media.

J and J Records

Email: 16.jjrecords@gmail.com
Website: http://16jjrecords.wixsite.com/jjrecords

Genres: All types of music

A record company based in Poole, Dorset. The company mainly produces music but does create other types of media alongside that. Please take a look around the site. We would be happy to answer any questions you may have in the concats section of the page.

Jeepers! Music

Brighton
Email: nick@jeepersmusic.co.uk
Email: info@jeepersmusic.co.uk
Website: http://jeepersmusic.com
Website: https://www.facebook.com/jeepersmusic/

Genres: House

Contact: Nick Hook

House label based in Brighton.Send submissions by email with demos as MP3s or private Soundcloud links.

Jost Music

Email: info@jostmusic.co.uk
Website: https://www.jostmusic.co.uk
Website: https://www.soundcloud.com/user-883894064

Genres: All types of music

Record label and artist management. Send query by email with links to music online.

Kaneda Records

Newcastle
Email: kanedarecords@hotmail.com
Website: http://www.kanedarecords.com
Website: https://soundcloud.com/kanedarecords

Genres: Electronic; Dance; Hip-Hop

Record label based in Newcastle. Send demos by email.

Keep Me Young (KMY)

Email: Dan@keepmeyoung.uk
Website: https://www.keepmeyoung.uk
Website: https://www.facebook.com/KeepMeYoungUK

Genres: All types of music

Mainly a music management company, but also run an indie label. Open to all genres, but particularly interested in acoustic and pop. Send query by email with links to music online.

Kokeshi

London
Email: kokeshi@iheartkokeshi.com
Website: http://iheartkokeshi.com
Website: https://www.facebook.com/iheartkokeshi

Genres: Electronic; Dubstep; Garage; Grime; Chill

Record label based in London. Send query by email with links to music online.

Lapsang House

Email: hello@lapsanghouse.com
Website: https://lapsanghouse.com
Website: https://www.facebook.com/LapsangHouse/

Genres: All types of music

Record label based in South East London. Send query by email with links to music online.

Last Night From Glasgow

Email: ian@lastnightfromglasgow.com
Website: http://www.lastnightfromglasgow.com
Website: https://www.facebook.com/LastNightFromGlasgow

Genres: All types of music

Describes itself as the world's first crowd funded not-for-profit record label. Send query by email with soundcloud / dropbox links.

Less is More Music Ltd

Unit 36, 88-90
Hatton Garden
London
EC1N 8PN
Email: info@lessismoremusic.co.uk
Website: http://lessismoremusic.co.uk
Website: http://soundcloud.com/limm_uk/dropbox

Genres: Grime; Hip-Hop; Jazz; R&B; Soul

Independent, soul-orientated record company based in London. Send demos via soundcloud dropbox.

LGM Records

52 Tottenham Court Road
London
W1T 2EH
Email: info@lgmrecords.co.uk
Website: http://lgmrecords.co.uk
Website: https://www.facebook.com/LGMRecordsUK/

Genres: All types of music

A record label and music publisher based in London.

The label have been featured in The Times and on BBC World News and their artists have been enjoyed widespread exposure on BBC Radio 1, Radio 2, 6Music, Radio X, Amazing Radio and Manchester XS, as well as, articles and excellent reviews in The NME, The Times, The Metro, The Guardian, Mojo, UNCUT, the Evening Standard and many more.

Libertino

Email: gruff.owen@libertinorecords.com
Website: https://www.libertinorecords.com
Website: https://www.facebook.com/Libertinorecords/

Genres: Alternative

Alternative label releasing both Welsh and English language bands. Send query by email with MP3s or links to music online.

Lo Recordings
2(b) Swanfield Street
London
E2 7DS
Email: info@hub100.com
Email: jon@hub100.com
Website: https://www.lorecordings.com
Website: https://soundcloud.com/lo-recordings

Genres: Electronic

Contact: Jon Tye

Record label with offices in London and Millbrook, Cornwall. Send demo by email as links or MP3 attachment.

Loner Noise
Email: michael@lonernoise.com
Website: https://www.lonernoise.com
Website: https://soundcloud.com/lonernoise

Genres: Rock; Alternative

Contact: Michael Edward

Send demos as streams by email or through online form. No files.

Lost in the Manor
Email: chris@lostinthemanor.co.uk
Email: nick@lostinthemanor.co.uk
Website: http://www.lostinthemanor.co.uk

Genres: Acoustic; Alternative; Dance; Folk; Hip-Hop; Jazz; Pop; Reggae; Rock

Always seeking new bands and artists. See website for details on how to approach.

Mayfield Records
2A Down End Road
Drayton
Hampshire
PO6 1HT
Email: info@mayfieldrecords.com
Website: https://mayfieldrecords.com
Website: https://www.facebook.com/mayfieldrecordsltd

Genres: All types of music

Recording studio, record label, and video production. Send query by email with links to music online.

Me & You Music
Email: meandyoumusic@yahoo.co.uk
Website: https://www.facebook.com/meandyoumusic1

Genres: All types of music

Artist management, record label, promotions, and online PR. Send query by email with MP3s or links to music online.

Melee Recording Group
Birmingham
Email: info@mrg-group.co.uk
Website: http://mrg-group.co.uk

Genres: Hip-Hop; Urban

Contact: Chris Brown; Nathaniel Thompson

Hip hop label based in Birmingham. Specialises in urban music but willing to consider music from any genre.

Mellowtone Records
Static Gallery
23 Roscoe Lane
Liverpool
L1 9JD
Email: info@mellowtonerecords.com
Website: http://mellowtonerecords.com/
Website: https://www.facebook.com/mellowtoneclub

Genres: Acoustic; Roots; Singer-Songwriter; Country; Folk; Blues

Contact: David McTague

Record label based in Liverpool. Send query by email with links to music online or MP3 attachments.

MHM
Email: hq@mhmmusic.com
Website: http://www.mhmmusic.com
Website: https://www.facebook.com/mhmmusichq/

Genres: All types of music

Records, publishing, distribution and management.

Midnineties

1st Floor
32 Queens Terrace
Southampton
SO14 3BQ

Email: sikmon@midnineties.co
Email: jay@midnineties.co
Website: http://midnineties.co
Website: https://www.instagram.com/midnineties/

Genres: Electronic Club Underground Urban Garage Glitch House

Contact: Simon Hassett

Record label out of Southampton, UK. Specialising in deep house, bass house, garage, future bass & trap and more.

Modern Sky

Email: info@modernsky.uk
Website: http://modernsky.uk
Website: https://soundcloud.com/modernsky-uk

Genres: All types of music

Music entertainment and events company based in the North of England.

Musical Bear Records

Email: info@musicalbearrecords.co.uk
Website: http://www.musicalbearrecords.co.uk

Genres: All types of music

Provides artists with a platform to further their careers by offering digital / CD / Vinyl distribution across the globe. Send query by email or through contact form on website, with links to music online.

musicXart

Email: info@musicxart.co.uk
Website: http://www.musicxart.co.uk

Genres: Acoustic; Experimental

Contact: Francis

Willing to consider all genres but particularly interested in acoustic and experimental material. Send query by email with MP3 attachments.

My Little Empire

London
Email: hello@mylittleempirerecords.com
Website: http://www.mylittleempirerecords.com
Website: https://twitter.com/MLE_Records

Genres: Americana; Country; Guitar based; Indie; Roots

DIY indie label based in London. Send query by email with links to music online. No MP3 attachments or submissions by post.

NB Audio

Manchester
Email: info@nbaudio.tv
Email: dance@nbaudio.tv
Website: http://nbaudio.tv
Website: https://soundcloud.com/nbaudio

Genres: Alternative; Electronic; Dance; Drum and Bass; Dub; Dubstep; Hip-Hop; Reggae

Record label based in Manchester, UK. Send query by email with links to music online.

Never Fade Records

London
Email: info@neverfaderecords.com
Website: http://neverfaderecords.com
Website: https://www.facebook.com/NeverFadeRecordsUK/

Genres: All types of music

Independent record label based in London. Send query by email with MP3s or links to music online.

New Street Records

Email: hello@newstreetrecords.com
Website: http://www.newstreetrecords.com
Website: https://www.facebook.com/newstreetrecords/

Genres: All types of music

University record label run by students, for students. Send query by email with MP3s or links to music online.

Nice Swan Records

Email: info@niceswanrecords.com
Website: http://www.niceswanrecords.com
Website: https://soundcloud.com/NiceSwanRecords/

Genres: Garage; Indie; Rock

Independent record label specialising in vinyl releases, which are also made available via the usual online digital music outlets. Send query by email with links to music online.

101BPM

Email: leon@101bpm.com
Website: https://www.facebook.com/101BPM

Genres: Electronic; Urban

Music agency and record label. Send query by email with link to your latest music or showreel. Aims to respond within two weeks.

Organ Records

Email: demo@organrecords.com
Website: http://www.organrecords.com
Website: https://www.facebook.com/OrganRecords/?fref=ts

Genres: Alternative; Guitar based; Indie; Soul; Underground

A label for underground music. Send query by email with MP3s or links to music online.

OXRecordings

Email: demos@oxrecordings.com
Email: info@oxrecordings.com
Website: https://oxrecordings.com
Website: https://soundcloud.com/oxrecordings

Genres: Drum and Bass

Handles drum & bass and neurofunk only. No house. Send private soundcloud link by email. No attachments.

Partisan Records

Email: info@partisanrecords.com
Website: https://www.partisanrecords.com
Website: https://www.facebook.com/partisanrecords

Genres: Alternative

Record label based in Brooklyn and London. Send query by email with links to music online.

Perfect Havoc Limited

Flat 7
46 De Beauvoir Crescent
London
N1 5RY
Email: info@perfecthavoc.com
Website: https://www.perfecthavoc.com

Genres: Disco; House

Submit demos via online form on website.

Phantasy

PO Box 56972
London
N10 9BR
Email: demos@phantasysound.co.uk
Email: phantasyhq@gmail.com
Website: https://shop.phantasysound.co.uk/
Website: https://soundcloud.com/phantasysound

Genres: Alternative Dance; Dance; Electronic

Record label based in London. Send demo by email. See website for full guidelines.

Pink Lane Records

Newcastle Upon Tyne
Email: pinklanerecords@gmail.com
Website: https://pinklanerecords.bandcamp.com

Genres: All types of music

Record label based in Newcastle. Send query by email with bio and links to music online and social media presence.

Portfolio Music

Email: info@theportfoliomusic.com
Website: http://www.theportfoliomusic.com
Website: https://www.facebook.com/theportfoliomusic

Genres: Electronic; Grime; Hip-Hop; House; R&B; Rap; Urban

London-based record and publishing label.

Project Allout Records

Sheffield
Email: projectalloutinfo@gmail.com
Website: https://www.facebook.com/projectalloutrecords
Website: https://soundcloud.com/projectalloutrecords

Genres: Garage; Grime; Underground; Dubstep

Record label based in Sheffield. Send submissions by email.

Psymmetry Collective

Email: psymmetryrecords@gmail.com
Website: https://www.facebook.com/psymmetrycollective/

Genres: Garage; Psychedelic Rock; Punk; Punk Rock

Record label working with acts across the North West of England. Send query by email with MP3s, WAVs, or links to music online.

QM Records

Email: contact@qmrecords.com
Email: bookings@qmrecords.com
Website: https://www.qmrecords.com

Genres: Acoustic; Funk; Jazz; Grime; Hip-Hop; Soul

Send demos by email as links to music online.

Ramajam Recordings

Website: http://ramajamrecordings.com
Website: https://soundcloud.com/ramajam-recordings

Genres: Drum and Bass

Record label founded in Bristol in 2011. Send query by email with MP3 links.

Reckless Yes

Email: pete@recklessyes.com
Email: sarah@recklessyes.com
Website: http://recklessyes.com
Website: https://www.facebook.com/RecklessYes/

Genres: All types of music

Contact: Pete Darrington; Sarah Lay

An independent record label, artist management, live music agency and publishing house. Send demos by email to both addresses. See website for full details and specific subject line to include to prove you have read the submission guidelines.

Regent Street Records

71-75 Shelton Street
Covent Garden
London
Email: admin@regentstreetrecords.com
Website: https://regentstreetrecords.com
Website: https://www.facebook.com/regentstreetrecords/

Genres: Grime; Punk; Rock

UK Based Record Label, Publisher and Sync Rep. See website for submission guidelines.

Restless Bear

Chester
Email: info@restlessbear.com
Website: https://restlessbear.com
Website: https://soundcloud.com/user-804547797

Genres: Garage; Punk

Record label based in Chester. Send query by email with links to music online.

Riff Rock Records

Email: leigh@riffrockrecords.co.uk
Website: https://www.riffrockrecords.co.uk
Website: https://www.facebook.com/pg/RiffRockMusic/about/?ref=page_internal

Genres: Psychedelic Rock; Rock; Doom

Rock label launched in 2015. Send query by email or Facebook message with links to music online.

Robot Needs Home

Email: info@robotneedshome.com
Website: http://www.robotneedshome.com

Genres: All types of music

DIY collective involved in promoting shows, releasing records, and providing assistance to bands.

Rolla Records

London
Email: info@rollarecords.com
Website: http://www.rollarecords.com
Website: https://soundcloud.com/rolla-records

Genres: All types of music

Independent Record Label and Promotions company based in Easy London. Send query by email with links to music online.

Rooftop Records

Liverpool
Email: emily@parrstreetstudios.com
Website: http://www.rooftoprecs.com
Website: https://www.facebook.com/RooftopRecordsLimited

Genres: All types of music

Independent label based in Liverpool, set on developing emerging artists.

Rose Coloured Records

Email: records@rosecoloured.com
Website: https://www.facebook.com/RoseColouredRecords/

Genres: All types of music

Independent record label based in the South of England. Genre not important. Send query by email with SoundCloud links.

Rough Trade Records

66 Golborne Road
London
W10 5PS
Fax: +44 (0) 20 8968 6715
Email: demos@roughtraderecords.com
Website: http://www.roughtraderecords.com
Website: https://www.facebook.com/roughtraderecords

Genres: Indie; Rock

Contact: Paul Jones

Record label based in London. Send demos by email as MP3s or streaming links, or on CD by post.

RU:Listening

Email: matt@ru-listening.com
Email: T@ru-listening.com
Website: https://ru-listening.com
Website: https://www.facebook.com/RUlisteningLtd/

Genres: All types of music

Record label and international talent management company based in the UK and UAE. Formed in 2014. Send query by email with Soundcloud links.

Run Tingz Recordings

Email: info@runtingzrecordings.co.uk
Website: http://www.runtingzrecordings.co.uk
Website: https://soundcloud.com/runtingzrecordings

Genres: Drum and Bass; Jungle

Send query by email with MP3 attachments or links to music online.

Sad Club Records

London / Leeds
Email: sadclubrecords@gmail.com
Website: https://www.sadclubrecords.com
Website: https://www.facebook.com/sadclubrecords

Genres: All types of music

Contact: Tallulah Webb

Independent cassette label founded in 2016, based in Leeds and London. Send demos by email.

Safe Suburban Home

79 Alness Drive
York
Email: safesuburbanhome@gmail.com
Website: https://www.facebook.com/safesuburbanhome
Website: https://safesuburbanhomerecords.bandcamp.com

Genres: Alternative; Indie; Psychedelic Rock; Shoegaze

Small independent record label specialising in physical limited edition singles for up and coming artists around the UK and Europe. Contact by email.

Saffron Records

Email: info@saffronrecords.co.uk
Website: https://saffronrecords.co.uk
Website: https://www.facebook.com/Saffronrecords/

Genres: Electronic; Jazz; R&B

Artist development platform and record label.

Sain

Canolfan Sain
Llandwrog
Caenarfon
Gwynedd
LL54 5TG
Email: sain@sainwales.com
Email: dmr@sainwales.com
Website: https://www.sainwales.com
Website: https://www.facebook.com/SainRecordiau

Genres: All types of music

Contact: Dafydd Roberts; Ellen Davies

Record label based in Caenarfon. Send demo with bio by post or by email.

Salute the Sun

Email: info@salutethesunrecords.com
Website: https://www.salutethesunrecords.com
Website: https://soundcloud.com/wesalutethesun

Genres: Electronic; Hip-Hop; Pop; R&B; Soul

Send query by email with links to music online.

Salvation Records

Liverpool
Email: info@salvationrecords.co.uk
Website: http://salvationrecords.co.uk
Website: https://soundcloud.com/salvationrecords

Genres: Electronic; Garage; Psychedelic Rock; Punk; Underground

Contact: Anthony Nyland

Record label, publisher, and management company based in Liverpool, releasing physical product, lost classics and the current underground sounds.

Sapien Records Limited

35c Framwellgate Bridge
Durham
DH1 4SJ
Email: info@sapienrecords.com
Email: david@sapienrecords.com
Website: http://www.sapienrecords.com

Genres: Hip-Hop; Metal; Pop; Punk; Rock; R&B

Contact: David Smith; Ollie Rillands; Michael Hall

Independent record label based in Durham. Send links to music online via form on website. Listens to all submissions and tries to respond to as many as possible.

Saraseto Records

Glasgow
Email: sarasetorecords@hotmail.co.uk
Website: http://www.sarasetorecords.com
Website: https://www.facebook.com/SarasetoRecords

Genres: Alternative; Pop; Rock; Indie

Contact: Andrew

Record label based in Glasgow. Send demo by email.

Saved Records

Maidstone, Kent
Email: saveddemos@gmail.com
Website: http://www.savedrecords.com
Website: https://soundcloud.com/savedrecords

Genres: House; Techno; Electronic

Record label based in Maidstone. Send demos by email.

Saving Grace Music

Huddersfield
West Yorkshire
Email: info@saving-grace.co.uk
Email: bookings@saving-grace.co.uk
Website: http://www.saving-grace.co.uk
Website: http://www.soundcloud.com/saving-grace-music

Genres: Grime; Hip-Hop; House; Garage; Indie; Folk; Rock; Soul; Pop; Drum and Bass; Dubstep

Record label based in Huddersfield. Send demos via soundcloud.

Schnitzel Records Ltd

London
Email: talent@schnitzel.co.uk
Email: info@schnitzel.co.uk
Website: http://www.schnitzel.co.uk
Website: https://www.facebook.com/schnitzelrecords

Genres: Alternative; Rock

Record label based in London. Send submissions by email.

Sci Fi Ltd

18 Carlton Road
London
E17 5RE
Email: hello@scifirecords.co.uk
Website: http://www.scifirecords.co.uk
Website: https://soundcloud.com/scifirecords

Genres: Break Beat; Electronic; House; Techno; Trip Hop

Record label based in London, influenced by the future, science and technology. Send demos via soundcloud.

Scotdisc

Newtown Street
Kilsyth
Glasgow
G65 OLY
Fax: +44 (0) 1236 826900
Email: info@scotdisc.co.uk
Website: http://www.scotdisc.co.uk

Genres: Regional

Record label based in Glasgow, specialising in Scottish music. Send demo by post.

Scottish Fiction

Glasgow
Email: scottishfiction@mail.com
Website: http://scottishfiction.co.uk
Website: https://scottishfiction.bandcamp.com

Genres: Alternative Rock; Electronic; Folk; Pop; Hip-Hop

DIY independent record label based in Glasgow. Send query by email with links to music online.

ScreamLite Records

Cheltenham
Email: screamliterecordsuk@gmail.com
Website: https://screamliterecords.bandcamp.com
Website: https://twitter.com/screamliterecs

Genres: Folk; Metal; Punk; Rock

Record label based in Cheltenham. Send demos by email.

Scruff of the Neck (SOTN)

Manchester
Email: info@scruffoftheneck.com
Website: http://scruffoftheneck.com
Website: https://twitter.com/SOTNRecords

Genres: All types of music

Independent record label and music collective promoting concerts and tours, releasing records and developing artists. Approach via Artist Contact Form on website.

Seed Records

Email: demos@seedrecords.co.uk
Email: contact@seedrecords.co.uk
Website: http://www.seedrecords.co.uk
Website: https://soundcloud.com/seed-records

Genres: Alternative; Electronic; Techno; Folk

Record label handling Electronics, Folk, Noise, Techno, Italo, Golf, No-wave, and Weird. Send demos by email.

Sentosa Records

18 Firshaw Rroad
Meols
Wirral
Email: contact@sentosarecords.com
Website: https://www.sentosarecords.com

Genres: Mainstream Club; Mainstream; House; Modern

Contact: Dan

A record label guided by a team of successful producers who have a vast experience in a Major label setup from being part of UK number one campaigns to building club level tracks into commercial success. The approach is to break new music and develop new artists from the ground up along with signing high calibre established artists/producers and getting music heard in all four corners of the globe.

Serotone Recordings

Website: http://serotonednb.co.uk
Website: https://www.facebook.com/SerotoneRecordings

Genres: Drum and Bass

Send query by email with links to your music online.

Shabby Doll Records

Email: hello@shabbydoll.co.uk
Website: http://www.shabbydoll.co.uk
Website: https://soundcloud.com/shabby-doll-records

Genres: Underground House

Record label specialising in bespoke underground house music. Send query by email with MP3 attachments or links to music online.

Sharpe Music

9A Irish Street
Dungannon
Co. Tyrone
BT70 1DB
Fax: +44 (0) 2887 752195
Email: imd@sharpemusic.com
Website: https://www.sharpemusicireland.com

Genres: Regional; Celtic; Traditional

Record label based in Northern Ireland, releasing traditional Irish music. Send demo by post or by email.

Shogun Audio Ltd

Brighton
Email: shogunaudio@label-engine.com
Email: info@shogunaudio.co.uk
Website: http://www.shogunaudio.co.uk
Website: https://soundcloud.com/shogunaudio

Genres: Electronic; Drum and Bass

Record label based in Brighton. Send demos by email.

Sister 9 Recordings

Email: contact@sister9.com
Website: http://www.sister9.com
Website: http://www.facebook.com/Sister9Recordings

Genres: Alternative; Lo-fi; Post Punk Rock; Psychedelic Rock

Specialise in Alternative and Lo-Fi recordings and sessions.

The label also puts on gig nights and is home to a label set up to release previously recorded material by artists from anywhere in the world.

Interested in sourcing new artists to work with. Make contact via the website with links to music online.

SLAM Productions

c/o 3 Thesiger Road
Abingdon
OX14 2DX
Email: slamprods@aol.com
Website: http://www.slamproductions.net

Genres: Contemporary Jazz; Experimental

Independent CD label based in Abingdon, and founded in 1989. Send demo by post.

Slapped Up Soul Records

Bristol
Email: info@circleoffunk.com
Website: https://www.facebook.com/slappedupsoul/
Website: https://twitter.com/slappedupsouluk

Genres: Soul

Independent record label based in Bristol, specialising in music with soul. Send CD or vinyl by post, or MP3s, WAVs, or links to music online by email.

Sliced Note Recordings

Email: silentcodeuk@gmail.com
Website: http://www.slicednoterecordings.com
Website: https://soundcloud.com/slicednoterecordings

Genres: Drum and Bass; Jungle

Send query by email with private SoundCloud links.

Small Bear Records

Isle of Man
Email: smallbearrecords@gmail.com
Website: http://www.smallbearrecords.com
Website: https://www.facebook.com/Small-Bear-Records-290549551024394/

Genres: All types of music

Small independent record label, based in the Isle of Man.

Small Pond Record Label

27 Castle Street
Brighton
BN1 2HD
Email: label@smallpondrec.co.uk
Website: http://smallpondrec.co.uk
Website: https://soundcloud.com/small-pond

Genres: All types of music

Record label based in Brighton. Send query by email with links to streaming music online.

Small Town Records

Email: pete@smalltownrecords.co.uk
Email: ben@smalltownrecords.co.uk
Website: http://smalltownrecords.co.uk
Website: http://www.facebook.com/smalltownuk

Genres: Emo; Hardcore; Metal; Punk; Rock

Contact: Pete; Ben; Alex

Record label based in Leeds. Send email with info about your band and links to music online. Do not contact via social media, or send music file attachments. Works only with bands that do a substantial amount of touring. See website for full details.

Snapper Music

1st Floor
52 Lisson Street
London
NW1 5DF
Email: sales@snappermusic.co.uk
Website: http://www.snappermusic.com

Genres: Alternative; Rock; Metal; Post Progressive

Record label based in London. Send demo with brief bio by post.

Snatch! Records

7 Bourne Court
Southend Road
Woodford Green
London
IG8 8HD
Email: demos@snatchrecords.com
Email: contact@snatchrecords.com
Website: http://www.snatchrecords.com
Website: http://www.soundcloud.com/snatchrecords

Genres: House

Record label dealing in House music, based in London. "Expect slamming fresh house cuts from some of the most exciting talent in the scene." Send query via form on website with links to music online (wetransfer, dropbox, or soundcloud with active download).

So Recordings

3 Prowse Place
Camden Town
London
NW1 9PH
Email: info@sorecordings.com
Website: http://sorecordings.com
Website: https://soundcloud.com/sorecords

Genres: Alternative; Indie; Rock

Contact: Adam Greenup

Record label based in Camden, London.

Something in Construction

Email: misterlaurie@gmail.com
Website: http://somethinginconstruction.com
Website: https://soundcloud.com/sicrecords

Genres: Leftfield Pop

Management stable and record label based in London and started in 2005. Send query via website with links to music online.

Somewhere Records

Email: enquiry@somewhererecords.co.uk
Website: https://www.somewhererecords.co.uk
Website: https://www.facebook.com/somewhererecordsuk

Genres: All types of music

Independent record label based in Market Harborough, Leicestershire. Contact via form on website.

SOMM Recordings

13 Riversdale Road
Thames Ditton
Surrey
KT7 0QL
Email: soke@somm-recordings.com
Email: sales@somm-recordings.com
Website: http://www.somm-recordings.com
Website: https://soundcloud.com/siva-oke

Genres: Classical

Classical label based in Thames Ditton, Surrey. Send demo by post, or send email with links to music online.

Sonic Bear

Email: sonicbearlabel@gmail.com
Website: https://www.sonic-bear.com
Website: https://www.facebook.com/sonicbearlabel

Genres: Electronic; House

Record label specialising in electronic house music / deep house. Send query by email with links to music online.

Sonic Cathedral

PO Box 57718
London
NW11 1DR
Email: info@soniccathedral.co.uk
Website: http://www.soniccathedral.co.uk
Website: http://soundcloud.com/sonic-cathedral

Genres: Electronic; Psychedelic Rock; Shoegaze

Record label based in London. Send demo on CD by post, or use soundcloud dropbox (see website).

Sony Music UK & Ireland

9 Derry Street
London
W8 5HY
Email: reception.enquiries@sonymusic.com
Website: http://www.sonymusic.co.uk

Genres: All types of music

London office of large international record label.

Sotones Music Co-Operative

13 Mansion Road
Southampton
SO15 3BQ
Email: demos@sotones.co.uk

Email: andy@sotones.co.uk
Website: http://sotones.co.uk
Website: https://soundcloud.com/sotones

Genres: All types of music

Contact: Andy Harris (Managing Director)

Music collective based in Southampton, generally only working with local acts. Will accept demos, however. See website for more details.

Soul II Soul

PO Box 67934
NW1W 8ZB
Email: info@soul2soul.co.uk
Email: press@soul2soul.co.uk
Website: http://www.soul2soul.co.uk
Website: https://soundcloud.com/soul2souluk

Genres: R&B; Rap; Urban

Record label based in London. Send demos and mixes by post or email.

Soulvent Records

London
Email: info@soulventrecords.co.uk
Website: http://soulventrecords.com
Website: http://soulventrecords.label-engine.com/demos

Genres: Drum and Bass

Independent East London record label. Send demo via online submission system.

Sound House Records

Email: Enquiries@soundhouserecords.co.uk
Website: http://www.soundhouserecords.co.uk
Website: https://soundcloud.com/soundhouserecords

Genres: Metal; Rock

UK based independent record label and music services company. Send query via online form on website.

Sound-Hub Records

7 King Street
Belper
Derbyshire
DE56 1PS
Email: info@sound-hub.com
Email: barrington@sound-hub.com
Website: http://www.sound-hub.com
Website: https://www.facebook.com/SoundHubStudio

Genres: All types of music

Describe themselves as "The UK's fastest growing Independent Record Label, Recording Studio's and Band Development Facility". Send details with YouTube or Soundcloud link via online web form, available on website. Only accepts submissions from the UK and Europe.

Soundplate

London
Email: label@soundplate.com
Website: http://soundplate.com
Website: https://www.submithub.com/label/soundplate-records-label

Genres: Electronic; House

Record label and online music platform based in London.

Sounds Like Vinyl

Email: shawndavis22@hotmail.com
Website: https://milwaukie2003.wixsite.com/sounds-like-vinyl
Website: https://www.facebook.com/soundslikevinyl/

Genres: Electronic; Acid; Techno; Underground

Record label that seeks to capture the sound of vinyl in digital format.

Sour Grapes

Manchester
Email: info@sourgrapesrecords.co.uk
Website: http://www.sourgrapesrecords.co.uk
Website: https://www.facebook.com/sourgrapesmanchester/

Genres: Psychedelic; Garage; Punk; Rock; Rock and Roll

DIY record label and promoter based in Manchester. Send demos by email only.

Southern Fried Records

(A&R) Southern Fried Records
Fulham Palace
Bishops Avenue
London
SW6 6EA
Fax: +44 (0) 20 7384 7392
Email: cameron@southernfriedrecords.com
Email: info@southernfriedrecords.com
Website: http://www.southernfriedrecords.com
Website: https://soundcloud.com/southernfriedrecords

Genres: Electronic; Dance

A London-based independent electronic dance music record label. Send demos by email.

Southpoint

18 Cambridge Road, Flat 4
Hove
East Sussex
BN3 1DF
Email: info@southpointmusic.co.uk
Email: josh@southpointmusic.co.uk
Website: http://southpointmusic.co.uk
Website: https://soundcloud.com/southpointmusic

Genres: Dubstep; Garage; Grime

Contact: Josh Gunston; Jay McDougall

Record label based in Hove, dedicated to promoting local and lesser known talent and reviving Brighton's fading bass and grime scene. Send submissions by email.

Speedowax

Birmingham
Email: speedowax@gmail.com
Website: https://www.facebook.com/speedowax
Website: https://twitter.com/Speedowax

Genres: Hardcore; Indie; Rock; Post Rock; Thrash; Punk

Non-profit record label based in Birmingham. Send query by email with links to music online. No MP3 attachments.

Speedy Enix Records

Email: info@se-records.co.uk
Website: http://www.se-records.co.uk
Website: https://www.facebook.com/speedyenixrecords

Genres: All types of music

Record label catering for raw, unsigned talent and independent musicians of all genres. Send links to music online via contact form on website.

Speedy Wunderground

Email: info@speedywunderground.com
Website: http://speedywunderground.com
Website: https://www.facebook.com/speedywunder/

Genres: All types of music

Contact: Dan Carey

Record label focusing on speed to market. All recordings will be done on one day; all mixing the next. Records will be in the shops as soon as humanly possible. Send query by email with links to music online.

Spiritual Records

4 Ferdinand Street
Camden
NW1 8ER
Fax: +44 (0) 7748 593758
Email: rafael@spiritualrecords.co.uk
Email: louise@spiritualrecords.co.uk
Website: https://www.spiritualrecords.co.uk

Genres: Alternative Blues; Acoustic; Folk; Rock; Singer-Songwriter

Born in September 2015, in Camden.

We started to record some of our best featured artists in our own studio upstairs at the Bar.

Our hope is that we can bring out the best of our artists musically and support them long and short term. We encourage all our artists to help each other and help us build the label and to make it stand out in an industry that continues to be plagued by false hope and promises.

Square Leg

Email: info@squarelegrecords.co.uk
Website: http://www.squarelegrecords.co.uk
Website: https://www.facebook.com/squarelegrecords/

Genres: All types of music

Contact: Charlie Andrew

Record label set up by award-winning record producer. Send query by email with links to music online.

STA – Small Town America

Bay Road
Derry, Northern Ireland
Email: info@smalltownamerica.co.uk
Website: http://www.smalltownamerica.co.uk
Website: http://www.facebook.com/smalltownamerica

Genres: Indie; Pop; Punk; Rock; Alternative

Record label based in Londonderry. Send query by email with links to music online.

Standby

Email: demos@standbyrecords.co.uk
Website: http://www.standbyrecords.co.uk
Website: https://soundcloud.com/standby_records

Genres: Progressive House

Record label based in London, releasing Deep Tech Progressive House. Always looking to sign quality new music. Contact via Soundcloud with links to music online.

State51 Conspiracy

17 Hereford Street
London
E2 6EX
Email: support@state51.com
Website: http://state51.com
Website: https://www.facebook.com/thestate51conspiracy/

Genres: All types of music

Ethical music company based in London. Send demos by post or send query by email with links to music online.

Staylittle Music

Email: press@staylittlemusic.com
Email: shows@staylittlemusic.com
Website: http://www.staylittlemusic.com
Website: https://soundcloud.com/staylittlemusic

Genres: Acoustic; Folk; Indie

Record label with strong DIY ethos.

Stoa Sounds

London
Email: james@stoasounds.co.uk
Website: http://www.stoasounds.co.uk

Genres: Indie; Pop; Singer-Songwriter

Management company and record label based in London. Send query by email with links to music online.

Stolen Recordings

Email: stolen@stolenrecordings.co.uk
Website: http://www.stolenrecordings.co.uk
Website: https://soundcloud.com/stolenrecordings

Genres: Alternative; Indie

Record label, management, and publishing company. Send demos as links to music online via form on website.

Strawberry Moon Records

3B, 48 Comercial Road
Wolverhampton
Email: groundcontrol@strawberrymoonrecords.co.uk
Website: https://www.facebook.com/strawberrymoonrecordsltd

Genres: All types of music

Describes itself as one of the UK's most innovative independent record labels. Send query by email with links to your music online.

Strong Island Recordings

Email: INFO@
STRONGISLANDRECORDINGS.com
Website: https://strongislandrecordings.
tumblr.com
Website: https://soundcloud.com/
strongislandrecordings

Genres: Psychedelic; Shoegaze; Garage Rock; Post Punk; Indie

Send query by email with link to music online.

Sub Cube Records

11 Rose Mews
Hull
HU2 9AG
Email: info@subcuberecords.com
Website: http://www.subcuberecords.com
Website: https://soundcloud.com/sub-cube-records

Genres: Electronic Dance; Drum and Bass; Dubstep; Break Beat; House

Contact: Dainis Vitols

Independent record label based in Hull, releasing electronic dance music in the form of Drum & Bass, Dub-Step, Break-beat and House. Send demos by email.

Subdust Music

Office 459
275 Deansgate
Manchester
M3 4EL
Email: info@subdust.com
Website: http://www.subdust.com
Website: https://spaces.hightail.com/uplink/
subdustmusic

Genres: Alternative; Electronic; Experimental; Mainstream; Urban; Commercial

Contact: Jason Holmes

An evolution of the normal record label model with collaborative production and artist releases with artist services including distribution and consultation. Submit demo files via Hightail dropbox.

SubSoul

London
Email: demos@subsoul.co.uk
Email: rich@subsoul.co.uk
Website: http://www.subsoul.com
Website: https://soundcloud.com/subsoul

Genres: Dance; Electronic; Garage; House

Record label based in London. Send query by email with links to music online.

Sunbird Records

4 The Circus
Darwen
BB3 1BS
Email: info@sunbirdrecords.co.uk
Website: http://www.sunbirdrecords.co.uk
Website: https://www.facebook.com/
SunbirdRecords

Genres: All types of music

Independent record label and live music venue, based in Darwen.

Sunday Best Recordings

Unit 1
50-52 Hanbury Street
London
E1 5JL
Email: info@sundaybest.net
Website: http://www.sundaybest.net
Website: https://www.facebook.com/
sundaybestrecordings
Website: http://www.myspace.com/
sundaybestrecordings

Genres: Indie; Electronic; Alternative

Send query by email with links to music online.

Sunstone Records Ltd

Website: http://www.sunstonerecords.co.uk
Website: https://soundcloud.com/sunstone-records-uk

Genres: Electronic Psychedelic; Progressive; Twisted Folk

Independent record label based in the North West of England, with a taste in electronics, psychedelia, prog, twisted folk and more. Send query via form on website.

Super Fan 99
London
Email: iamsuperfan99@outlook.com
Website: https://soundcloud.com/SUPERFAN99

Genres: Americana; Indie; Pop; Psychedelic Rock

"A small but perfectly formed record label". Send query by email with links to music online.

Supermarine Music
North Wiltshire
Email: hello@supermarinemusic.co.uk
Email: jon@supermarinemusic.co.uk
Website: https://www.supermarinemusic.co.uk
Website: https://www.facebook.com/supermarinemusic

Genres: Acoustic; Electronic; Alternative Rock; Folk

Start-up independent record label based in North Wiltshire, supporting new and original artists in the region and beyond. Send query by email with links to music online. No MP3 attachments.

Supersonic Media
London
Email: demos@supersonic-media.co.uk
Email: info@supersonic-media.co.uk
Website: https://www.supersonic-media.co.uk
Website: https://soundcloud.com/supersonicmedia

Genres: Alternative; Dance; Drum and Bass; House; Post Hardcore

Independent record label and publisher, based in London. Send query by email with streaming links and artist bio.

Superstar Destroyer Records
Email: bookings@superstardestroyer.co.uk
Website: http://www.superstardestroyer.co.uk
Website: https://www.facebook.com/ssdrecords

Genres: Alternative; Progressive; Post Rock; Shoegaze

Contact: Alex; Anderson; Tom; Jake; Jonny

Record label based in Manchester. Make contact by email with links to music online.

Swallow Song Records
Email: swallowsongrecords@gmail.com
Website: http://www.swallowsongrecords.com
Website: https://twitter.com/swallowsongrec

Genres: All types of music

Record label based in Northern Ireland, handling Irish bands and artists of all genres. Prefers to receive submissions by email.

Talking Elephant
PO Box 376
Bexleyheath
Kent
DA7 9LF
Email: info@talkingelephant.co.uk
Website: http://www.talkingelephant.co.uk
Website: https://www.facebook.com/talkingelephant

Genres: Blues; Folk; Classic Rock

Record label based in Bexleyheath, Kent. Send demo by post.

Tangled Talk Records
London
Email: info@tangledtalk.com
Website: http://www.tangledtalk.com
Website: https://www.facebook.com/tangledtalk

Genres: All types of music

Independent record label based in London. Only releases music they are passionate about, by artists they love. Send query by email with links to music online. No MP3s or hard copy submissions by post.

Tape Club Records
London
Email: info@tapeclubrecords.com
Website: http://www.tapeclubrecords.com

Website: https://soundcloud.com/tapeclubrecords

Genres: Electronic; Pop

Record label based in London.

TeaPot Records

Email: contactteapotrecords@gmail.com
Website: http://teapotrecs.com
Website: https://www.facebook.com/teapotrecs

Genres: All types of music

Independent Record Label and Music Production House. Send query by email with links to music online.

These Bloody Thieves Records

Sheffield
Email: info@fansforbands.com
Website: https://www.thesebloodythievesrecords.com
Website: https://www.facebook.com/thesebloodythieves

Genres: Alternative; Acoustic; Indie; Folk; Metal; Rock

Indie label based in Sheffield. Send query by email with links to music online.

37 Adventures

London
Email: hello@37adventures.co.uk
Website: http://37adventures.co.uk
Website: https://soundcloud.com/37adventures

Genres: Electronic; Dance; Indie; Pop

Record label based in London. Send query by email with links to music online.

This Is It Forever

Email: thisisitforeverrecords@gmail.com
Website: http://www.thisisitforever.co.uk
Website: https://soundcloud.com/thisisitforeverrecords

Genres: Experimental; Electronic

Contact: Gavin / Tom

A small record label, releasing experimental / electronic music. Send query by email with Soundcloud links.

Thumbhole Records

Reading
Email: Admin@thumbholerecords.com
Website: http://www.thumbholerecords.com/
Website: https://www.facebook.com/thumbholerecords

Genres: Alternative Emo Hardcore Metal Punk Rock Ska

Contact: Dan Allman

Independent record label compiling compilations of upcoming punk rock and alternative bands from around the world.

Tigertrap Records

14 Pixley Street
London
E14 7DF
Email: info@tigertrap.co.uk
Website: http://www.tigertrap.co.uk
Website: https://www.facebook.com/tigertraprecords

Genres: Alternative Electronic; Rock

Record label based in London. Send query by email with links to music online.

Tight Lines

Leeds
Email: will@tightlinesmusic.co.uk
Website: https://www.tightlinesmusic.co.uk
Website: https://www.facebook.com/tightlinesmusic

Genres: Hip-Hop; Jazz; Leftfield; Punk; Soul

Independent record label presenting emerging bands from Leeds.

TNS (That's Not Skanking) Records

Manchester
Email: info@tnsrecords.co.uk
Email: bev@tnsrecords.co.uk
Website: http://www.tnsrecords.co.uk
Website: http://www.facebook.com/group.

php?gid=5735058846
Website: http://www.myspace.com/tnsrecords_uk

Genres: Punk; Ska; Underground

Not-for-profit label based in Manchester. Send query by email in first instance.

Tone Artistry

Manchester
Email: brigitte@toneartistry.co.uk
Website: http://www.toneartistry.co.uk
Website: https://soundcloud.com/tone-artistry-record-label

Genres: House

Record label and marketing company based in Manchester, specialising in all genres of House Music.

ToneTrade Productions

70 Minet Avenue
London
NW10 8AP
Email: francescoaccurso@tonetrade.co.uk
Website: http://www.tonetrade.co.uk

Genres: Jazz; Urban Blues; Alternative Blues; Blues; Roots

Independent production company and management based in London. Send query by email with short bio and links to streaming music online.

Tonotopic Records

4 Capricorn Centre
Cranes Farm Road
Basildon
Essex
United Kingdom
SS14 3JJ
Email: laura@tonotopicrecords.com
Website: https://www.tonotopicrecords.com

Genres: Avant-Garde Alternative Acoustic Electronic Experimental Melodic

Contact: Laura Evans

An independent UK record label founded in 2015. We work closely with artists of all genres to record, publish and promote their music internationally.

Run by musicians and music lovers, we sign every artist with long term development in mind. We don't drop an act once their music stops selling, we support and grow their creative output so they can continue to write amazing music. We look for raw talent we can work with, not hits handed to us on a silver platter. If you are interested in becoming an artist, send us a demo and we'll get back to you as soon as possible.

Tontena Music

Email: info@tontenamusic.com
Website: http://www.tontenamusic.com
Website: https://soundcloud.com/tontena

Genres: All types of music

Record label and studio (also production and music publishing). Send queries by email with links to music online. No attachments.

Too Pure Records

17-19 Alma Road
London
SW18 1AA
Fax: +44 (0) 20 8871 1766
Email: paulriddlesworth@beggars.com
Website: http://www.toopure.com
Website: https://www.facebook.com/Too-Pure-Singles-Club-9333833636/
Website: http://www.myspace.com/toopure

Genres: Alternative; Rock

Contact: Paul Riddlesworth

Accepts demos by post or by email.

Toolroom Records

Top Floor
Raglan House
St Peters Street
Maidstone
Kent
ME16 0SN
Email: demos@toolroomrecords.com
Website: http://www.toolroomrecords.com
Website: http://www.soundcloud.com/toolroomrecords
Website: http://www.myspace.com/toolroomrecords

Genres: House

House record label based in Maidstone, Kent. Send demos via online submission system. Endeavours to listen to all of them, but cannot guarantee a response.

TOR Records

Those Old Records
Brewery St
Rugeley
Staffordshire
WS15 2DY
Email: info@torrecords.com
Website: http://torrecords.com
Website: https://www.facebook.com/Those-Old-Records-Rugeley-172161069606675/

Genres: All types of music

Independent vinyl-only record label based in Rugeley, Staffordshire.

Tough Love Records

Email: info@toughloverecords.com
Website: http://toughloverecords.com
Website: https://soundcloud.com/tough-love

Genres: All types of music

Record label based in London. Send query by email with links to music online.

Traffic Cone Records

Glasgow
Email: traffic.cone.records@gmail.com
Website: https://www.facebook.com/Traffic.Cone.Records
Website: https://www.youtube.com/user/TrafficConeLive

Genres: All types of music

No-for-profit based in Glasgow, involved in management, recording, distribution, and events. Send query by email.

Trancespired Recordings

Email: demos@trancespired.com
Email: contact@trancespired.com
Website: https://trancespired.com
Website: https://soundcloud.com/trancespiredrecordings

Genres: Trance; Progressive

UK-based Trance Label, aspiring to release the best in Uplifting, Progressive, Tech and Vocal trance. Submit your demo by email as a link to your music online.

Transgressive Records

London
Email: demos@transgressiverecords.com
Website: http://www.transgressiverecords.co.uk
Website: https://soundcloud.com/transgressive-records
Website: http://www.myspace.com/transgressiverecords

Genres: All types of music

Record label based in London. Send query by email or through website contact form, with links to music online.

Trashmouth Records

London
Website: https://trashmouthrecords.bandcamp.com
Website: https://www.facebook.com/trashmouthrecs

Genres: All types of music

Record label based in London. Prefers to hear demos rather than finished EPs / albums.

Trellis Music

Email: chris@trellismusic.co.uk
Website: http://www.trellismusic.co.uk
Website: https://twitter.com/trellismusicuk

Genres: All types of music

Record label / artist management company. Send query by email with links to music online.

Trestle Records

Email: info@trestlerec.com
Website: http://www.trestlerec.com
Website: https://www.facebook.com/trestlerecords

Genres: Electronic; Classical; Pop; Contemporary; Instrumental

Record label dedicated to putting out new instrumental music.

Triassic Tusk

Email: Stephen@triassictuskrecords.com
Website: https://www.triassictuskrecords.com
Website: https://www.facebook.com/triassictuskrecords/

Genres: All types of music

Contact: Lucy Hine; Stephen Marshall

Small record label based in a brewery in the East Neuk of Fife. Send queries by email with links to music online.

TRNS Records

Email: info@trnsrecords.com
Website: http://www.trnsrecords.com
Website: https://www.facebook.com/trnsrecords

Genres: Alternative Guitar based

Contact: Luke Riffiths

UK based record label and live music series. Send query by email with links to music online.

Tru Thoughts

PO Box 2818
Brighton
East Sussex
BN1 4RL
Email: demos@tru-thoughts.co.uk
Email: info@tru-thoughts.co.uk
Website: http://www.tru-thoughts.co.uk
Website: https://www.facebook.com/truthoughts

Genres: Funk; Hip-Hop; Break Beat; Jazz; Soul

Contact: Robert Luis

Contact by email.

Tu-kay Records

Bridge Road
Stoke Bruerne
Northampton
NN12 7SB
Email: contact@tu-kayrecords.com
Website: http://www.tu-kayrecords.com
Website: http://soundcloud.com/tu-kayrecords
Website: http://www.myspace.com/tukayrecords

Genres: All types of music

Contact: Ash Woodward

Independent record label established in 2006. Send demos as MP3s by email, or send links to music online. Due to the high level of emails I receive, unfortunately I cannot ensure a response to them all.

Tumi Music Ltd

Mill Cottage
St Catherine
Bath
BA1 8EU
Fax: +44 (0) 1225 858545
Email: info@tumimusic.com
Website: http://www.tumimusic.com

Genres: Latin; World

Record label based in Bristol, specialising in Latin American and Caribbean music. Send query by email with links to music online or as MP3 attachments.

21st Century Music

23 Collyer Road
London Colney
St Albans
Hertfordshire
AL2 1PD
Email: clifford.white@21newmedia.com
Website: https://www.21stcentury.co.uk
Website: http://www.21newmedia.com

Genres: Electronic Alternative Atmospheric Downtempo Funky Melodic New Wave Psychedelic

Contact: Clifford White

Incredible electronic music. That's what we bring you. Our music will inspire you. Uplift you. Enrich you. Top-quality, superbly melodic, rich and full of originality. That's 21st Century Music. Electronic music for the next generation...!

Twin City Records

Website: http://www.twincityrecords.com
Website: https://www.facebook.com/twincityrecord/

Genres: Indie; Guitar based

Independent record label based in Scotland.

Two Piece Records

Email: twopiecerecords@gmail.com
Website: http://www.twopiecerecords.bigcartel.com
Website: https://www.facebook.com/twopiecerecords

Genres: Garage; Rock; Underground

London/Nottingham based independent record label. Send query by email with MP3s or links to music online.

Tye Die Tapes

Sheffield
Email: contact@tyedietapes.com
Website: http://www.tyedietapes.com

Genres: Alternative; Experimental; Indie

Record label and recording studio based in Sheffield. Send demos by email as MP3s or links to music online.

Ubiquity Project Records

Email: admin@theubiquityproject.co.uk
Email: graeme@graemerawson.co.uk
Website: http://ubiprorec.wordpress.com

Genres: All types of music

Non-profit, non-exclusive record label based in Reading, UK. Send email with links to music online. Also offers professional recording services.

Universal Music Group

364-366 Kensington High Street
London
W14 8NS
Fax: +44 (0) 20 8910 3224
Email: contact@umusic.com
Website: https://www.umusic.co.uk

Genres: All types of music

No direct approaches. Accepts queries for new material via well-known managers, agents, producers, radio DJs or other music industry professional only.

Upbeat Recordings

Waverley House
6 The Bramblings
Rustington
West Sussex
BN16 2DA
Email: info@upbeat.co.uk
Website: http://www.upbeatrecordings.co.uk

Genres: Jazz

Jazz record label based in Rustington, West Sussex. Query by phone in first instance.

Vallance Records

East London
Email: elliott@vallancerecords.com
Website: http://www.vallancerecords.com
Website: https://www.facebook.com/VALLANCERECORDS/

Genres: Garage; Indie; Psychedelic Rock; Punk

Record label based in East London, founded in 2016. Send query by email with MP3s or links to music online.

Venn Records

London
Email: houseofvenn@gmail.com
Website: https://vennrecords.com
Website: https://www.facebook.com/vennrecords

Genres: Metal; Punk; Rock

Record label based in London. Send query by email with links to music online. Response not guaranteed.

Vertical Records

16 Woodlands Terrace
Glasgow
G3 6DF
Email: info@verticalrecords.co.uk
Website: http://www.verticalrecords.co.uk

Genres: Celtic; Roots

Celtic and roots label based in Glasgow, Scotland. Closed to demos as at November 2017.

Vertigo Records

364-366 Kensington High Street
London
W14 8NS
Email: contact@umusic.com
Website: http://www.umusic.co.uk

Genres: All types of music

Record label based in London. Send demo by post.

Virgin EMI Records

364–366
Kensington High Street
London W14 8NS
Email: contact@virginemirecords.com
Website: http://www.virginemirecords.com
Website: https://www.facebook.com/VirginEmiRecords

Genres: All types of music

Record label based in London. Recommends approaching through an industry professional with an established relationship with the company, but will accept submissions by post, marked for the attention of the A&R department.

Voltage Records

Units 7,8,10,11
St. Stephen's Mill
Newton Place
Ripley Street
Bradford
West Yorkshire
BD5 7JW
Email: enquiries@voltagerecords.com
Email: info@voltagerecords.com
Website: http://www.voltagerecords.com
Website: https://www.facebook.com/voltagerecords1
Website: http://www.myspace.com/voltagerecords

Genres: Guitar based; Electronic

Contact: Tim Walker

Send demos on audio CDs only – no MP3s. Include brief bio, one or two photos, and contact details on the CD itself.

Vox Humana

Email: colin@voxhumanarecords.co.uk
Website: http://www.voxhumanarecords.co.uk

Genres: Acoustic; Electronic; Experimental; Pop

Contact: Colin

Small label supporting new artists. Specialises in abstract pop. Send query by email with details about you and your music, with a streaming link to one song (Soundcloud, Bandcamp or YouTube preferred). Response not guaranteed.

Wagg Records

25 Commercial Street
Brighouse
HD6 1AF
Fax: +44 (0) 1484 717247
Email: john@now-music.com
Website: http://www.now-music.com

Genres: All types of music

Contact: John

A small independent label used mainly for nurturing new artists. Parent company also offers music management and music publishing services, as well as operating another record label. Send demo by post.

Wah Wah 45s

London
Email: dom@wahwah45s.com
Email: adam@wahwah45s.com
Website: http://www.wahwah45s.com
Website: https://www.facebook.com/WahWah45s

Genres: Soul; Funk; Acoustic; Jazz; Electronic; Dub; Reggae

Contact: Dom Servini; Adam Scrimshire

Record label based in London. Send email with MP3 attachments or links to music online, or submit material in the post.

Wall of Sound Recordings Ltd

Email: info@wallofsound.net
Website: https://www.facebook.com/wallofsound.net
Website: https://www.twitter.com/wallofsounduk

Genres: All types of music

Record label based in London. Send query by email with links to music online.

War Room Records

Liverpool
Email: info@warroomrecords.co.uk
Website: http://www.warroomrecords.co.uk
Website: https://www.facebook.com/warroomrecordsliverpool

Genres: All types of music

Independent record label based in Liverpool. Send query by email with MP3s or links to music online.

Warner / Chappell Music

WARNER/CHAPPELL MUSIC LTD
Hammersmith
Griffin House
161 Hammersmith Road
London
W6 8BS
Fax: +44 (0) 20 8563 5801
Website: http://www.warnerchappell.co.uk

Genres: All types of music

Contact: Mike Smith

Use contact form on website to get in touch with the A&R department. No unsolicited material / demos.

Warner Music Group UK

27 Wrights Lane
London
W8 5SW
Website: https://www.wmg.com

Genres: All types of music

UK arm of major international label. No unsolicited submissions.

Warp Records

PO Box 25378
London
NW5 1GL
Email: info@warprecords.com
Email: international@warprecords.com
Website: http://warp.net
Website: https://soundcloud.com/warp-records/
Website: http://www.myspace.com/warprecords

Genres: Alternative; Ambient; Electronic; Experimental; Guitar based; Dance; Shoegaze

Contact: Nicola Fairchild

Query in first instance, describing your act, then send demo upon request only.

Wasted Years

Email: submissions@wastedyearsrecords.com
Email: contact@wastedyearsrecords.com
Website: https://wastedyearsrecords.com
Website: https://www.facebook.com/wastedyearsrecords

Genres: Electronic; Indie; Psychedelic Rock; Rock; Shoegaze

Describes itself as a label for a new era. Send demos by email with links to music online. No attachments.

Watercolour Music

Ardgour
Fort William
Scotland
PH33 7AH
Email: info@watercolourmusic.co.uk
Website: http://www.watercolourmusic.com
Website: https://www.facebook.com/watercolourmusicuk

Genres: Alternative; Singer-Songwriter; Acoustic; Indie

Contact: Nick Turner; Mary Ann Kennedy

Music company based in the Highlands, offering a studio, radio suite, and a complete design service. Send query by email with MP3 attachments.

When Planets Collide

Email: whenplanetscollide@hotmail.co.uk
Website: https://whenplanetscollide.bigcartel.com
Website: https://www.facebook.com/whenplanetscollideuk

Genres: Gothic; Heavy Metal; Underground

Contact: Gareth Kelly

Send query by email with links to music online.

Wichita Recordings

120 Curtain Road
London
EC2A 3SQ
Email: info@wichita-recordings.com
Website: http://www.wichita-recordings.com
Website: https://soundcloud.com/wichita-recordings
Website: http://www.myspace.com/wichitarecordings

Genres: All types of music

Record label based in London. Send query by email with links to music online. No MP3 attachments. Response not guaranteed.

Wire & Wool Records

Email: info@imnotfromlondon.com
Website: http://www.imnotfromlondon.com/event-category/wire-and-wool/

Genres: Acoustic; Americana; Country

Label based in Nottingham, putting on gigs and putting out releases.

Wobbly Music

Bakehouse Studio
52, Willows Lane
Accrington
Lancashire
BB5 0RT
Email: info@wobblymusic.net
Email: lynn@wobblymusic.net
Website: http://www.wobblymusic.net
Website: https://www.facebook.com/WobblyMusic.net

Genres: Acoustic; Blues; Classic Dance; Classical; Country; Dance; Ethnic; Folk; Funk; Fusion; Pop; Reggae; Rock; Singer-Songwriter

Contact: Lynn Monk

An independent music production, recording, and internet marketing company dedicated to the advancement of mature independent musicians.

Wolf Tone

The Church Studios
145h Crouch Hill
N8 9QH
Email: info@wolf-tone.com
Website: http://www.wolf-tone.com
Website: https://www.facebook.com/wolftoneHQ/

Genres: All types of music

London-based record label and publishing company launched in 2012. Send query by email with links to music online.

Wrong Way Records

Email: info@wrongwayrecords.com
Website: http://wrongwayrecords.com
Website: https://www.facebook.com/wrongwayrecords/

Genres: Psychedelic; Shoegaze; Space Rock; Leftfield; Kraut Rock

Independent record label with a passion for vinyl, specialising in psychedelia, shoegaze, spacerock, leftfield and krautrock. Not taking on bands for the foreseeable future.

WW Records

London
Email: info@wwrecords.co.uk
Website: http://www.wwrecords.co.uk
Website: https://soundcloud.com/wwrecords

Genres: Alternative Dance

Record label based in London. Send query by email with soundcloud links or MP3s.

XL Recordings

UK OFFICE:
FAO A&R
1 Codrington Mews

London
W11 2EH

US OFFICE:
304 Hudson Street, 7th Floor
New York, 10013
Fax: +44 (0) 20 8871 4178
Email: xl@xlrecordings.com
Website: http://www.xlrecordings.com
Website: https://www.facebook.com/xlrecordings

Genres: Alternative; Electronic

Contact: Matt Thornhill

Closed to submissions as at January 2018. Approach via manager only.

XVII Music Group

Brighton
Email: info@xviimusic.com
Website: https://www.xviimusic.com
Website: https://soundcloud.com/xviimusicgroup

Genres: All types of music

Artist development, record label, and recording studio based in Brighton.

Yala! Records

London
Email: info@yalarecords.com
Website: http://www.yalarecords.com
Website: https://www.facebook.com/yalarecords

Genres: Alternative; Electronic; Indie; Pop; Punk; Punk Rock; Rock

London-based label/club night founded in 2016. Send queries by email with links to music online.

ZTT Records

Sarm Studios
8-10 Basing Street
London
W11 1ET
Email: stephen@spz.com
Website: http://www.ztt.com
Website: https://www.facebook.com/zttrecords

Genres: Alternative; Acoustic; Indie; Electronic

Record label based in London. Send demo with contact details and SAE if return required, or send links to music online by email. Listens to every demo but responds only if interested.

ZyNg Tapes

Newcastle Upon Tyne
Email: info@zyngtapes.co.uk
Website: http://www.zyngtapes.co.uk
Website: https://www.facebook.com/zyngtapes

Genres: Indie; Lo-fi; Punk; Rock

Record label based in Newcastle. Send query through form on website with link to your music online.

Canadian Record Labels

For the most up-to-date listings of these and hundreds of other record labels, visit https://www.musicsocket.com/recordlabels

*To claim your **free** access to the site, please see the back of this book.*

Alert Music Inc.

Toronto, ON
Email: gabriella@alertmusic.com
Website: http://alertmusic.com
Website: https://www.facebook.com/AlertMusicInc

Genres: Jazz; Roots

Independent recording, publishing, producing and managing company, based in Toronto, Ontario.

Anthem Records

120 Bremner Blvd, Suite 2900
Toronto, ON M5J 0A8
Email: info@anthementertainmentgroup.com
Website: http://www.anthementertainmentgroup.com
Website: https://www.facebook.com/oleismajorlyindie/?fref=ts

Genres: Rock

Record label with offices in Toronto, Nashville, Los Angeles, New York, and London.

Aquarius Records

57-B Hymus Boulevard
Montreal, QC H9R 4T2
Email: francis@unidisc.com
Website: http://www.aquariusrecords.com
Website: https://twitter.com/aquariusrec
Website: https://myspace.com/aquariusrecordsltd

Genres: All types of music

Record label based in Montreal, formed in the summer of 69.

Battle Axe

Vancouver
Website: http://www.battleaxemusic.com

Genres: Hip-Hop

Hip-hop label based in Vancouver, Canada.

Bonsound

160, Saint-Viateur Street East, suite 400
Montreal, QC
H2T 1A8
Fax: +1 (514) 700-1307
Email: nextbigthing@bonsound.com
Email: info@bonsound.com
Website: http://www.bonsound.com

Genres: Alternative; Rock

An artist management company, a record label, a booking agency, a concert producer and a promotion and publicity agency. Not actively looking to expand its roster, but willing to listen. Send query by email with links to music online. No physical submissions or MP3 attachments.

Chacra Music

262 Rang 1
St. Etienne De Bolton
Quebec, J0E 2E0
Fax: +1 (450) 297-4616
Email: info@chacramusic.com
Website: http://www.chacramusic.com

Genres: New Age; Celtic; Guitar based; World

Record label based in St Etienne De Bolton, Quebec. Send demos by post on CD or cassette.

Coalition Music

1731 Lawrence Avenue East
Toronto, ON M1R 2X7
Email: info@coalitionmusic.com
Website: http://coalitionmusic.com
Website: https://www.facebook.com/CoalitionMUS

Genres: All types of music

Record label based in Toronto, Ontario. Send demos by email.

Constellation

PO Box 55012
CSP Fairmount
Montreal, Québec
H2T 3E2
Fax: +1 (253) 736-1966
Email: demos@cstrecords.com
Email: info@cstrecords.com
Website: http://cstrecords.com
Website: https://www.facebook.com/cstrecords

Genres: Alternative; Rock

Have released bands from the Canadian west coast, the United States, and Europe, but main artist focus remains predominantly regional, i.e. projects based in Montreal, the province of Quebec, or Central/Eastern Canada. Send query by email with links to music online. No attachments. Response not guaranteed.

Curve Music

714 Gerrard Street East
Toronto, Ontario
Email: luckj@curvemusic.com
Website: http://curvemusic.com
Website: https://www.facebook.com/curvemusiccanada

Genres: Alternative; Rock; Punk; Pop Rock

Record label based in Toronto, Ontario.

Distort

1111 Privet Place
Oakville, ON
L6J 7J6
Email: demos@teamdistort.com
Email: info@teamdistort.com
Website: http://www.distortent.com
Website: https://www.facebook.com/Distort

Genres: Metal

Independent metal label based in Toronto. Send query by email with links to music online.

Funktasy

#120-1055 Lucien L'Allier
Montreal, QC, Canada
H3G 3C4
Email: demos@funktasy.com
Website: http://funktasy.com

Genres: Commercial Electronic Experimental Funky Dancehall Dance Club Break Beat Dubstep Hip-Hop House Latin Pop R&B Rap Reggae Reggaeton Remix Rock Rhythm and Blues Synthpop Techno Trance Trip Hop World Soul New Age

Contact: Amir Hoss

A Canadian-based mainstream music label, originally established in 2010. Featuring various international artists, the prominent label continues to grow its roster of talent in the categories of EDM, Dance, Hip Hop, R&B, and Pop. As the company has continued to target different markets domestically and internationally, it has branched out to include sub-labels, each its own brand.

Last Gang Records

134 Peter St, Suite 700
Toronto, Canada
M5V 2H2

Email: info@lastgang.com
Website: https://lastgang.com

Genres: Electronic; Rock

Entertainment company based in Toronto, Ontario, including label, publishing, licensing, management, and promotions. Submit demos through Soundcloud.

Mint Records

PO Box 3613
Vancouver, BC
V6B 3Y6
Email: info@mintrecs.com
Website: https://www.mintrecs.com
Website: https://www.facebook.com/mintrecords

Genres: Indie

Record label based in Vancouver. Send demo on CD by post with your contact information. No fancy packaging required. Response if interested.

Seventh Fire Records

459 George St North
Peterborough, ON K9H 3R6
Email: t.street@seventhfirerecords.com
Website: https://seventhfirerecords.com

Genres: All types of music

Fiercely independent, artist-run music company.

604 Records

20 3 Ave E
Vancouver, BC V5T 1C3
Email: info@604records.com
Website: http://www.604records.com
Website: https://www.facebook.com/604records

Genres: Rock; Pop; Country; Electronic

Known for hard rock but willing to consider any style of music, as long as it's good. Send physical submissions only – preferably CDs. Does not respond to emails directing to online music clips. In submissions of more than 3 songs, indicate which are the most likely to be commercially successful, and ensure band details are on the CD itself. See website for full details.

Warner Music Canada

155 Gordon Baker Road, Suite 401
Toronto, Ontario
M2H 3N5
Website: http://www.warnermusic.ca
Website: https://www.facebook.com/warnermusiccanada

Genres: All types of music

Canadian arm of international music label, based in Toronto. Unsolicited music will not be listened to, and will be disposed of without record or response. Music is accepted through entertainment lawyers, managers, publishers, promoters and branch offices. Contact A&R team for more info.

Australian Record Labels

For the most up-to-date listings of these and hundreds of other record labels, visit https://www.musicsocket.com/recordlabels

*To claim your **free** access to the site, please see the back of this book.*

Cooking Vinyl Australia

Melbourne
Email: info@cookingvinylaustralia.com
Website: https://www.cookingvinylaustralia.com
Website: https://www.facebook.com/cookingvinylAU/

Genres: All types of music

Record label based in Melbourne, Australia, home to local and international acts.

Inertia

Email: info@inertiamusic.com
Website: http://inertiamusic.com
Website: https://www.facebook.com/inertiamusic

Genres: All types of music

Describes itself as Australia's leading music company.

Liberation Records

Email: info@liberationrecords.com.au
Website: http://www.liberationrecords.com.au
Website: https://soundcloud.com/liberationrecords

Genres: All types of music

Record label based in Albert Park, Australia.

Secret Service

PO Box 401
Fortitude Valley
QLD, 4006
Email: stacey@secret-service.com.au
Website: http://www.secret-service.com.au
Website: https://www.facebook.com/secretservicePR

Genres: All types of music

Contact: Stacey Piggott; Shari Hindmarsh

Management company based in Fortitude Valley, Queensland.

Warner Music Australia

39-47 Albany St
Crows Nest
NSW, 2065

MELBOURNE:
36 Wellington Street
Collingwood
VIC 3066
Website: http://www.warnermusic.com.au
Website: https://www.facebook.com/WarnerMusicAU

Genres: All types of music

Australian arm of international record label.

Record Labels Index

This section lists record labels by their genres, with directions to the section of the book where the full listing can be found.

You can create your own customised lists of record labels using different combinations of these subject areas, plus over a dozen other criteria, instantly online at https://www.musicsocket.com.

*To claim your **free** access to the site, please see the back of this book.*

All types of music
A-Blake Records (*US*)
Acorn Records (*UK*)
Alive Naturalsound (*US*)
Alya Records (*UK*)
American Eagle Recordings (*US*)
Anchorage Records (*UK*)
Aquarius Records (*Can*)
Associated Music International (AMI) Media (*UK*)
Atlantic Records (*UK*)
Atlantic Records (*US*)
Avenoir Records (*UK*)
Ba Da Bing Records & Management (*US*)
Battle Worldwide (*UK*)
Beluga Heights (*US*)
Bespoke Records (*UK*)
BFS Records (*UK*)
Big Noise (*US*)
Blackheart Records Group (*US*)
Bluesky Pie Records (*UK*)
BMG (*US*)
Brash Music (*US*)
Brushfire Records (*US*)
Canvasback Music (*US*)
Carved Records (*US*)
Cheap Lullaby Records (*US*)
Cherrytree Records (*US*)
Chicago Kid Records (*US*)
Coalition Music (*Can*)
Collect Records (*US*)
Columbia Records (*UK*)
Columbia Records (*US*)
Come Play With Me (*UK*)
Communion Records US (*US*)
Cooking Vinyl Australia (*Aus*)
Daptone Records (*US*)
DCD2 Records (*US*)
Decca Records (*UK*)
Deek Recordings (*UK*)
DigSin (*US*)
Discovering Arts Music Group (DAMG) (*UK*)
Disney Music Group (*US*)
DO IT Records (*US*)
Downtown Records (*US*)
Droma Records (*UK*)
Electric Honey Music (*UK*)
Elektra Music Group (*US*)
Elm City Music (*US*)
Emblem Music Group (*US*)
Entertainment One (eOne) (*US*)
Epic Records Group (*US*)
Eromeda Records (*UK*)
Everloving (*US*)
Evil Genius Records (*UK*)
Fade To Silence (*US*)
Fame Throwa Records (*UK*)
Famous Records (*US*)
Flowers in the Dustbin (*UK*)

Fool's Gold (*US*)
Frenchkiss Records (*US*)
Friendly Fire Recordings (*US*)
Fueled By Ramen (*US*)
G1 Muzic (*US*)
Gameplan Records (*UK*)
Glassnote (*US*)
Hollywood Records (*US*)
Iamsound (*US*)
Inertia (*Aus*)
Infidel Records (*US*)
Innovative Leisure (*US*)
Inspired Studios Inc. (*US*)
Intelligent Noise (*US*)
J and J Records (*UK*)
Jost Music (*UK*)
K Records (*US*)
Keep Me Young (KMY) (*UK*)
Killroom Records (*US*)
Lapsang House (*UK*)
Last Night From Glasgow (*UK*)
Lava Records (*US*)
LGM Records (*UK*)
Liberation Records (*Aus*)
Lightyear Entertainment (*US*)
Loma Vista (*US*)
Loyalty Over Royalty Records (*US*)
Machin Entertainment (*US*)
Mandala Records (*US*)
Mascot Label Group (*US*)
Mayfield Records (*UK*)
Me & You Music (*UK*)
MHM (*UK*)
Middle West (*US*)
Modern Sky (*UK*)
Musical Bear Records (*UK*)
Never Fade Records (*UK*)
New Street Records (*UK*)
Pink Lane Records (*UK*)
Rampage Records (*US*)
Reckless Yes (*UK*)
Robot Needs Home (*UK*)
Rolla Records (*UK*)
Rooftop Records (*UK*)
Rose Coloured Records (*UK*)
RU:Listening (*UK*)
Sad Club Records (*UK*)
Sain (*UK*)
Scruff of the Neck (SOTN) (*UK*)
Secret Service (*Aus*)
Seventh Fire Records (*Can*)
Sick House Entertainment (*US*)
Small Bear Records (*UK*)
Small Pond Record Label (*UK*)
Somewhere Records (*UK*)
Sony Music UK & Ireland (*UK*)
Sotones Music Co-Operative (*UK*)
Sound-Hub Records (*UK*)
Speedy Enix Records (*UK*)
Speedy Wunderground (*UK*)
Square Leg (*UK*)
State51 Conspiracy (*UK*)
Strawberry Moon Records (*UK*)
Sunbird Records (*UK*)
Sunset Music Supervision (*US*)
Sunset Recordings (*US*)
Sunset Special Markets (SSM) (*US*)
Swallow Song Records (*UK*)
Tama Industries (*US*)
Tangled Talk Records (*UK*)
TeaPot Records (*UK*)
37 Records & Management (*US*)
300 Entertainment (*US*)
Tonally Records (*US*)
Tontena Music (*UK*)
TOR Records (*UK*)
Tough Love Records (*UK*)
Traffic Cone Records (*UK*)
Transgressive Records (*UK*)
Trashmouth Records (*UK*)
Trellis Music (*UK*)
Triassic Tusk (*UK*)
Tu-kay Records (*UK*)
Ubiquity Project Records (*UK*)
Universal Music Group (*UK*)
Velour Music Group (*US*)
Vertigo Records (*UK*)
Virgin EMI Records (*UK*)
Wagg Records (*UK*)
Wall of Sound Recordings Ltd (*UK*)
War Room Records (*UK*)
Warner / Chappell Music (*UK*)
Warner Bros. Records (*US*)
Warner Music Australia (*Aus*)
Warner Music Canada (*Can*)
Warner Music Group (WMG) (*US*)
Warner Music Group UK (*UK*)
Washington Square Music (*US*)
Wichita Recordings (*UK*)
Wolf Tone (*UK*)
XVII Music Group (*UK*)
Yamaha Entertainment Group of America (*US*)

Acid
Brock Wild (*UK*)
Futurist Recordings (*UK*)
Sounds Like Vinyl (*UK*)

Acoustic
Acoustic Disc (*US*)
ATO Records (*US*)

DJD Music Ltd (*UK*)
Everyday Records (*UK*)
Harbourtown Records (*UK*)
Haystack Records (*UK*)
Heist or Hit Records (*UK*)
Lost in the Manor (*UK*)
Maggie's Music (*US*)
Mellowtone Records (*UK*)
Moth Man Records (*US*)
musicXart (*UK*)
QM Records (*UK*)
Spiritual Records (*UK*)
Staylittle Music (*UK*)
Supermarine Music (*UK*)
Tama Industries Record Label (*US*)
These Bloody Thieves Records (*UK*)
Tonotopic Records (*UK*)
Vox Humana (*UK*)
Wah Wah 45s (*UK*)
Watercolour Music (*UK*)
Wire & Wool Records (*UK*)
Wobbly Music (*UK*)
ZTT Records (*UK*)

Alternative

0114 Records (*UK*)
A&M Records (*US*)
Abattoir Blues (*UK*)
The Adult Teeth Recording Company (*UK*)
American Laundromat Records (*US*)
AnalogueTrash Ltd (*UK*)
Asthmatic Kitty Records (*US*)
Astralwerks Records (*US*)
ATO Records (*US*)
Bad Bat Records (*UK*)
Bar/None Records (*US*)
Bear Love Records (*UK*)
Beggars Group (US) (*US*)
Black Bleach Records (*UK*)
Blak Hand Records (*UK*)
Bloodshot Records (*US*)
Bonsound (*Can*)
Box Records (*UK*)
Brightonsfinest (*UK*)
Bubblewrap Collective (*UK*)
Burnt Toast Vinyl (*US*)
Carpark Records (*US*)
Cascine (*US*)
Castle Records (*US*)
CCT Records (*UK*)
Chalkpit Records Ltd (*UK*)
Compass Records (*US*)
Constellation (*Can*)
Curve Music (*Can*)
Dangerbird Records (*US*)
Demon Music Group (*UK*)
Dewey Dog Records (*US*)
Dirty Bingo Records (*UK*)
Dirty Canvas Music (*US*)
DJD Music Ltd (*UK*)
Doghouse Records (*US*)
Doing Life Records (*UK*)
Don't Try (*UK*)
Drag City (*US*)
Easy Life Records (*UK*)
The End Records (*US*)
Epitaph (*US*)
Equal Vision Records (*US*)
Everyday Records (*UK*)
Fearless Records (*US*)
Ferret Music (*US*)
Fox Records (*UK*)
Freaks R Us (*UK*)
Frontier Records (*US*)
Ganbei Records (*UK*)
Graphite Records (*UK*)
Headliner Records / George Tobin Music (*US*)
Heist or Hit Records (*UK*)
Highwheel Records (*US*)
Hit City USA (*US*)
Jagjaguwar (*US*)
Kirtland Records (*US*)
Le Grand Magistery, LLC (*US*)
Libertino (*UK*)
Loner Noise (*UK*)
Lost in the Manor (*UK*)
Mad Dragon Music Group (*US*)
Metropolis Records (*US*)
Moth Man Records (*US*)
NB Audio (*UK*)
Organ Records (*UK*)
Partisan Records (*UK*)
Phantasy (*UK*)
Safe Suburban Home (*UK*)
Saraseto Records (*UK*)
Schnitzel Records Ltd (*UK*)
Scottish Fiction (*UK*)
Seed Records (*UK*)
Sister 9 Recordings (*UK*)
Skate Mountain Records (*US*)
Snapper Music (*UK*)
So Recordings (*UK*)
Spiritual Records (*UK*)
STA – Small Town America (*UK*)
Stolen Recordings (*UK*)
Subdust Music (*UK*)
Sunday Best Recordings (*UK*)
Supermarine Music (*UK*)
Supersonic Media (*UK*)

Superstar Destroyer Records (*UK*)
These Bloody Thieves Records (*UK*)
Thumbhole Records (*UK*)
Tigertrap Records (*UK*)
ToneTrade Productions (*UK*)
Tonotopic Records (*UK*)
Too Pure Records (*UK*)
TRNS Records (*UK*)
21st Century Music (*UK*)
00:02:59 LLC (*US*)
Tye Die Tapes (*UK*)
Warm Electronic Recordings (*US*)
Warp Records (*UK*)
Watercolour Music (*UK*)
WW Records (*UK*)
XL Recordings (*UK*)
Yala! Records (*UK*)
ZTT Records (*UK*)

Ambient

The Adult Teeth Recording Company (*UK*)
Bad Bat Records (*UK*)
Canigou Records (*UK*)
CCT Records (*UK*)
Clickpop Records (*US*)
Cold Spring (*UK*)
Delved in Dreams, inc. (*US*)
DJD Music Ltd (*UK*)
DOMO Records, Inc. (*US*)
Warp Records (*UK*)
Waveform Records (*US*)

Americana

Alligator Records (*US*)
At the Helm Records (*UK*)
Aveline Records (*UK*)
Bear Love Records (*UK*)
Carnival Music (*US*)
Compass Records (*US*)
Dualtone Records (*US*)
Funzalo Records (*US*)
Idol Records (*US*)
Landslide Records (*US*)
Lightning Rod Records (*US*)
Little Fish Records (*US*)
Lost Highway Records (*US*)
Moth Man Records (*US*)
My Little Empire (*UK*)
Skate Mountain Records (*US*)
Super Fan 99 (*UK*)
00:02:59 LLC (*US*)
Wire & Wool Records (*UK*)

Atmospheric

21st Century Music (*UK*)

Avant-Garde

Dewey Dog Records (*US*)
DJD Music Ltd (*UK*)
Focused Silence (*UK*)
Tonotopic Records (*UK*)

Black Metal

Century Media Records (US) (*US*)
Mad Decent (*US*)

Blues

Abattoir Blues (*UK*)
Acoustic Disc (*US*)
Alligator Records (*US*)
Big Bear Records (*UK*)
The Birdman Recording Group, Inc. (*US*)
Blind Pig Records (*US*)
Bloodshot Records (*US*)
Castle Records (*US*)
CMH Records (*US*)
Compass Records (*US*)
Concord Music Group (*US*)
Delmark Records (*US*)
Delta Groove Music (*US*)
Dewey Dog Records (*US*)
Earache Records Inc. (*US*)
Earwig Music Company, Inc. (*US*)
Everyday Records (*UK*)
Fat Possum Records (*US*)
Lamon Records (*US*)
Landslide Records (*US*)
Little Fish Records (*US*)
Lovelane Music Group (*US*)
Mellowtone Records (*UK*)
Skate Mountain Records (*US*)
Spiritual Records (*UK*)
Stryker Records, Inc. (*US*)
Talking Elephant (*UK*)
Tama Industries Record Label (*US*)
ToneTrade Productions (*UK*)
00:02:59 LLC (*US*)
Wild Records (*US*)
Wobbly Music (*UK*)
Yep Roc Records (*US*)

Break Beat

Forward Motion Records (UK) (*UK*)
Funktasy (*Can*)
Sci Fi Ltd (*UK*)
Sub Cube Records (*UK*)
Tru Thoughts (*UK*)

Celtic

Chacra Music (*Can*)
Compass Records (*US*)
Green Linnet (*US*)
Maggie's Music (*US*)
Sharpe Music (*UK*)
Vertical Records (*UK*)

Chill

Kokeshi (*UK*)

Waveform Records (*US*)
Christian
Ardent Records (*US*)
Black River Entertainment (*US*)
Capitol Christian Music Group (*US*)
Curb Records (*US*)
Delved in Dreams, inc. (*US*)
Dove Records (*UK*)
Fair Trade (*US*)
Lamon Records (*US*)
Maranatha Music (*US*)
Tama Industries Record Label (*US*)
Vineyard Worship (*US*)
VSR Music Group (*US*)
Word Records (*US*)
Classic
Delved in Dreams, inc. (*US*)
Everyday Records (*UK*)
Frontier Records (*US*)
1-2-3-4 Go! Records (*US*)
Skate Mountain Records (*US*)
Talking Elephant (*UK*)
Tama Industries Record Label (*US*)
Wobbly Music (*UK*)
Classical
Acoustic Disc (*US*)
API Records (*US*)
Arabesque Recordings (*US*)
The Birdman Recording Group, Inc. (*US*)
Cantaloupe Music (*US*)
Chesky Records (*US*)
Concord Music Group (*US*)
Curb Records (*US*)
Delos (*US*)
Delved in Dreams, inc. (*US*)
DOMO Records, Inc. (*US*)
Everyday Records (*UK*)
SOMM Recordings (*UK*)
Trestle Records (*UK*)
Wobbly Music (*UK*)
Club
Alex King Records (*UK*)
Funktasy (*Can*)
Midnineties (*UK*)
Sentosa Records (*UK*)
Tama Industries Record Label (*US*)
Commercial
Amathus Music (*US*)
ChillnBass (*UK*)
Funktasy (*Can*)
Skate Mountain Records (*US*)
Subdust Music (*UK*)
Tama Industries Record Label (*US*)
Contemporary
Appleseed Recordings (*US*)
Aware Records (*US*)
DOMO Records, Inc. (*US*)
Dove Records (*UK*)
Everyday Records (*UK*)
Fervor Records (*US*)
LML Music (*US*)
SLAM Productions (*UK*)
Trestle Records (*UK*)
The Verve Music Group (*US*)
Word Records (*US*)
Country
Alternative Tentacles Records (*US*)
Aveline Records (*UK*)
Average Joes Entertainment (*US*)
Big Loud Records (*US*)
Big Machine Records (*US*)
The Birdman Recording Group, Inc. (*US*)
Black River Entertainment (*US*)
Bloodshot Records (*US*)
Capitol Records Nashville (*US*)
Carnival Music (*US*)
Castle Records (*US*)
CMH Records (*US*)
Curb Records (*US*)
Delved in Dreams, inc. (*US*)
DM Music Group (*US*)
Dreamscope Media Group (DMG) (*UK*)
Lamon Records (*US*)
Lost Highway Records (*US*)
Mellowtone Records (*UK*)
My Little Empire (*UK*)
1-2-3-4 Go! Records (*US*)
604 Records (*Can*)
Skate Mountain Records (*US*)
Stryker Records, Inc. (*US*)
Tama Industries Record Label (*US*)
00:02:59 LLC (*US*)
Warner Bros. Records Nashville (*US*)
Wire & Wool Records (*UK*)
Wobbly Music (*UK*)
Word Records (*US*)
Yep Roc Records (*US*)
Cuban
Delved in Dreams, inc. (*US*)
Dance
Alex King Records (*UK*)
Amathus Music (*US*)
Astralwerks Records (*US*)
Axtone (*UK*)
Bad Bat Records (*UK*)
Beatphreak (*UK*)
Beggars Group (US) (*US*)
Big Beat (*US*)
Brightonsfinest (*UK*)
Capitol Music Group (*US*)

ChillnBass (*UK*)
Curb Records (*US*)
Dauman Music (*US*)
Defenders Ent (*UK*)
Delved in Dreams, inc. (*US*)
Dewey Dog Records (*US*)
Disruptor Records (*US*)
DJD Music Ltd (*UK*)
DM Music Group (*US*)
Eton Messy Records (*UK*)
Explosive Beatz Records (*UK*)
Funktasy (*Can*)
Incessant Records (*UK*)
Kaneda Records (*UK*)
Lost in the Manor (*UK*)
LoveCat Music (*US*)
NB Audio (*UK*)
Phantasy (*UK*)
Southern Fried Records (*UK*)
Sub Cube Records (*UK*)
SubSoul (*UK*)
Supersonic Media (*UK*)
Tama Industries Record Label (*US*)
37 Adventures (*UK*)
Warp Records (*UK*)
Wobbly Music (*UK*)
WW Records (*UK*)

Dancehall

Funktasy (*Can*)

Deep Funk

Dewey Dog Records (*US*)

Disco

Alex King Records (*UK*)
Axtone (*UK*)
Coloursounds (*UK*)
DFA Records (*US*)
Perfect Havoc Limited (*UK*)

Doom

Box Records (*UK*)
Cold Spring (*UK*)
Riff Rock Records (*UK*)

Downtempo

21st Century Music (*UK*)
Waveform Records (*US*)

Drum and Bass

Alex King Records (*UK*)
Elevate Records (*UK*)
NB Audio (*UK*)
OXRecordings (*UK*)
Ramajam Recordings (*UK*)
Run Tingz Recordings (*UK*)
Saving Grace Music (*UK*)
Serotone Recordings (*UK*)
Shogun Audio Ltd (*UK*)
Sliced Note Recordings (*UK*)
Soulvent Records (*UK*)
Sub Cube Records (*UK*)
Supersonic Media (*UK*)

Dub

Alex King Records (*UK*)
NB Audio (*UK*)
Wah Wah 45s (*UK*)

Dubstep

Alex King Records (*UK*)
Axtone (*UK*)
CCT Records (*UK*)
Funktasy (*Can*)
Kokeshi (*UK*)
NB Audio (*UK*)
Project Allout Records (*UK*)
Saving Grace Music (*UK*)
Southpoint (*UK*)
Sub Cube Records (*UK*)
Tama Industries Record Label (*US*)

Electronic

!K7 Records (*UK*)
The Adult Teeth Recording Company (*UK*)
Akira (*UK*)
Alex King Records (*UK*)
Alias Records (*US*)
Amathus Music (*US*)
Aphagia Recordings (*US*)
Astralwerks Records (*US*)
Asylum Arts (*US*)
Axtone (*UK*)
Babygrande Records, Inc. (*US*)
Bad Bat Records (*UK*)
Beggars Group (US) (*US*)
Big Beat (*US*)
Black Bleach Records (*UK*)
Brightonsfinest (*UK*)
Bubblewrap Collective (*UK*)
Canigou Records (*UK*)
Cantaloupe Music (*US*)
Cascine (*US*)
CCT Records (*UK*)
Cleopatra Records (*US*)
Clickpop Records (*US*)
Cold Spring (*UK*)
Coloursounds (*UK*)
Delved in Dreams, inc. (*US*)
Dewey Dog Records (*US*)
DFA Records (*US*)
Dirty Bingo Records (*UK*)
DJD Music Ltd (*UK*)
Domino Record Co. Ltd (*US*)
DOMO Records, Inc. (*US*)
Double Denim Records (*UK*)
Eton Messy Records (*UK*)

Focused Silence (*UK*)
Forward Motion Records (UK) (*UK*)
Freaks R Us (*UK*)
Funktasy (*Can*)
Ghostly International (*US*)
Harbour Records (*US*)
HQ Familia (*UK*)
Hyperdub Records (*UK*)
Kaneda Records (*UK*)
Keyframe Music (*US*)
Kokeshi (*UK*)
Last Gang Records (*Can*)
Lo Recordings (*UK*)
Midnineties (*UK*)
Milan Records (*US*)
NB Audio (*UK*)
101BPM (*UK*)
Phantasy (*UK*)
Portfolio Music (*UK*)
Saffron Records (*UK*)
Salute the Sun (*UK*)
Salvation Records (*UK*)
Saved Records (*UK*)
Sci Fi Ltd (*UK*)
Scottish Fiction (*UK*)
Seed Records (*UK*)
Shogun Audio Ltd (*UK*)
604 Records (*Can*)
Sonic Bear (*UK*)
Sonic Cathedral (*UK*)
Soundplate (*UK*)
Sounds Like Vinyl (*UK*)
Southern Fried Records (*UK*)
Sub Cube Records (*UK*)
Subdust Music (*UK*)
SubSoul (*UK*)
Sunday Best Recordings (*UK*)
Sunstone Records Ltd (*UK*)
Supermarine Music (*UK*)
Tape Club Records (*UK*)
37 Adventures (*UK*)
This Is It Forever (*UK*)
Tigertrap Records (*UK*)
Tonotopic Records (*UK*)
Trestle Records (*UK*)
21st Century Music (*UK*)
Voltage Records (*UK*)
Vox Humana (*UK*)
Wah Wah 45s (*UK*)
Warp Records (*UK*)
Wasted Years (*UK*)
Waveform Records (*US*)
XL Recordings (*UK*)
Yala! Records (*UK*)
ZTT Records (*UK*)

Emo
Bullet Tooth (*US*)
Deep Elm Records (*US*)
Disconnect Disconnect Records (*UK*)
Doing Life Records (*UK*)
Epitaph (*US*)
Geilston Records (*UK*)
Moth Man Records (*US*)
Small Town Records (*UK*)
Thumbhole Records (*UK*)

Ethnic
Delved in Dreams, inc. (*US*)
Dewey Dog Records (*US*)
Wobbly Music (*UK*)

Experimental
The Adult Teeth Recording Company (*UK*)
Alex King Records (*UK*)
Aphagia Recordings (*US*)
Audio Vendor (*UK*)
Bad Bat Records (*UK*)
Box Records (*UK*)
Cold Spring (*UK*)
Dance To The Radio (*UK*)
DJD Music Ltd (*UK*)
Drag City (*US*)
Fire Records (*UK*)
Focused Silence (*UK*)
Freaks R Us (*UK*)
Funktasy (*Can*)
Futurist Recordings (*UK*)
God Unknown Records (*UK*)
Hydra Head Records (*US*)
Morphius Records (*US*)
musicXart (*UK*)
SLAM Productions (*UK*)
Subdust Music (*UK*)
T&R Recordings (*US*)
This Is It Forever (*UK*)
Tonotopic Records (*UK*)
Tye Die Tapes (*UK*)
Vox Humana (*UK*)
Warp Records (*UK*)

Extreme
Earache Records Inc. (*US*)

Folk
0114 Records (*UK*)
Acoustic Disc (*US*)
Akira (*UK*)
American Laundromat Records (*US*)
Appleseed Recordings (*US*)
Audio Vendor (*UK*)
Aveline Records (*UK*)
Bear Love Records (*UK*)
Box Records (*UK*)

Breakfast Records LLP (*UK*)
Brightonsfinest (*UK*)
Bubblewrap Collective (*UK*)
Canigou Records (*UK*)
Clickpop Records (*US*)
Compass Records (*US*)
Delved in Dreams, inc. (*US*)
Dewey Dog Records (*US*)
DJD Music Ltd (*UK*)
DOMO Records, Inc. (*US*)
Dreamscope Media Group (DMG) (*UK*)
Dualtone Records (*US*)
Everyday Records (*UK*)
Funzalo Records (*US*)
Ganbei Records (*UK*)
Get Hip Recordings (*US*)
Green Linnet (*US*)
Harbourtown Records (*UK*)
Haystack Records (*UK*)
Hudson Records (*UK*)
Jagjaguwar (*US*)
Lamon Records (*US*)
Landslide Records (*US*)
Little Fish Records (*US*)
Lost Highway Records (*US*)
Lost in the Manor (*UK*)
Mellowtone Records (*UK*)
Saving Grace Music (*UK*)
Scottish Fiction (*UK*)
ScreamLite Records (*UK*)
Seed Records (*UK*)
Spiritual Records (*UK*)
Staylittle Music (*UK*)
Sunstone Records Ltd (*UK*)
Supermarine Music (*UK*)
Talking Elephant (*UK*)
These Bloody Thieves Records (*UK*)
00:02:59 LLC (*US*)
Wobbly Music (*UK*)
Yep Roc Records (*US*)

Funk
Chalkpit Records Ltd (*UK*)
Dewey Dog Records (*US*)
Lovelane Music Group (*US*)
Moth Man Records (*US*)
1-2-3-4 Go! Records (*US*)
QM Records (*UK*)
Tru Thoughts (*UK*)
Wah Wah 45s (*UK*)
Wobbly Music (*UK*)

Funky
Dewey Dog Records (*US*)
Forward Motion Records (UK) (*UK*)
Funktasy (*Can*)
Moth Man Records (*US*)
Stryker Records, Inc. (*US*)
21st Century Music (*UK*)

Fusion
Delved in Dreams, inc. (*US*)
Wobbly Music (*UK*)

Garage
0114 Records (*UK*)
Abattoir Blues (*UK*)
Alex King Records (*UK*)
The Birdman Recording Group, Inc. (*US*)
Black Bleach Records (*UK*)
Blak Hand Records (*UK*)
Bomp Records (*US*)
Breakfast Records LLP (*UK*)
Epitaph (*US*)
God Unknown Records (*UK*)
In the Red Records (*US*)
Kokeshi (*UK*)
Midnineties (*UK*)
Moth Man Records (*US*)
Nice Swan Records (*UK*)
1-2-3-4 Go! Records (*US*)
Project Allout Records (*UK*)
Psymmetry Collective (*UK*)
Restless Bear (*UK*)
Salvation Records (*UK*)
Saving Grace Music (*UK*)
Skate Mountain Records (*US*)
Sour Grapes (*UK*)
Southpoint (*UK*)
Strong Island Recordings (*UK*)
SubSoul (*UK*)
Two Piece Records (*UK*)
Vallance Records (*UK*)
Wild Records (*US*)

Glam
Mad Decent (*US*)

Glitch
Alex King Records (*UK*)
Aphagia Recordings (*US*)
Midnineties (*UK*)

Gospel
Blackberry Records (*US*)
Capitol Christian Music Group (*US*)
Castle Records (*US*)
CMH Records (*US*)
Delved in Dreams, inc. (*US*)
Dove Records (*UK*)
Hacienda Records (*US*)
Hidden Beach Recordings (*US*)
Lamon Records (*US*)
Maranatha Music (*US*)
Tama Industries Record Label (*US*)
00:02:59 LLC (*US*)

Gothic
Century Media Records (US) (*US*)
Cleopatra Records (*US*)
Tama Industries Record Label (*US*)
When Planets Collide (*UK*)
Grime
Alex King Records (*UK*)
i/o Recordings (*UK*)
Kokeshi (*UK*)
Less is More Music Ltd (*UK*)
Portfolio Music (*UK*)
Project Allout Records (*UK*)
QM Records (*UK*)
Regent Street Records (*UK*)
Saving Grace Music (*UK*)
Southpoint (*UK*)
Guitar based
Abattoir Blues (*UK*)
Blak Hand Records (*UK*)
Breakfast Records LLP (*UK*)
Chacra Music (*Can*)
Copro Productions (*UK*)
DJD Music Ltd (*UK*)
Everyday Records (*UK*)
Moth Man Records (*US*)
My Little Empire (*UK*)
Organ Records (*UK*)
TRNS Records (*UK*)
Twin City Records (*UK*)
Voltage Records (*UK*)
Warp Records (*UK*)
Hard
0114 Records (*UK*)
Bieler Bros. Records (*US*)
Century Media Records (US) (*US*)
DJD Music Ltd (*UK*)
Drag City (*US*)
Ferret Music (*US*)
Forward Motion Records (UK) (*UK*)
Moth Man Records (*US*)
Stryker Records, Inc. (*US*)
T&R Recordings (*US*)
Tama Industries Record Label (*US*)
Hardcore
Alex King Records (*UK*)
Alternative Tentacles Records (*US*)
Bridge Nine Records (*US*)
Bullet Tooth (*US*)
Century Media Records (US) (*US*)
Disconnect Disconnect Records (*UK*)
Doghouse Records (*US*)
Epitaph (*US*)
Fearless Records (*US*)
Hopeless Records (*US*)
Hydra Head Records (*US*)
Metal Blade Records, Inc. (*US*)
Moth Man Records (*US*)
1-2-3-4 Go! Records (*US*)
Small Town Records (*UK*)
Speedowax (*UK*)
Supersonic Media (*UK*)
T&R Recordings (*US*)
Tama Industries Record Label (*US*)
Thumbhole Records (*UK*)
Victory Records (*US*)
Heavy
Copro Productions (*UK*)
DJD Music Ltd (*UK*)
Hydra Head Records (*US*)
Moth Man Records (*US*)
T&R Recordings (*US*)
When Planets Collide (*UK*)
Hip-Hop
Activate Entertainment (*US*)
Babygrande Records, Inc. (*US*)
Bad Boy Entertainment (*US*)
Barbarian Productions (*US*)
Battle Axe (*Can*)
Big Beat (*US*)
Cash Money Records (*US*)
CCT Records (*UK*)
Cleopatra Records (*US*)
Derrty Entertainment (*US*)
Dewey Dog Records (*US*)
DJD Music Ltd (*UK*)
Dose Entertainment (*UK*)
Duck Down Music (*US*)
Epitaph (*US*)
Explosive Beatz Records (*UK*)
Funktasy (*Can*)
Ghostly International (*US*)
Hidden Beach Recordings (*US*)
i/o Recordings (*UK*)
Idol Records (*US*)
Interscope Geffen A&M (*US*)
Jaggo Records, LLC (*US*)
Kaneda Records (*UK*)
Less is More Music Ltd (*UK*)
Lost in the Manor (*UK*)
LoveCat Music (*US*)
Melee Recording Group (*UK*)
Morphius Records (*US*)
NB Audio (*UK*)
1-2-3-4 Go! Records (*US*)
Portfolio Music (*UK*)
QM Records (*UK*)
Salute the Sun (*UK*)
Sapien Records Limited (*UK*)
Saving Grace Music (*UK*)
Scottish Fiction (*UK*)

Skate Mountain Records (*US*)
Stryker Records, Inc. (*US*)
Tama Industries Record Label (*US*)
Tight Lines (*UK*)
Tru Thoughts (*UK*)
Viper Records (*US*)
Waxploitation Records (*US*)
Word Records (*US*)

House

Alex King Records (*UK*)
Amathus Music (*US*)
Axtone (*UK*)
Big Beat (*US*)
Brock Wild (*UK*)
Circus Recordings (*UK*)
Coloursounds (*UK*)
DFA Records (*US*)
Forward Motion Records (UK) (*UK*)
Funktasy (*Can*)
Futurist Recordings (*UK*)
Jeepers! Music (*UK*)
Mad Decent (*US*)
Midnineties (*UK*)
Perfect Havoc Limited (*UK*)
Portfolio Music (*UK*)
Saved Records (*UK*)
Saving Grace Music (*UK*)
Sci Fi Ltd (*UK*)
Sentosa Records (*UK*)
Shabby Doll Records (*UK*)
Snatch! Records (*UK*)
Sonic Bear (*UK*)
Soundplate (*UK*)
Standby (*UK*)
Sub Cube Records (*UK*)
SubSoul (*UK*)
Supersonic Media (*UK*)
Tone Artistry (*UK*)
Toolroom Records (*UK*)

House

Alex King Records (*UK*)
Amathus Music (*US*)
Axtone (*UK*)
Big Beat (*US*)
Brock Wild (*UK*)
Circus Recordings (*UK*)
Coloursounds (*UK*)
DFA Records (*US*)
Forward Motion Records (UK) (*UK*)
Funktasy (*Can*)
Futurist Recordings (*UK*)
Jeepers! Music (*UK*)
Mad Decent (*US*)
Midnineties (*UK*)
Perfect Havoc Limited (*UK*)
Portfolio Music (*UK*)
Saved Records (*UK*)
Saving Grace Music (*UK*)
Sci Fi Ltd (*UK*)
Sentosa Records (*UK*)
Shabby Doll Records (*UK*)
Snatch! Records (*UK*)
Sonic Bear (*UK*)
Soundplate (*UK*)
Standby (*UK*)
Sub Cube Records (*UK*)
SubSoul (*UK*)
Supersonic Media (*UK*)
Tone Artistry (*UK*)
Toolroom Records (*UK*)

IDM

Alex King Records (*UK*)

Indie

0114 Records (*UK*)
4AD (*US*)
6/8 Records (*US*)
A&M Records (*US*)
The Adult Teeth Recording Company (*UK*)
Akira (*UK*)
Alias Records (*US*)
Alternative Tentacles Records (*US*)
American Laundromat Records (*US*)
Anti (*US*)
ATO Records (*US*)
Audio Vendor (*UK*)
Aware Records (*US*)
Babygrande Records, Inc. (*US*)
Bar/None Records (*US*)
Barsuk Records (*US*)
Beggars Group (US) (*US*)
Black Bleach Records (*UK*)
Bloodshot Records (*US*)
Bomp Records (*US*)
Breakfast Records LLP (*UK*)
Brightonsfinest (*UK*)
Bubblewrap Collective (*UK*)
Capitol Music Group (*US*)
Carnival Music (*US*)
Chalkpit Records Ltd (*UK*)
Coloursounds (*UK*)
Copro Productions (*UK*)
Dance To The Radio (*UK*)
Dangerbird Records (*US*)
Deep Elm Records (*US*)
Delved in Dreams, inc. (*US*)
Demon Music Group (*UK*)
Dewey Dog Records (*US*)
DFA Records (*US*)
Dirty Bingo Records (*UK*)

DJD Music Ltd (*UK*)
Doing Life Records (*UK*)
Domino Record Co. Ltd (*US*)
DOMO Records, Inc. (*US*)
Don't Try (*UK*)
Donut Records (*UK*)
Dovecote Records (*US*)
Dualtone Records (*US*)
The End Records (*US*)
Endearment Records (*UK*)
Epitaph (*US*)
Equal Vision Records (*US*)
Everyday Records (*UK*)
Fat Possum Records (*US*)
Fearless Records (*US*)
Fervor Records (*US*)
Funzalo Records (*US*)
Geilston Records (*UK*)
Get Hip Recordings (*US*)
Ghostly International (*US*)
Heist or Hit Records (*UK*)
Hopeless Records (*US*)
Idol Records (*US*)
Interscope Geffen A&M (*US*)
Jagjaguwar (*US*)
Kanine Records (*US*)
Kill Rock Stars (*US*)
Matador Records (*US*)
Merge Records (*US*)
Metropolis Records (*US*)
Mint Records (*Can*)
Moth Man Records (*US*)
My Little Empire (*UK*)
Nice Swan Records (*UK*)
1-2-3-4 Go! Records (*US*)
Organ Records (*UK*)
Rough Trade Records (*UK*)
Safe Suburban Home (*UK*)
Saraseto Records (*UK*)
Saving Grace Music (*UK*)
So Recordings (*UK*)
Speedowax (*UK*)
STA – Small Town America (*UK*)
Staylittle Music (*UK*)
Stoa Sounds (*UK*)
Stolen Recordings (*UK*)
Strong Island Recordings (*UK*)
Stryker Records, Inc. (*US*)
Sunday Best Recordings (*UK*)
Super Fan 99 (*UK*)
Tama Industries Record Label (*US*)
These Bloody Thieves Records (*UK*)
37 Adventures (*UK*)
Twin City Records (*UK*)
00:02:59 LLC (*US*)
Tye Die Tapes (*UK*)
Vallance Records (*UK*)
Victory Records (*US*)
Wasted Years (*UK*)
Watercolour Music (*UK*)
Yala! Records (*UK*)
ZTT Records (*UK*)
ZyNg Tapes (*UK*)

Industrial

Aphagia Recordings (*US*)
Cleopatra Records (*US*)
Cold Spring (*UK*)
Delved in Dreams, inc. (*US*)
DJD Music Ltd (*UK*)

Instrumental

Aphagia Recordings (*US*)
Babygrande Records, Inc. (*US*)
CMH Records (*US*)
Curb Records (*US*)
Delved in Dreams, inc. (*US*)
DJD Music Ltd (*UK*)
Everyday Records (*UK*)
Idol Records (*US*)
Tama Industries Record Label (*US*)
Trestle Records (*UK*)

Jazz

Acoustic Disc (*US*)
Alert Music Inc. (*Can*)
Arabesque Recordings (*US*)
Big Bear Records (*UK*)
The Birdman Recording Group, Inc. (*US*)
Blue Note Label Group (*US*)
Bolero Records (*US*)
Cantaloupe Music (*US*)
Chesky Records (*US*)
Cleopatra Records (*US*)
Compass Records (*US*)
Concord Music Group (*US*)
Curb Records (*US*)
Delmark Records (*US*)
Delved in Dreams, inc. (*US*)
Dewey Dog Records (*US*)
Earwig Music Company, Inc. (*US*)
Everyday Records (*UK*)
Focused Silence (*UK*)
Hidden Beach Recordings (*US*)
Jaggo Records, LLC (*US*)
Landslide Records (*US*)
Less is More Music Ltd (*UK*)
Little Fish Records (*US*)
Lost in the Manor (*UK*)
LoveCat Music (*US*)
Marsalis Music (*US*)
1-2-3-4 Go! Records (*US*)
QM Records (*UK*)

Saffron Records (*UK*)
SLAM Productions (*UK*)
Tama Industries Record Label (*US*)
Tight Lines (*UK*)
ToneTrade Productions (*UK*)
Tru Thoughts (*UK*)
Upbeat Recordings (*UK*)
The Verve Music Group (*US*)
Wah Wah 45s (*UK*)

Jungle

Run Tingz Recordings (*UK*)
Sliced Note Recordings (*UK*)

Kraut

Wrong Way Records (*UK*)

Latin

Acoustic Disc (*US*)
Bloodshot Records (*US*)
Bolero Records (*US*)
Concord Music Group (*US*)
Dewey Dog Records (*US*)
Funktasy (*Can*)
Hacienda Records (*US*)
Lamon Records (*US*)
LoveCat Music (*US*)
Tama Industries Record Label (*US*)
Tumi Music Ltd (*UK*)

Leftfield

Hyperdub Records (*UK*)
Something in Construction (*UK*)
Tight Lines (*UK*)
Wrong Way Records (*UK*)

Lo-fi

Canigou Records (*UK*)
Moth Man Records (*US*)
Sister 9 Recordings (*UK*)
ZyNg Tapes (*UK*)

Lounge

DJD Music Ltd (*UK*)

Mainstream

Delved in Dreams, inc. (*US*)
Everyday Records (*UK*)
Sentosa Records (*UK*)
Skate Mountain Records (*US*)
Subdust Music (*UK*)

Melodic

Everyday Records (*UK*)
Moth Man Records (*US*)
Stryker Records, Inc. (*US*)
Tonotopic Records (*UK*)
21st Century Music (*UK*)

Melodicore

Alex King Records (*UK*)
Moth Man Records (*US*)

Metal

ALM Records (*UK*)
Alternative Tentacles Records (*US*)
Asylum Arts (*US*)
Bieler Bros. Records (*US*)
Bullet Tooth (*US*)
Century Media Records (US) (*US*)
Cleopatra Records (*US*)
Clickpop Records (*US*)
Copro Productions (*UK*)
Distort (*Can*)
DJD Music Ltd (*UK*)
Earache Records Inc. (*US*)
The End Records (*US*)
Equal Vision Records (*US*)
Ferret Music (*US*)
Graphite Records (*UK*)
Hopeless Records (*US*)
Hydra Head Records (*US*)
Magna Carta Records (*US*)
Metal Blade Records, Inc. (*US*)
Sapien Records Limited (*UK*)
ScreamLite Records (*UK*)
Small Town Records (*UK*)
Snapper Music (*UK*)
Sound House Records (*UK*)
T&R Recordings (*US*)
Tama Industries Record Label (*US*)
These Bloody Thieves Records (*UK*)
Thumbhole Records (*UK*)
Venn Records (*UK*)
Victory Records (*US*)
When Planets Collide (*UK*)

Modern

The Birdman Recording Group, Inc. (*US*)
Castle Records (*US*)
Ernest Jenning Record Co. (*US*)
Moth Man Records (*US*)
Sentosa Records (*UK*)
Tama Industries Record Label (*US*)

MOR

Everyday Records (*UK*)

New Age

Bolero Records (*US*)
Cantaloupe Music (*US*)
Chacra Music (*Can*)
Delved in Dreams, inc. (*US*)
DOMO Records, Inc. (*US*)
Everyday Records (*UK*)
Funktasy (*Can*)
Tama Industries Record Label (*US*)

New Wave

Bomp Records (*US*)
DJD Music Ltd (*UK*)
Fire Records (*UK*)
Tama Industries Record Label (*US*)
21st Century Music (*UK*)

Noise Core
Cold Spring (*UK*)
T&R Recordings (*US*)
Non-Commercial
Tama Industries Record Label (*US*)
Nostalgia
Delved in Dreams, inc. (*US*)
Pop
A&M Records (*US*)
The Adult Teeth Recording Company (*UK*)
Alex King Records (*UK*)
Alternative Tentacles Records (*US*)
American Laundromat Records (*US*)
API Records (*US*)
Asthmatic Kitty Records (*US*)
ATO Records (*US*)
Aware Records (*US*)
Bad Boy Entertainment (*US*)
Barbarian Productions (*US*)
Big Deal Records (*US*)
Blue Note Label Group (*US*)
Bomp Records (*US*)
Brightonsfinest (*UK*)
Cantora (*US*)
Capitol Music Group (*US*)
Carnival Music (*US*)
Cascine (*US*)
Cash Money Records (*US*)
Castle Records (*US*)
Chalkpit Records Ltd (*UK*)
Cleopatra Records (*US*)
Clickpop Records (*US*)
CMH Records (*US*)
Coloursounds (*UK*)
Compass Records (*US*)
Compound Entertainment (*US*)
Concord Music Group (*US*)
Crush Music (*US*)
Curb Records (*US*)
Curve Music (*Can*)
Delved in Dreams, inc. (*US*)
Dirty Bingo Records (*UK*)
Dirty Canvas Music (*US*)
Disconnect Disconnect Records (*UK*)
Disruptor Records (*US*)
DJD Music Ltd (*UK*)
DM Music Group (*US*)
DOMO Records, Inc. (*US*)
Don Rubin Productions (*US*)
Don't Try (*UK*)
Double Denim Records (*UK*)
Drag City (*US*)
Dreamscope Media Group (DMG) (*UK*)
ECR Music Group (*US*)
Ernest Jenning Record Co. (*US*)
Everyday Records (*UK*)
Fearless Records (*US*)
Funktasy (*Can*)
Ghostly International (*US*)
Harbour Records (*US*)
Headliner Records / George Tobin Music (*US*)
Hit City USA (*US*)
Hit World Records (*US*)
Idol Records (*US*)
Incessant Records (*UK*)
Interscope Geffen A&M (*US*)
Jaggo Records, LLC (*US*)
Kanine Records (*US*)
Kirtland Records (*US*)
LML Music (*US*)
Lost in the Manor (*UK*)
LoveCat Music (*US*)
Moth Man Records (*US*)
Salute the Sun (*UK*)
Sapien Records Limited (*UK*)
Saraseto Records (*UK*)
Saving Grace Music (*UK*)
Scottish Fiction (*UK*)
604 Records (*Can*)
Skate Mountain Records (*US*)
Something in Construction (*UK*)
STA – Small Town America (*UK*)
Stoa Sounds (*UK*)
Stryker Records, Inc. (*US*)
Super Fan 99 (*UK*)
T&R Recordings (*US*)
Tama Industries Record Label (*US*)
Tape Club Records (*UK*)
37 Adventures (*UK*)
Trestle Records (*UK*)
00:02:59 LLC (*US*)
The Verve Music Group (*US*)
Vox Humana (*UK*)
Wax Records Inc. (*US*)
We Are Free (*US*)
Wobbly Music (*UK*)
Yala! Records (*UK*)
Yep Roc Records (*US*)
Post
Black Bleach Records (*UK*)
Deep Elm Records (*US*)
Disconnect Disconnect Records (*UK*)
Epitaph (*US*)
Fire Records (*UK*)
Freaks R Us (*UK*)
Ganbei Records (*UK*)
Moth Man Records (*US*)
Sister 9 Recordings (*UK*)

Snapper Music (*UK*)
Speedowax (*UK*)
Strong Island Recordings (*UK*)
Supersonic Media (*UK*)
Superstar Destroyer Records (*UK*)

Power
Bomp Records (*US*)
Cold Spring (*UK*)

Progressive
Aphagia Recordings (*US*)
Cantora (*US*)
Delved in Dreams, inc. (*US*)
Dewey Dog Records (*US*)
DJD Music Ltd (*UK*)
Everyday Records (*UK*)
Magna Carta Records (*US*)
Moth Man Records (*US*)
Snapper Music (*UK*)
Standby (*UK*)
Stryker Records, Inc. (*US*)
Sunstone Records Ltd (*UK*)
Superstar Destroyer Records (*UK*)
Trancespired Recordings (*UK*)

Psychedelic
Abattoir Blues (*UK*)
Alex King Records (*UK*)
Blak Hand Records (*UK*)
Box Records (*UK*)
Donut Records (*UK*)
Fire Records (*UK*)
Ganbei Records (*UK*)
God Unknown Records (*UK*)
Moth Man Records (*US*)
Psymmetry Collective (*UK*)
Riff Rock Records (*UK*)
Safe Suburban Home (*UK*)
Salvation Records (*UK*)
Sister 9 Recordings (*UK*)
Sonic Cathedral (*UK*)
Sour Grapes (*UK*)
Strong Island Recordings (*UK*)
Sunstone Records Ltd (*UK*)
Super Fan 99 (*UK*)
21st Century Music (*UK*)
Vallance Records (*UK*)
Wasted Years (*UK*)
Wrong Way Records (*UK*)

Punk
0114 Records (*UK*)
A-F Records (*US*)
Abattoir Blues (*UK*)
Alternative Tentacles Records (*US*)
Beggars Group (US) (*US*)
Black Bleach Records (*UK*)
Blak Hand Records (*UK*)
Bloodshot Records (*US*)
Bomp Records (*US*)
Box Records (*UK*)
Breakfast Records LLP (*UK*)
Bullet Tooth (*US*)
Cantaloupe Music (*US*)
Cleopatra Records (*US*)
Clickpop Records (*US*)
Copro Productions (*UK*)
Crush Music (*US*)
Curve Music (*Can*)
Deep Elm Records (*US*)
Dewey Dog Records (*US*)
Disconnect Disconnect Records (*UK*)
DJD Music Ltd (*UK*)
Doghouse Records (*US*)
Domino Record Co. Ltd (*US*)
Don Giovanni Records (*US*)
Epitaph (*US*)
Equal Vision Records (*US*)
Fearless Records (*US*)
Fire Records (*UK*)
Freaks R Us (*UK*)
Frontier Records (*US*)
Ganbei Records (*UK*)
Geilston Records (*UK*)
Get Hip Recordings (*US*)
Hopeless Records (*US*)
Idol Records (*US*)
In the Red Records (*US*)
Kanine Records (*US*)
Kill Rock Stars (*US*)
Morphius Records (*US*)
Moth Man Records (*US*)
1-2-3-4 Go! Records (*US*)
Psymmetry Collective (*UK*)
Regent Street Records (*UK*)
Restless Bear (*UK*)
Salvation Records (*UK*)
Sapien Records Limited (*UK*)
ScreamLite Records (*UK*)
Sister 9 Recordings (*UK*)
Skate Mountain Records (*US*)
Small Town Records (*UK*)
Sour Grapes (*UK*)
Speedowax (*UK*)
STA – Small Town America (*UK*)
Strong Island Recordings (*UK*)
T&R Recordings (*US*)
Tama Industries Record Label (*US*)
Thumbhole Records (*UK*)
Tight Lines (*UK*)
TNS (That's Not Skanking) Records (*UK*)
00:02:59 LLC (*US*)
Vallance Records (*UK*)

Venn Records (*UK*)
Victory Records (*US*)
Yala! Records (*UK*)
ZyNg Tapes (*UK*)

Ragga

Tama Industries Record Label (*US*)

R&B

A&M Records (*US*)
Alex King Records (*UK*)
Alternative Tentacles Records (*US*)
Barbarian Productions (*US*)
Bloodshot Records (*US*)
Blue Note Label Group (*US*)
Castle Records (*US*)
Concord Music Group (*US*)
Curb Records (*US*)
Defenders Ent (*UK*)
Dewey Dog Records (*US*)
DJD Music Ltd (*UK*)
DM Music Group (*US*)
Dose Entertainment (*UK*)
Dreamscope Media Group (DMG) (*UK*)
Everyday Records (*UK*)
Explosive Beatz Records (*UK*)
Funktasy (*Can*)
Gotee Records (*US*)
Headliner Records / George Tobin Music (*US*)
Hidden Beach Recordings (*US*)
Hit City USA (*US*)
i/o Recordings (*UK*)
Incessant Records (*UK*)
Jaggo Records, LLC (*US*)
Less is More Music Ltd (*UK*)
LoveCat Music (*US*)
Lovelane Music Group (*US*)
1-2-3-4 Go! Records (*US*)
Portfolio Music (*UK*)
Saffron Records (*UK*)
Salute the Sun (*UK*)
Sapien Records Limited (*UK*)
Skate Mountain Records (*US*)
Soul II Soul (*UK*)
Tama Industries Record Label (*US*)
The Verve Music Group (*US*)

Rap

Bad Boy Entertainment (*US*)
Cleopatra Records (*US*)
Defenders Ent (*UK*)
Dewey Dog Records (*US*)
DJD Music Ltd (*UK*)
DM Music Group (*US*)
Dose Entertainment (*UK*)
Dove Records (*UK*)
Funktasy (*Can*)
Ghostly International (*US*)
Gotee Records (*US*)
Hidden Beach Recordings (*US*)
i/o Recordings (*UK*)
Idol Records (*US*)
Interscope Geffen A&M (*US*)
LoveCat Music (*US*)
Portfolio Music (*UK*)
Skate Mountain Records (*US*)
Soul II Soul (*UK*)
Stryker Records, Inc. (*US*)
Tama Industries Record Label (*US*)
Viper Records (*US*)
Word Records (*US*)

Reggae

0114 Records (*UK*)
Defenders Ent (*UK*)
Delved in Dreams, inc. (*US*)
DJD Music Ltd (*UK*)
Dove Records (*UK*)
Funktasy (*Can*)
Gotee Records (*US*)
Little Fish Records (*US*)
Lost in the Manor (*UK*)
NB Audio (*UK*)
1-2-3-4 Go! Records (*US*)
Tama Industries Record Label (*US*)
00:02:59 LLC (*US*)
VP Records (*US*)
Wah Wah 45s (*UK*)
Wobbly Music (*UK*)

Reggaeton

Cleopatra Records (*US*)
Funktasy (*Can*)
LoveCat Music (*US*)
Tama Industries Record Label (*US*)

Regional

Canyon (*US*)
Delved in Dreams, inc. (*US*)
Little Fish Records (*US*)
Scotdisc (*UK*)
Sharpe Music (*UK*)

Relaxation

Tama Industries Record Label (*US*)

Remix

Alex King Records (*UK*)
Dewey Dog Records (*US*)
Funktasy (*Can*)

Rhythm and Blues

Delved in Dreams, inc. (*US*)
Everyday Records (*UK*)
Funktasy (*Can*)
Tama Industries Record Label (*US*)

Rock and Roll

Donut Records (*UK*)

Everyday Records (*UK*)
In the Red Records (*US*)
Moth Man Records (*US*)
Skate Mountain Records (*US*)
Sour Grapes (*UK*)
Stryker Records, Inc. (*US*)
Tama Industries Record Label (*US*)
Wicked Cool Records (*US*)

Rock

0114 Records (*UK*)
4AD (*US*)
A&M Records (*US*)
A-F Records (*US*)
Abattoir Blues (*UK*)
Activate Entertainment (*US*)
The Adult Teeth Recording Company (*UK*)
Akira (*UK*)
Alias Records (*US*)
ALM Records (*UK*)
Alternative Tentacles Records (*US*)
American Laundromat Records (*US*)
Anthem Records (*Can*)
Anti (*US*)
Aphagia Recordings (*US*)
API Records (*US*)
Ardent Records (*US*)
ATO Records (*US*)
Audio Vendor (*UK*)
Aware Records (*US*)
Babygrande Records, Inc. (*US*)
Bar/None Records (*US*)
Barsuk Records (*US*)
Beggars Group (US) (*US*)
Bieler Bros. Records (*US*)
Big Deal Records (*US*)
Black Bleach Records (*UK*)
Blak Hand Records (*UK*)
Bloodshot Records (*US*)
Bomp Records (*US*)
Bonsound (*Can*)
Box Records (*UK*)
Breakfast Records LLP (*UK*)
Bright Antenna Records (*US*)
Brightonsfinest (*UK*)
Bullet Tooth (*US*)
Cantaloupe Music (*US*)
Capitol Music Group (*US*)
Carnival Music (*US*)
Carpark Records (*US*)
Castle Records (*US*)
Century Media Records (US) (*US*)
CMH Records (*US*)
Concord Music Group (*US*)
Constellation (*Can*)
Copro Productions (*UK*)
Crush Music (*US*)
Curb Records (*US*)
Curve Music (*Can*)
Dangerbird Records (*US*)
Deep Elm Records (*US*)
Deep South Records (*US*)
Dirty Canvas Music (*US*)
Disconnect Disconnect Records (*UK*)
Doghouse Records (*US*)
Doing Life Records (*UK*)
Domino Record Co. Ltd (*US*)
DOMO Records, Inc. (*US*)
Don Rubin Productions (*US*)
Donut Records (*UK*)
Dovecote Records (*US*)
Drag City (*US*)
Dreamscope Media Group (DMG) (*UK*)
Dualtone Records (*US*)
Earache Records Inc. (*US*)
ECR Music Group (*US*)
The End Records (*US*)
Epitaph (*US*)
Equal Vision Records (*US*)
Ernest Jenning Record Co. (*US*)
Fearless Records (*US*)
Ferret Music (*US*)
Fervor Records (*US*)
Fire Records (*UK*)
Frontier Records (*US*)
Funktasy (*Can*)
Funzalo Records (*US*)
Ganbei Records (*UK*)
Get Hip Recordings (*US*)
Ghostly International (*US*)
God Unknown Records (*UK*)
Gotee Records (*US*)
Graphite Records (*UK*)
Harbour Records (*US*)
Highwheel Records (*US*)
Hopeless Records (*US*)
Idol Records (*US*)
Incessant Records (*UK*)
Interscope Geffen A&M (*US*)
Ipecac Recordings (*US*)
Jaggo Records, LLC (*US*)
Kanine Records (*US*)
Kirtland Records (*US*)
Landslide Records (*US*)
Last Gang Records (*Can*)
Le Grand Magistery, LLC (*US*)
Lightning Rod Records (*US*)
Little Fish Records (*US*)
Loner Noise (*UK*)
Lost Highway Records (*US*)

Lost in the Manor (*UK*)
LoveCat Music (*US*)
Mad Dragon Music Group (*US*)
Magna Carta Records (*US*)
Merge Records (*US*)
Metal Blade Records, Inc. (*US*)
Morphius Records (*US*)
Moth Man Records (*US*)
Nice Swan Records (*UK*)
1-2-3-4 Go! Records (*US*)
Psymmetry Collective (*UK*)
Regent Street Records (*UK*)
Riff Rock Records (*UK*)
Rough Trade Records (*UK*)
Safe Suburban Home (*UK*)
Salvation Records (*UK*)
Sapien Records Limited (*UK*)
Saraseto Records (*UK*)
Saving Grace Music (*UK*)
Schnitzel Records Ltd (*UK*)
Scottish Fiction (*UK*)
ScreamLite Records (*UK*)
Sister 9 Recordings (*UK*)
604 Records (*Can*)
Skate Mountain Records (*US*)
Small Town Records (*UK*)
Snapper Music (*UK*)
So Recordings (*UK*)
Sonic Cathedral (*UK*)
Sound House Records (*UK*)
Sour Grapes (*UK*)
Speedowax (*UK*)
Spiritual Records (*UK*)
STA – Small Town America (*UK*)
Strong Island Recordings (*UK*)
Stryker Records, Inc. (*US*)
Super Fan 99 (*UK*)
Supermarine Music (*UK*)
Superstar Destroyer Records (*UK*)
T&R Recordings (*US*)
Talking Elephant (*UK*)
Tama Industries Record Label (*US*)
These Bloody Thieves Records (*UK*)
Thumbhole Records (*UK*)
Tigertrap Records (*UK*)
Too Pure Records (*UK*)
00:02:59 LLC (*US*)
Two Piece Records (*UK*)
Vallance Records (*UK*)
Venn Records (*UK*)
Victory Records (*US*)
VSR Music Group (*US*)
Warm Electronic Recordings (*US*)
Wasted Years (*UK*)
Wax Records Inc. (*US*)
Wobbly Music (*UK*)
Word Records (*US*)
Wrong Way Records (*UK*)
Yala! Records (*UK*)
Yep Roc Records (*US*)
ZyNg Tapes (*UK*)

Rockabilly

Everyday Records (*UK*)
Moth Man Records (*US*)
Wild Records (*US*)

Roots

Acoustic Disc (*US*)
Alert Music Inc. (*Can*)
Alligator Records (*US*)
Appleseed Recordings (*US*)
Blind Pig Records (*US*)
Bloodshot Records (*US*)
Compass Records (*US*)
Delta Groove Music (*US*)
Delved in Dreams, inc. (*US*)
DJD Music Ltd (*UK*)
Everyday Records (*UK*)
Harbourtown Records (*UK*)
Lamon Records (*US*)
Lightning Rod Records (*US*)
Lost Highway Records (*US*)
Mellowtone Records (*UK*)
My Little Empire (*UK*)
Skate Mountain Records (*US*)
ToneTrade Productions (*UK*)
00:02:59 LLC (*US*)
Vertical Records (*UK*)
Yep Roc Records (*US*)

Shoegaze

Black Bleach Records (*UK*)
Canigou Records (*UK*)
Moth Man Records (*US*)
Safe Suburban Home (*UK*)
Sonic Cathedral (*UK*)
Strong Island Recordings (*UK*)
Superstar Destroyer Records (*UK*)
Warp Records (*UK*)
Wasted Years (*UK*)
Wrong Way Records (*UK*)

Singer-Songwriter

0114 Records (*UK*)
A&M Records (*US*)
Alias Records (*US*)
American Laundromat Records (*US*)
Aveline Records (*UK*)
Barbarian Productions (*US*)
Beggars Group (US) (*US*)
Birdland Records (*UK*)
Bloodshot Records (*US*)
Burnt Toast Vinyl (*US*)

Crush Music (*US*)
Delved in Dreams, inc. (*US*)
Dewey Dog Records (*US*)
DJD Music Ltd (*UK*)
Doing Life Records (*UK*)
DOMO Records, Inc. (*US*)
Dualtone Records (*US*)
Everyday Records (*UK*)
Mellowtone Records (*UK*)
Merge Records (*US*)
Skate Mountain Records (*US*)
Spiritual Records (*UK*)
Stoa Sounds (*UK*)
Tama Industries Record Label (*US*)
00:02:59 LLC (*US*)
Watercolour Music (*UK*)
Wobbly Music (*UK*)

Ska
0114 Records (*UK*)
Hopeless Records (*US*)
1-2-3-4 Go! Records (*US*)
Thumbhole Records (*UK*)
TNS (That's Not Skanking) Records (*UK*)

Soul
Big Crown Records (*US*)
Bloodshot Records (*US*)
Chalkpit Records Ltd (*UK*)
Concord Music Group (*US*)
Delved in Dreams, inc. (*US*)
Dewey Dog Records (*US*)
DJD Music Ltd (*UK*)
Dreamscope Media Group (DMG) (*UK*)
Everyday Records (*UK*)
Funktasy (*Can*)
Jaggo Records, LLC (*US*)
Less is More Music Ltd (*UK*)
1-2-3-4 Go! Records (*US*)
Organ Records (*UK*)
QM Records (*UK*)
Salute the Sun (*UK*)
Saving Grace Music (*UK*)
Skate Mountain Records (*US*)
Slapped Up Soul Records (*UK*)
Tight Lines (*UK*)
Tru Thoughts (*UK*)
Wah Wah 45s (*UK*)
Wild Records (*US*)

Soulful
Delved in Dreams, inc. (*US*)
Dewey Dog Records (*US*)
Everyday Records (*UK*)
Skate Mountain Records (*US*)
Tama Industries Record Label (*US*)

Soundtracks
Aphagia Recordings (*US*)
Barbarian Productions (*US*)
Cold Spring (*UK*)
Curb Records (*US*)
DOMO Records, Inc. (*US*)
DRG Records Incorporated (*US*)
Everyday Records (*UK*)
Lakeshore Entertainment (*US*)
Milan Records (*US*)
Skate Mountain Records (*US*)
Watertower Music (*US*)

Space
Wrong Way Records (*UK*)

Spoken Word
DJD Music Ltd (*UK*)
Tama Industries Record Label (*US*)

Surf
Wild Records (*US*)

Swing
Big Bear Records (*UK*)
Delved in Dreams, inc. (*US*)
Everyday Records (*UK*)

Synthpop
DJD Music Ltd (*UK*)
Funktasy (*Can*)

Techno
Alex King Records (*UK*)
Astralwerks Records (*US*)
Axtone (*UK*)
CCT Records (*UK*)
Circus Recordings (*UK*)
Delved in Dreams, inc. (*US*)
Dewey Dog Records (*US*)
Funktasy (*Can*)
Futurist Recordings (*UK*)
Saved Records (*UK*)
Sci Fi Ltd (*UK*)
Seed Records (*UK*)
Sounds Like Vinyl (*UK*)
Tama Industries Record Label (*US*)

Thrash
Moth Man Records (*US*)
Speedowax (*UK*)

Traditional
Bomp Records (*US*)
Castle Records (*US*)
Century Media Records (US) (*US*)
Delved in Dreams, inc. (*US*)
Fervor Records (*US*)
Harbourtown Records (*UK*)
LML Music (*US*)
Sharpe Music (*UK*)

Trance
Alex King Records (*UK*)
Amathus Music (*US*)
Axtone (*UK*)

Funktasy (*Can*)
Keyframe Music (*US*)
Trancespired Recordings (*UK*)
Tribal
Delved in Dreams, inc. (*US*)
Dewey Dog Records (*US*)
Forward Motion Records (UK) (*UK*)
Trip Hop
Funktasy (*Can*)
Sci Fi Ltd (*UK*)
Tama Industries Record Label (*US*)
Twisted
Sunstone Records Ltd (*UK*)
Underground
Amathus Music (*US*)
The Birdman Recording Group, Inc. (*US*)
Box Records (*UK*)
Futurist Recordings (*UK*)
Mad Decent (*US*)
Midnineties (*UK*)
Organ Records (*UK*)
Project Allout Records (*UK*)
Salvation Records (*UK*)
Shabby Doll Records (*UK*)
Sounds Like Vinyl (*UK*)
Tama Industries Record Label (*US*)
TNS (That's Not Skanking) Records (*UK*)
Two Piece Records (*UK*)
When Planets Collide (*UK*)
Uptempo
Alex King Records (*UK*)
Urban
Affluent Records (*US*)
Alex King Records (*UK*)
Bad Boy Entertainment (*US*)
Capitol Music Group (*US*)
Cash Money Records (*US*)
Compound Entertainment (*US*)
Curb Records (*US*)
Derrty Entertainment (*US*)
Dewey Dog Records (*US*)
Disturbing Tha Peace Records (DTP) (*US*)
Duck Down Music (*US*)
Hit World Records (*US*)
HQ Familia (*UK*)
i/o Recordings (*UK*)
Javotti Media (*US*)
Melee Recording Group (*UK*)
Midnineties (*UK*)
101BPM (*UK*)
Portfolio Music (*UK*)
Soul II Soul (*UK*)
Subdust Music (*UK*)
Tama Industries Record Label (*US*)
ToneTrade Productions (*UK*)
Visionary Music Group (*US*)
World
Acoustic Disc (*US*)
Beggars Group (US) (*US*)
Bolero Records (*US*)
Cantaloupe Music (*US*)
Canyon (*US*)
Chacra Music (*Can*)
Chesky Records (*US*)
Compass Records (*US*)
Concord Music Group (*US*)
DOMO Records, Inc. (*US*)
Everyday Records (*UK*)
Funktasy (*Can*)
Green Linnet (*US*)
Jaggo Records, LLC (*US*)
Little Fish Records (*US*)
LoveCat Music (*US*)
Milan Records (*US*)
Tama Industries Record Label (*US*)
Tumi Music Ltd (*UK*)
00:02:59 LLC (*US*)

US Managers

For the most up-to-date listings of these and hundreds of other managers, visit https://www.musicsocket.com/managers

*To claim your **free** access to the site, please see the back of this book.*

25 Artist Agency

25 Music Square West
Nashville, TN 37203
Fax: +1 (615) 687-6699
Email: david@25ent.com
Email: dara@25ent.com
Website: http://www.25ccm.com

Represents: Artists/Bands

Genres: Christian

Contact: David Breen; Dara Easterday; Todd Thomas

Christian record label, based in Nashville, Tennessee.

Abba-Tude Entertainment

311 North Robertson Avenue, Suite 505
Beverly Hills, CA 90211
Email: kingabba@aol.com

Represents: Artists/Bands

Genres: All types of music

Contact: Mark Abbattista

Management company based in California. Accepts unsolicited material.

ACA Music & Entertainment

21005 Watertown Road, Suite A
Waukesha, WI 53186
Fax: +1 (262) 790-9149
Email: info@acaentertainment.com
Website: http://acaentertainment.com
Website: https://www.facebook.com/AcaMusicEntertainment/

Represents: Artists/Bands; DJs

Genres: All types of music

Describes itself as the oldest and largest provider of live entertainment in the Midwest

Act 1 Entertainment

28 Price Street
Patchogue, NY 11772
Email: info@act1entertainment.net
Email: karl@act1entertainment.net
Website: http://act1entertainment.net
Website: https://www.facebook.com/Act1Inc/

Represents: Artists/Bands; Comedians; DJs; Tribute Acts

Genres: Jazz; R&B; Soul; Blues; Swing; Roots; Rockabilly; Country; Reggae; Classic Rock

Contact: Karl BD Reamer

Management company based in Patchogue, New York.

Advanced Alternative Media (AAM)

270 Lafayette Street, Suite 605
New York, NY 10012

LOS ANGELES
5979 West 3rd Street, Suite 204
Los Angeles, CA 90036

NASHVILLE
1600 17th Avenue South
Nashville, TN 37212
Email: info@aaminc.com
Website: http://www.aaminc.com
Website: https://www.facebook.com/AdvancedAlternativeMedia

Represents: Artists/Bands; Producers; Songwriters; Sound Engineers

Genres: Alternative; Pop; Rock; Indie

Contact: Matthew Clayman

Management company with offices in New York, Nashville, London, and Los Angeles.

Aesthetic V

Email: aestheticv@gmail.com
Website: http://www.vickyhamilton.com

Represents: Artists/Bands

Genres: All types of music

Contact: Vicky Hamilton

Management by long time Grammy Award-Winning music industry executive and personal manager, responsible for developing or managing such acts as Guns 'N' Roses, Mötley Crüe, Poison, Faster Pussycat and many others. Also offers consultancy service.

American Artists Corporation

8500 Wilshire Boulevard, Suite 525
Beverly Hills, CA 90211
Fax: +1 (310) 277-9697
Email: Mike@AmericanArtists.net
Website: http://www.americanartists.net

Represents: Artists/Bands

Genres: Country; Classic Rock; Rock; R&B; Swing

Contact: Michael Weinstein

Exclusive music booking agency based in Beverly Hills, California.

American Artists Entertainment Group

29 Royal Palm Pointe Suite 5
Vero Beach, Florida 32960

NEW YORK OFFICE
245 E 63rd St suite 1701
New York, NY 10065

Fax: +1 (954) 251-4602
Email: online@aaeg.com
Website: http://www.aaeg.com
Website: http://www.facebook.com/pages/American-Artists-Entertainment-Group/147738265237919?ref=info
Website: https://myspace.com/aaeg

Represents: Artists/Bands

Genres: Country; Pop; R&B; Rock

Management company with offices in Vero Beach, Florida, New York, and Hollywood. Has a 45-year history in the performing arts, and today serves over 16 countries and over 100 cities worldwide. Submit via form on website.

AMW Group Inc.

337 Garden Oaks Blvd. #8295
Houston, TX 77018

LOS ANGELES:
8605 Santa Monica Blvd
West Hollywood, CA 90069

NEW YORK:
228 Park Ave. South
New York City, NY 10003
Website: https://www.amworldgroup.com
Website: https://facebook.com/amwgrp

Represents: Artists/Bands

Genres: All types of music

Management company with offices in Texas, LA, and New York. No unsolicited submissions.

Angelica Arts & Entertainment

Nashville, TN
Fax: +1 (615) 591-1463
Email: mgmt@angelica.org
Website: http://www.angelica.org

Represents: Artists/Bands

Genres: Ambient; Lounge; New Age; Pop; World

Management company based in Nashville, Tennessee.

APA (Agency for the Performing Arts)

405 S. Beverly Drive
Beverly Hills, CA 90212
Website: http://apa-agency.com

Represents: Artists/Bands

Genres: All types of music

Management company with offices in Los Angeles, Nashville, New York, Atlanta, Toronto, and London. Accepts new clients by referral only. No submissions.

Arslanian & Associates, Inc.

6671 Sunset Boulevard, Suite 1502
Hollywood, CA 90028
Email: oscar@discoverhollywood.com
Website: http://www.arslanianassociates.com

Represents: Artists/Bands

Genres: Classic Rock

Contact: Oscar Arslanian; Nyla Arslanian

Management company based in Hollywood, California.

Artist in Mind

14100 Dickens Street, Suite 1
Sherman Oaks, CA 91423
Fax: +1 (818) 924-1000
Email: info@artistinmind.com

Represents: Artists/Bands; Film / TV Composers; Producers; Songwriters

Genres: Contemporary; Indie; Pop; Rock; Singer-Songwriter; Alternative; Americana; Folk; Modern Rock

Contact: Doug Buttleman

Management company based in Sherman Oaks, California. Not currently accepting submissions as at March 2019.

Artist Representation and Management (ARM) Entertainment

1257 Arcade Street
St Paul, MN 55106
Fax: +1 (651) 776-6338
Email: jd@armentertainment.com
Website: http://www.armentertainment.com

Represents: Artists/Bands

Genres: Blues; Country; Classic Rock; Metal

Contact: John Domagall, President

Entertainment business with a focus on 70s, 80s, and 90s rock. No unsolicited material.

Azoff Music Management

1100 Glendon Ave., Ste. 2000
Los Angeles, CA 90024

Represents: Artists/Bands

Genres: All types of music

Management company based in Los Angeles, California.

Backstage Entertainment

Email: staff@backstageentertainment.net
Website: https://backstageentertainment.net
Website: https://www.facebook.com/BackstageEntertainment

Represents: Artists/Bands

Genres: All types of music

Contact: Paul Loggins

Artist management/marketing firm which specialises in working with independent artists, and aims to bridge the gap between radio, print and social media.

Bandguru Management

PO Box 11192
Denver, CO 80211

Fax: +1 (303) 561-1496
Email: mark@bandguru.com
Website: http://www.bandguru.com

Represents: Artists/Bands

Genres: All types of music

Contact: Mark Bliesener

Management and consulting company. Offers consultancy services at $100 an hour.

BBA Management & Booking

Email: info@bbabooking.com
Website: http://www.bbabooking.com
Website: https://www.facebook.com/bbabooking

Represents: Artists/Bands

Genres: Jazz; Classical; Rock; Latin

Management and booking for jazz, classical, and versatile party bands in Central Texas.

Big Beat Productions, Inc.

1515 University Drive, Suite 106
Coral Springs, FL 33071
Fax: +1 (954) 755-8733
Email: talent@bigbeatproductions.com
Email: rlloyd@bigbeatproductions.com
Website: http://www.bigbeatproductions.com
Website: https://www.facebook.com/Big-Beat-Productions-Inc-Worldwide-Representation-146226482073192/?ref=ts

Represents: Artists/Bands; Comedians; DJs

Genres: Contemporary; Classic Rock; R&B; Disco; Regional; Jazz; Country

Contact: Richard Lloyd; Gary Ladka; Elissa Solomon

Management company based in Coral Springs, Florida. Send promotional kit including CD or DVD, 8x10 photos, bio, resume, lyric sheets, and copyright dates (if available), by post or by email.

Big Hassle Management

NEW YORK:
40 Exchange Pl, Ste. 1900
New York, NY 10005

LA:
3685 Motor Avenue, Suite 240
Los Angeles, CA 90034
Email: weinstein@bighassle.com
Email: jim@bighassle.com
Website: http://www.bighassle.com

Represents: Artists/Bands

Genres: Indie; Pop; Rock; Alternative

Contact: Ken Weinstein

Management company with offices in New York and Los Angeles.

Big Noise

11 South Angell Street, Suite 336
Providence, RI 02906
Email: algomes@bignoisenow.com
Email: al@bignoisenow.com
Website: http://www.bignoisenow.com

Represents: Artists/Bands

Genres: All types of music

Contact: Al Gomes; A. Michelle

Award-winning Music Firm specialising in artist development, project management, career strategies, and promotion and publicity. Based in Providence, Rhode Island. Looking for artists who are unique, talented, professional, and ready to launch. Considers all genres. Query by phone or email in first instance. Must be at least 18.

Bill Hollingshead Productions, Inc. Talent Agency

1010 Anderson Road
Davis, California 95616
Fax: +1 (530) 758-9777
Email: bhptalent@aol.com
Website: http://www.bhptalent.com

Represents: Artists/Bands

Genres: Classic Rock; Surf

Handles California surf music and classic 50s/60s rock.

Bitchin' Entertainment

1750 Collard Valley Road
Cedartown, GA 30125

Email: Ty@BitchinEntertainment.com
Email: Rodney@BitchinEntertainment.com
Website: http://www.bitchinentertainment.com

Represents: Artists/Bands; Tribute Acts

Genres: Rock; Pop; R&B; Funk; Urban; Hip-Hop; Rap; Instrumental; Jazz; Classical; Ambient; World; Experimental; House; Trance; Electronic; Techno; Alternative; Metal; Punk; Gothic; Country; Americana; Blues; Folk; Singer-Songwriter; Spoken Word

Management company based in Cedartown, Georgia. Send query by email with link to your music online. No MP3s or links to MP3s. See website for full submission guidelines, and details of who to approach regarding specific genres.

Black Dot Management

6820 La Tijera Boulevard, Suite 117
Los Angeles, CA 90045
Fax: +1 (323) 777-8169
Email: info@blkdot.com
Website: http://www.blkdot.com

Represents: Artists/Bands; Producers; Songwriters; Sound Engineers; Studio Musicians; Studio Technicians

Genres: Jazz; R&B; Urban; Contemporary

Contact: Raymond A. Shields II; Patricia Shields

Management company based in Los Angeles, California. Handles jazz, R&B, and urban.

Booking Entertainment

275 Madison Avenue 6th Floor
New York, NY 10016
Fax: +1 (212) 645-0333
Email: agents@bookingentertainment.com
Website: https://www.bookingentertainment.com

Represents: Artists/Bands

Genres: Pop; Rock; Jazz; R&B; Contemporary

Books big name entertainment for private parties, public concerts, corporate events, and fundraisers.

Brent Music Management

14431 Ventura Boulevard, Suite 306
Sherman Oaks, CA 91423

Represents: Artists/Bands; Songwriters

Genres: All types of music, except: Rap; Hip-Hop

Contact: Bobby Brent; Elysia Skye (A&R)

Management company based in Sherman Oaks, California. Accepts unsolicited submissions, but call first. No rap or hip-hop.

Brick Wall Management

39 West 32nd Street, Suite 1403
New York, NY 10001
Fax: +1 (212) 202-4582
Email: bwmgmt@brickwallmgmt.com
Website: http://www.brickwallmgmt.com

Represents: Artists/Bands; Producers

Genres: Country; Pop; Rock; Singer-Songwriter

Contact: Michael Solomon; Rishon Blumberg

Management company based in New York.

Brilliant Productions

Decatur, GA 30030
Email: nancy@brilliant-productions.com
Website: http://brilliant-productions.com
Website: https://www.youtube.com/user/itsbrilliant

Represents: Artists/Bands

Genres: Blues; Regional; Roots; Americana

Contact: Nancy Lewis-Pegel

Boutique agency based in Decatur, Georgia.

The Brokaw Company

4135 Bakman Avevenue
North Hollywood, CA 91602
Email: jobrok@aol.com

Email: db@brokawco.com
Website: http://brokawcompany.com

Represents: Artists/Bands

Genres: Country; Hip-Hop; Pop; Christian; Rock

Contact: Joel Brokaw; David Brokaw; Sanford Brokaw

Management company based in North Hollywood, California. As well as handling music artists, has also handled publicity for hit shows such as The Cosby Show and Roseanne.

Buddy Lee Attractions, Inc.

Nashville, TN
Website: https://buddyleeattractions.com
Website: https://www.facebook.com/BuddyLeeAttractions/

Represents: Artists/Bands

Genres: Country; Pop; Rock

One of Nashville's larges privately owned talent agencies, representing some of the biggest names in country music.

Bulletproof Artist Management

241 Main Street
Easthampton, MA 01027
Email: patty@bulletproofartists.com
Website: https://bulletproofartists.com

Represents: Artists/Bands; Producers

Genres: Country; Pop; Rock; Folk

Contact: Patty Romanoff

Management company based in Easthampton, Massachusetts.

Burgess World Co.

PO Box 646
Mayo, MD 21106-0646
Email: info@burgessworldco.com
Website: http://www.burgessworldco.com

Represents: Artists/Bands; Producers; Sound Engineers

Genres: Alternative; Blues; Jazz; Rock; Singer-Songwriter

Management company based in Mayo, Maryland. Originally founded to manage producers and engineers, but in the nineties expanded into artist management.

Cantaloupe Music Productions, Inc.

157 West 79 Street
New York, NY 10024-6415
Email: ellenazorin@gmail.com
Website: http://www.cantaloupeproductions.com

Represents: Artists/Bands

Genres: Regional; Latin; World; Jazz; Blues; Swing

Contact: Ellen Azorin, President

Handles Brazilian music, Argentine tango, and other Latin-American music.

Case Entertainment Group Inc.

102 E. Pikes Peak Ave., Ste. 200
Colorado Springs, CO 80903
Fax: +1 (719) 634-2274
Email: rac@crlr.net
Website: http://www.newpants.com
Website: http://www.oldpants.com

Represents: Artists/Bands

Genres: Rock; Pop; Country; Folk; R&B; Rap

Contact: Robert Case

Management company based in Colorado Springs, Colorado.

Celebrity Enterprises (CE) Inc.

Email: lisa@ent123.com
Website: http://ent123.com

Represents: Artists/Bands

Genres: All types of music

Provides acts for corporate events and fundraisers, performing arts centres and casinos, and other special events.

Celebrity Talent Agency Inc.

111 East 14th Street Suite 249
New York, NY 10003
Fax: +1 (201) 837-9011
Email: markg@celebritytalentagency.com
Email: alinak@celebritytalentagency.com
Website: http://www.celebritytalentagency.com
Website: https://www.facebook.com/CelebrityTalentAgency/

Represents: Artists/Bands; Comedians; DJs

Genres: Dance; Hip-Hop; R&B; Latin; Reggae; Jazz; Gospel

Contact: Mark Green; Alina Kim

Talent agency with offices in New York and London.

Chapman & Co. Management

14011 Ventura Boulevard #405
Sherman Oaks, CA 91423
Fax: +1 (818) 788-9525
Email: info@chapmanmanagement.com
Email: steve@chapmanmanagement.com
Website: http://chapmanmanagement.com

Represents: Artists/Bands

Genres: Contemporary Jazz

Contact: Steve Chapman

Management company based in Sherman Oaks, California. Concentrates on smooth, contemporary jazz.

Circle City Records USA

Email: circlecityrecordsusa@comcast.net
Website: https://www.circlecityrecords.com

Represents: Artists/Bands

Genres: Country; Gospel; Pop

Contact: Lincoln Plowman

A full service Musician Development and Artist Management company.

If you are just beginning your Music Career or are an established Artist, we can help.

Circle Talent Agency

5900 Wilshire Blvd. Suite 2200
Los Angeles, CA 90036
Fax: +1 (323) 424-4976
Email: info@circletalentagency.com
Email: kevin@circletalentagency.com
Website: http://www.circletalentagency.com

Represents: Artists/Bands

Genres: All types of music

Contact: Kevin Gimble

Talent agency based in Los Angeles.

Class Act Productions/Management

PO Box 55252
Sherman Oaks, CA 91413-0252
Fax: +1 (818) 903-6518
Email: peter.kimmel@sbcglobal.net

Represents: Artists/Bands

Genres: All types of music

Contact: Peter Kimmel

Management company based in Sherman Oaks, California. Query by phone before sending material.

Collin Artists

1099 N. Mar Vista Ave
Pasadena, CA 91104
Email: collinartists@gmail.com
Website: http://www.collinartists.com

Represents: Artists/Bands

Genres: Instrumental Jazz; Latin; World; Blues; R&B; Swing; Contemporary Jazz

Contact: Barbara Collin

Management company based in Pasadena, California.

Columbia Artists Management Inc. (CAMI)

5 Columbus Circle
@ 1790 Broadway
New York, NY 10019-1412
Fax: +1 (212) 841-9744

Email: info@columbia-artists.com
Website: http://www.cami.com

Represents: Artists/Bands; Film / TV Composers; Lyricists; Variety Artists

Genres: Contemporary; Blues; Classical; Country; Folk; Indie; Jazz; Latin; Pop; R&B; World; Instrumental; Celtic

Contact: Tim Fox

Represents classical, jazz, and popular musicians; orchestras, ensembles, etc. Offices in US and Europe.

Concerted Efforts

PO Box 440326
Somerville MA, 02144
Fax: +1 (617) 969-0810
Email: concerted@concertedefforts.com
Website: http://concertedefforts.com

Represents: Artists/Bands

Genres: Blues; Folk; Jazz; Gospel; Soul; Singer-Songwriter; Rock; World

Music booking agency based in Somerville, Massachusetts.

Creative Artists Agency (CAA)

2000 Avenue of the Stars
Los Angeles, CA 90067
Fax: +1 (424) 288-2900
Website: https://www.caa.com

Represents: Artists/Bands

Genres: All types of music

Talent agency with offices across the US, as well as in the UK, China, and Europe.

Crush Music Media Management

Email: info@crushmusic.com
Website: https://www.crushmusic.com

Represents: Artists/Bands; Producers; Songwriters

Genres: All types of music

Management company based in New York.

D. Bailey Management, Inc.

6607 Gunn Highway
Tampa, FL 33625
Fax: +1 (813) 960-4662
Email: info@dbaileymanagement.com
Website: http://dbaileymanagement.com
Website: https://www.facebook.com/dbaileymanagement

Represents: Artists/Bands

Genres: Pop; R&B; Rock

Contact: Dennis Bailey

Live entertainment, event management, and artist management, based in Tampa, Florida.

DAS Communications Ltd

83 Riverside Drive
New York, NY 10024-5713

Represents: Artists/Bands; Producers; Songwriters

Genres: Hip-Hop; Pop; Rock

Management company based in New York.

Dave Kaplan Management

1126 South Coast Highway 101
Encinitas, CA 92024
Fax: +1 (760) 944-7808
Email: demo@surfdog.com
Website: http://www.surfdog.com
Website: https://www.facebook.com/surfdogrecords/

Represents: Artists/Bands

Genres: Rock

Contact: Dave Kaplan; Scott Seine

Management company based in Encinitas, California. Also runs associated record label. Accepts submissions by post marked for the attention of A&R, but prefers links by email (no MP3 attachments).

Dawn Elder Management

Email: deworldmusic@aol.com
Website: https://dawnelderworldentertainment.com
Website: https://www.facebook.com/DawnElderWorldEntertainment

Represents: Artists/Bands

Genres: Classical; Jazz; Pop; Rock; Roots; Traditional; World

Have managed, represented and organised international tours for some of the most highly regarded international artists today.

DCA Productions

302A 12th Street, # 330
New York, NY 10014
Fax: +1 (609) 259-8260
Email: info@dcaproductions.com
Website: http://dcaproductions.com

Represents: Artists/Bands; Comedians; Variety Artists

Genres: Pop; Rock; Folk

Contact: Daniel C. Abrahmsen, President; Gerri Abrahamsen, Vice President

Management company founded in 1983, specialising in variety performers, comedians, musical performers, theatre productions, and producing live events.

Deep South Artist Management

RALEIGH
PO Box 17737
Raleigh, NC 27619

NASHVILLE
PO Box 121975
Nashville, TN 37212
Email: Hello@DeepSouthEntertainment.com
Website: http://www.deepsouthentertainment.com
Website: https://www.facebook.com/deepsouthent

Represents: Artists/Bands

Genres: Alternative; Country; Pop; Rock; Americana; Christian

Record label, artist management firm, talent agency, and concert production company based in Raleigh, North Carolina, with offices in both Raleigh and Nashville, Tennessee.

The Derek Power Company & Kahn Power Pictures

433 North Camden Drive, Suite 600 Beverly Hills, CA 90210
Email: Artists4Film@gmail.com
Email: iampower007@me.com
Website: https://www.artists4film.com

Represents: Artists/Bands; Film / TV Composers

Genres: All types of music

Contact: Derek Power; Ilene Kahn Power

Production and talent management company based in Beverly Hills, California.

Direct Management Group (DMG)

8332 Melrose Ave, Top Floor
Los Angeles, CA 90069
Email: info@directmanagement.com
Website: http://directmanagement.com

Represents: Artists/Bands

Genres: Pop

Contact: Martin Kirkup; Bradford Cobb; Steven Jensen

Management company based in West Hollywood, California. Founded in April 1985. Describes itself as an internationally oriented entertainment company with broad-based success in the representation of musical artists.

East Coast Entertainment (ECE)

Email: info@bookece.com
Website: https://www.bookece.com

Represents: Artists/Bands; DJs

Genres: All types of music

Describes itself as the largest full-service entertainment agency in the country.

East End Management

12441 Ventura Ct
Studio City, CA 91604

Website: https://www.linkedin.com/company/east-end-management

Represents: Artists/Bands

Genres: Rock; Pop

Management company based in Studio City, California.

Emcee Artist Management

Email: liz@emceeartist.com
Email: mfair@emceeartist.com
Website: https://www.emceeartist.com

Represents: Artists/Bands

Genres: Jazz; Blues; Rock

Contact: Liz Penta; Meagan Fair

Management company representing jazz, blues, and rock artists. No hip-hop.

Empire Artist Management

235 West 23rd Street, 6th Floor
New York, NY 10011
Email: info@empireartistmanagement.com
Website: http://www.empireartistmanagement.com

Genres: Electronic; Club; Techno

Management company based in New York.

Entertainment Services International

1819 South Harlan Circle
Lakewood, CO 80232
Fax: +1 (303) 936-0069
Email: randy@esientertainment.com
Website: http://www.esientertainment.com

Represents: Artists/Bands

Genres: Rock; Classic Rock

Contact: Randy Erwin

Manager based in Lakewood, Colorado.

Entourage Talent Associates, Ltd

150 West 28th Street, Suite 1503
New York, NY 10001
Fax: +1 (212) 633-1818
Email: info@entouragetalent.com
Website: http://www.entouragetalent.com
Website: https://www.facebook.com/EntourageTalentAssociates

Represents: Artists/Bands

Genres: Pop; Rock; Singer-Songwriter; Jazz

Send submissions by post or by email, or via form on website.

Fat City Artists

1906 Chet Atkins Place, Suite 502 Nashville, TN 37212
Fax: +1 (615) 321-5382
Website: http://fatcityartists.com

Represents: Artists/Bands

Genres: Acoustic; Blues; R&B; Celtic; Country; Folk; Funk; Gospel; Jazz; Pop; Reggae; Rockabilly; Rock and Roll; Ska; Swing; World

Artists management based in Nashville, Tennessee. Not signing new artists as at October 2018.

First Access Entertainment

New York / Los Angeles
Email: music@firstaccessent.com
Email: la@firstaccessent.com
Website: https://www.firstaccessent.com
Website: https://www.facebook.com/firstaccessent

Represents: Artists/Bands

Genres: Pop; Rap; R&B; Hip-Hop

Entertainment company with offices in New York, Los Angeles, and London, offering recorded music, management and publishing services as well as film, TV and tech development and acting and model management.

5B Artist Management

220 36th St, Suite B442
Brooklyn, NY 11232

LOS ANGELES:
12021 Jefferson Blvd,
Culver City, CA 90230

Email: hello@5bam.com
Website: http://5bam.com

Represents: Artists/Bands

Genres: Alternative; Metal; Rock

Management company with offices in New York, Los Angeles and Birmingham (UK). Not accepting submissions as at March 2019.

Fleming Artists

PO Box 1568
Ann Arbor, MI 48106
Fax: +1 (734) 662-6502
Email: jim@flemingartists.com
Email: cynthia@flemingartists.com
Website: http://www.flemingartists.com

Represents: Artists/Bands

Genres: Contemporary Roots Rock; Blues; Folk; Pop; Rock

Management company with a mission to "represent high quality performing artists by providing them with a unique, thoughtful and individualized approach to concert booking."

Fresh Flava Entertainment

2705 12th Street NE
Washington, DC 20018
Email: freshflava17@gmail.com
Website: http://www.freshflava.com

Represents: Artists/Bands

Genres: Hip-Hop; Jazz; Gospel; R&B; Rock

Management company based in Washington DC. Accepts unsolicited submissions.

Gary Stamler Management

PO Box 34575
Los Angeles, CA 90034
Email: garystamler@me.com
Email: nancysefton@gsmgmt.net
Website: https://www.gsmgmt.net

Represents: Artists/Bands; Producers

Genres: All types of music

Contact: Gary Stamler; Nancy Sefton

Management company based in Los Angeles.

The Gorfaine/Schwartz Agency, Inc.

4111 West Alameda Avenue, Suite 509
Burbank, CA 91505
Email: reception@gsamusic.com
Website: https://www.gsamusic.com

Represents: Artists/Bands; Producers

Genres: All types of music

Management agency based in Burbank, California.

Halfpipe Entertainment

PO Box 10534
Hollywood, CA 90213
Email: info@halfpipemusic.net
Website: http://www.halfpipe-entertainment.com
Website: http://www.halfpipemusic.net

Represents: Artists/Bands; Film / TV Composers; Songwriters

Genres: Alternative; Electronic; Indie; Pop; Rock; Lounge; Psychedelic; Remix; Hip-Hop; R&B; Soul; Jazz; Surf Pop

Management company based in Hollywood, California. Send query with links to online streaming audio, e.g. soundcloud.

Harmony Artists

3575 Cahuenga Blvd. W, #560
Los Angeles, CA 90068
Fax: +1 (323) 655-5154
Email: mdixon@harmonyartists.com
Email: jross@harmonyartists.com
Website: http://www.harmonyartists.com
Website: https://www.facebook.com/HarmonyArtistsLA/

Represents: Artists/Bands; Tribute Acts

Genres: Blues; Latin; Jazz; Swing

Specialises in providing top national headline and regional entertainment for venues throughout the world.

Heart & Soul Artist Management

St Paul, MN
Email: mvt@utrmusicgroup.com

Website: http://utrmusicgroup.com
Website: https://www.facebook.com/MikiMulvehill

Represents: Artists/Bands

Genres: All types of music

Contact: Miki Mulvehill

Management company based in St Paul, Minnesota.

Hello! Booking, Inc.

PO Box 18717
Minneapolis, MN 55418
Fax: +1 (763) 463-1264
Email: eric@hellobooking.com
Website: http://www.hellobooking.com
Website: https://www.facebook.com/hellobookingusa

Represents: Artists/Bands

Genres: Country; Folk; Indie; Jazz; Hip-Hop; Acoustic; Rockabilly; Rock; Pop

Contact: Eric Roberts

Show booking company based in Minneapolis.

HGRS Artist Management

208 commerce drive
Email: info@highergroundrehearsalstudios.com
Website: https://www.highergroundrehearsalstudios.com

Represents: Artists/Bands; Comedians; DJs; Producers; Songwriters; Studio Musicians; Studio Vocalists; Tribute Acts; Variety Artists

Genres: All types of music, except: Celtic Christian Horror Black Metal Doom Ethnic Gospel Rap Spoken Word

Contact: Jahna Eichel

For us, It's about the music. Our purpose is to sort through the business of the music industry so you have the time and space to create and develop the music you want out there. We work with musicians in virtually all genres of music and varying stages of career development. We are a full service, boutique entertainment company that focuses on career expansion, distribution, publicity, publishing and more. Our message is transparent and our goals are your goals.

Howard Rosen Promotion, Inc.

1129 Maricopa Highway
Ojai, CA 93023
Email: info@howiewood.com
Email: Howie@howiewood.com
Website: http://howiewood.com
Website: https://myspace.com/howardrosen

Represents: Artists/Bands

Genres: All types of music

Contact: Howard Rosen; Alex Louton

Full service radio promotion company based in Ojai, California. Submit music using online submissions system on website.

IMC Entertainment Group

19360 Rinaldi Street, Suite 217
Porter Ranch, CA 91326
Fax: +1 (206) 600-5534
Email: sr@imcentertainment.com
Website: http://www.imcentertainment.com

Represents: Artists/Bands

Genres: Pop; R&B

Management company based in Porter Ranch, California, providing entertainment and production services worldwide. Specialises in music performance, production, publishing and supervision services.

Impact Artist Management

275 Fair Street, Suite 10
Kingston, NY 12401
Website: http://www.impactartist.com
Website: https://www.facebook.com/impactartistmanagement

Represents: Artists/Bands; Film / TV Composers; Songwriters; Supervisors

Genres: Contemporary; Blues; Folk; Indie; Jazz; Latin; R&B; Rock; Roots; Singer-

Songwriter; World; Alternative; Alternative Country

Management company based in Kingston, New York.

In De Goot Entertainment

119 West 23rd Street, Suite 609
New York, NY 10011
Fax: +1 (212) 924-3242
Email: miurato@indegoot.com
Website: https://www.indegoot.com
Website: https://www.facebook.com/Indegoot/
Website: https://myspace.com/indegootentertainment

Represents: Artists/Bands

Genres: Indie; Metal; Pop; Rock; Underground

Contact: Michael Iurato

Management company based in New York.

Ina Dittke & Associates

770 N.E. 69th Street, Suite 7c
Miami, FL 33138
Email: ina@inadittke.com
Email: gina@inadittke.com
Website: https://inadittke.com
Website: https://www.facebook.com/inadittkeassociates/

Represents: Artists/Bands

Genres: Jazz; Latin; World

Music agency based in Miami, Florida, representing a varied and international roster of artists.

International Creative Management (ICM) Partners

LOS ANGELES
10250 Constellation Boulevard
Los Angeles, CA 90067

NEW YORK
65 East 55th Street
New York, NY 10022
Email: careersla@icmpartners.com
Website: http://www.icmtalent.com

Represents: Artists/Bands; Comedians

Genres: All types of music

Contact: Steve Levine

Concerts and live appearances department represents artists in all musical genres, including pop, rock, R&B, hip-hop, indie and adult contemporary. Arranges global engagements and tours in a wide variety of settings and venues.

Intrigue Music

New Haven, CT
Email: staff@intriguegroup.net
Website: http://intriguemusic.com
Website: https://www.facebook.com/intriguemusic

Represents: Artists/Bands

Genres: Pop; Rock

Full-service entertainment company based in New Haven, CT. Specialises in worldwide artist management, music publishing, and intellectual property rights management.

Invasion Group, Ltd

1133 Broadway Suite 919
New York, NY 10010
Fax: +1 (212) 414-0525
Email: info@invasiongroup.com
Website: http://www.invasiongroup.com
Website: https://facebook.com/invasiongroupltd

Represents: Artists/Bands; Film / TV Composers; Lyricists; Producers; Songwriters; Sound Engineers; Studio Musicians; Studio Technicians; Studio Vocalists; Supervisors

Genres: All types of music

Contact: Steven Saporta; Peter Casperson; Steve Dalmer

Management company based in New York.

Jampol Artist Management

Email: assistant@jamincla.com
Website: https://wemanagelegends.com
Website: https://www.facebook.com/jjampol

Represents: Artists/Bands

Genres: All types of music

Manages great legacy artists. Dedicated to the re-introduction of timeless art through modern means, and helps iconic artist legacies make the transition to the digital age with integrity. Does not manage new artists. If you are a legacy artist looking to extend your reach, use new technologies, or place your legacy in a modern context, send query by email.

Jeff Roberts & Associates

174 Saundersville Road, Ste 702
Hendersonville, TN
Website: http://www.jeffroberts.com
Website: https://www.facebook.com/jrabooking

Represents: Artists/Bands

Genres: Christian

Christina music booking agency, based in Tennessee.

Kari Estrin Management & Consulting

PO Box 60232
Nashville, TN 37206
Email: kari@kariestrin.com
Website: http://www.kariestrin.com
Website: https://www.facebook.com/Kari-Estrin-Management-118090355921/

Represents: Artists/Bands

Genres: Americana; Folk; Roots; Acoustic

Based in Nashville, Tennessee. Offers artist management and consulting.

KBH Entertainment

Los Angeles, CA
Email: support@kbhentertainment.com
Website: https://kbhentertainment.com
Website: https://www.facebook.com/KBHEntertainment

Represents: Artists/Bands; Film / TV Composers; Producers; Studio Musicians; Studio Vocalists

Genres: All types of music

Contact: Brent Harvey

A full service entertainment consulting, booking, event production, management and marketing company, based in Los Angeles, California.

KCA Artists

1025 17th Avenue South, 2nd Floor
Nashville, TN 37212
Fax: +1 (615) 327-4949
Email: keith@keithcase.com
Website: https://www.kcaartists.com
Website: https://www.facebook.com/KeithCaseAndAssociates

Represents: Artists/Bands

Genres: Blues; Folk; Roots; Singer-Songwriter; Pop; Gospel; Americana

Contact: Keith Case

Artist representation agency based in Nashville, Tennessee.

Kraft-Engel Management

15233 Ventura Boulevard, Suite 200
Sherman Oaks, CA 91403
Email: info@Kraft-Engel.com
Website: http://www.kraft-engel.com

Represents: Film / TV Composers; Songwriters; Supervisors

Genres: Soundtracks

Contact: Richard Kraft; Laura Engel; Sarah Kovacs; Jeff Jernigan; Jonathan Clark

Management company based in Sherman Oaks, California, specialising in representing film and theatre composers, songwriters and music supervisors.

Kragen & Company

Email: info@kragenandcompany.com
Website: https://www.kenkragen.com

Represents: Artists/Bands; Comedians; Songwriters; Variety Artists

Genres: Contemporary; Country; Singer-Songwriter

Contact: Ken Kragen

Management company based in Beverly Hills, California. Also offers consultancy services.

Kuper Personal Management

515 Bomar Street
Houston, TX 77006
Email: info@kupergroup.com
Website: http://www.kupergroup.com

Represents: Artists/Bands

Genres: Alternative; Americana; Folk; Roots Rock

Management company based in Houston, Texas. Accepts unsolicited submissions.

The Kurland Agency

173 Brighton Avenue
Boston, MA 02134-2003
Fax: +1 (617) 782-3577
Email: agents@thekurlandagency.com
Website: http://www.thekurlandagency.com

Represents: Artists/Bands

Genres: Jazz; Blues

Contact: Ted Kurland

Management company based in Boston, best known for representing jazz artists.

Len Weisman, Personal Manager

357 S. Fairfax Ave. #430
Los Angeles, Ca. 90036
Fax: +1 (323) 653-7670
Email: parlirec@aol.com
Website: http://www.parliamentrecords.com

Represents: Artists/Bands

Genres: Gospel; R&B; Hip-Hop; Rap; Soul; Blues

Manager based in Los Angeles.

Lippman Entertainment

Fax: +1 (805) 686-5866
Email: music@lippmanent.com
Email: info@lippmanent.com
Website: http://www.lippmanent.com
Website: https://www.facebook.com/lippmanent
Website: http://www.myspace.com/lippmanentertainment

Represents: Artists/Bands; Film / TV Composers; Producers; Sound Engineers; Studio Technicians

Genres: Pop; R&B; Rap; Hip-Hop; Rock; Singer-Songwriter; Urban

Contact: Michael Lippman; Nick Lippman

Management company based in California. Not accepting submissions as at September 2019.

Loggins Promotion

Nashville, TN
Email: staff@logginspromotion.com
Website: http://www.logginspromotion.com
Website: https://www.facebook.com/logginspromotion

Represents: Artists/Bands

Genres: R&B; Urban; Rap; Hip-Hop; Dance; Alternative; Rock; Americana; Jazz; Country; Pop

Full service promotion firm based in Nashville, Tennessee. Submit music using online form, or send email for permission to submit by post.

Lookout Management

1460 Fourth Street, Suite 300
Santa Monica, CA 90401
Fax: +1 (310) 319-5331
Email: webstar@lookoutmgmt.com

Represents: Artists/Bands

Genres: Alternative; Rock

Contact: Elliot Roberts; Frank Gironda

Management company founded in 1967 and based in Santa Monica, California.

Lupo Entertainment

725 River Road, Suite 32-388
Edgewater, NJ 07020
Email: steve@lupomusic.com
Email: nicklopiccolo@

lupoentertainment.com
Website: http://www.lupomusic.com

Represents: Artists/Bands

Genres: Country; Pop; R&B; Rock; Hip-Hop

Contact: Steve Corbin; Nick LoPiccolo

Management company and consulting service founded in 2003, based in Edgewater, New Jersey. Query before making submission.

M. Hitchcock Management

Nashville, TN
Email: info@mhmgmt.com
Website: http://www.mhmgmt.com

Represents: Artists/Bands

Genres: Alternative Country; Contemporary; Country; Folk; Rock

Contact: Monty Hitchcock

Management company based in Nashville, Tennessee.

Maine Road Management

PO Box 1412
Woodstock, NY 12498
Email: mailbox@maineroadmanagement.com
Website: http://www.maineroadmanagement.com

Represents: Artists/Bands; Producers

Genres: Country; Folk; Indie; Jazz; Rock

Contact: David Whitehead

New York-based management company.

Major Bob Music, Inc.

1111 17th Avenue South
Nashville, TN 37212
Website: http://www.majorbob.com
Website: https://www.facebook.com/majorbobmusic

Represents: Artists/Bands; Songwriters

Genres: Country; R&B; Soul; Pop

Contact: Bob Doyle; Michael Doyle

Management and publishing company based in Nashville, Tennessee.

The Management Ark, Inc.

Edward C. Arrendell, II
3 Bethesda Metro Center, Suite 700
Bethesda, MD 20814

Vernon H. Hammond III, CFP
116 Villiage Boulevard, Suite 200
Princeton, NJ 08540
Email: managearkeast@comcast.net
Email: rai@mngtark.com
Website: http://www.managementark.com

Represents: Artists/Bands

Genres: Jazz

Contact: Edward C. Arrendell, II; Vernon H. Hammond III, CFP

Jazz management company with offices in Bethesda, Maryland, and Princeton, New Jersey.

Mars Jazz

1006 Ashby Place
Charlottesville, VA 22901-4006
Fax: +1 (434) 979-6179
Email: reggie@marsjazz.com
Website: http://www.marsjazz.com

Represents: Artists/Bands

Genres: Jazz

Contact: Reggie Marshall

Jazz booking agency. Not currently accepting new clients or press kits, but happy to receive CDs and contact details and may contact further down the line if interested.

Mascioli Entertainment

319 Dillon Cir.
Orlando, FL 32822
Website: http://www.masciolientertainment.com

Represents: Artists/Bands

Genres: Country; Jazz; R&B; Swing; Rock

Contact: Paul Mascioli; Mike Mascioli

Full-service entertainment company based in Orlando, Florida, offering artists management and booking for conventions, casinos, arenas, theaters, night clubs, fairs, festivals, and special events.

Mauldin Brand Agency

Email: info@mauldinbrand.com
Website: https://www.mauldinbrandinc.com

Represents: Artists/Bands; Producers; Songwriters

Genres: Hip-Hop; R&B; Rap; Pop

Contact: Michael Mauldin

Management company based in Atlanta, Georgia.

McGhee Entertainment

8730 West Sunset Boulevard, Suite 200
West Hollywood, CA 90069

NASHVILLE OFFICE:
21 Music Square West
Nashville, TN 37203
Fax: +1 (310) 358-9299
Email: info@mcgheela.com
Website: http://www.mcgheela.com
Website: https://www.facebook.com/McGheeEntertainment

Represents: Artists/Bands; Songwriters

Genres: Country; Metal; Rock; Singer-Songwriter; World

Contact: Don McGhee; Scott McGhee

Management company with offices in Hollywood and Nashville. No unsolicited material.

MEGA Music Management

7295 Essex Dr
Douglasville, GA 30134
Email: goodmusicgoodmoney@gmail.com
Email: mmsonline2014@gmail.com
Website: http://www.megamusic.today/

Represents: Artists/Bands; Lyricists; Other Entertainers; Producers; Studio Musicians; Studio Technicians; Studio Vocalists; Variety Artists

Genres: All types of music

Contact: Jason Stokes

Helping independent artists get paid for your music. We can get your music heard all over the globe as well as receive royalties for your streaming and downloads! Get paid every time your music is played.

The MGMT Company

6906 Hollywood Blvd
Hollywood, CA 90028
Email: inquiries@themgmtcompany.com
Website: http://www.themgmtcompany.com

Represents: Artists/Bands

Genres: All types of music

Management company based in Hollywood, California.

Michael Anthony's Electric Events

Post Office Box 280848
Lakewood, CO 80228
Fax: +1 (303) 989-0037
Email: info2@electricevents.com
Website: http://www.electricevents.com

Represents: Artists/Bands

Genres: Rock; Country; Pop

Contact: Michael A Tolerico

Music entertainment booking agency based in Lakewood, Colorado.

Michael Hausman Artist Management Inc.

17A Stuyvesant Oval
New York, NY 10009
Fax: +1 (212) 505-1127
Email: info@michaelhausman.com
Website: http://www.michaelhausman.com

Represents: Artists/Bands

Genres: Contemporary; Pop; Rock; Singer-Songwriter

Contact: Michael Hausman

Management company based in New York.

Michael Kline Artists

PO Box 312
Cape May Point, NJ 08212
Email: info@michaelklineartists.com
Email: michael@michaelklineartists.com
Website: http://www.michaelklineartists.com
Website: https://www.facebook.com/Michaelklineartists

Represents: Artists/Bands

Genres: All types of music

Contact: Michael Kline

International management and booking agency based in New Jersey.

Mike's Artist Management

PO Box 571567
Tarzana, CA 91357
Email: mike@mikesmanagement.com
Email: dan@mikesmanagement.com
Website: http://funzalorecords.com/mikes-artist-management/
Website: https://www.facebook.com/funzalorecords

Represents: Artists/Bands

Genres: Americana; Pop; Rock

Contact: Mike Lembo; Dan Agnew

Record label and artist management based in Tarzana, California. Send submissions via contact form on website.

Million Dollar Artists

13001 Dieterle Lane
St. Louis, MO 63127
Fax: +1 (314) 984-0828
Email: info@americaneaglerecordings.com
Email: americaneaglerecordings@earthlink.net
Website: http://www.milliondollarartists.net
Website: http://americaneaglerecordings.com

Represents: Artists/Bands

Genres: All types of music

Contact: Dr. Charles Max E. Million

Management company based in St. Louis, Missouri. Send demos on CD only, with lyrics, bio, and photos / press coverage. Download and complete Preliminary Questionnaire from website. No submissions of MP3s or links by email – these will be ignored.

MM Music Agency

11 Island Avenue,Suite 1711
Miami, FL 33139
Fax: +1 (305) 831-4472
Email: maurice@mmmusicagency.com
Email: info@mmmusicagency.com
Website: http://www.mmmusicagency.com
Website: https://www.facebook.com/mmmusicagency

Represents: Artists/Bands

Genres: Jazz; Regional; Contemporary

Contact: Maurice Montoya

Music agency based in Florida, handling jazz, Afro-Caribbean, Brazilian and contemporary music.

MOB Agency

Los Angeles, CA
Fax: +1 (323) 653-0428
Email: Mitch@mobagency.com
Email: joy@mobagency.com
Website: http://www.mobagency.com

Represents: Artists/Bands

Genres: Alternative; Rock

Agency based in Los Angeles.

Monqui Presents

PO Box 5908
Portland, OR 97228
Email: monquipresents@gmail.com
Email: web@monqui.com
Website: http://www.monqui.com
Website: https://www.facebook.com/monquipresents

Represents: Artists/Bands

Genres: Alternative; Indie; Rock; Country; Pop

"Importers of fine live music", serving the Northwest since 1983. Send questions or comments by email and press kits by post.

MSH Management

Studio City, CA
Email: mshmgmt@yahoo.com
Website: http://mshmgmt.wixsite.com/music-management

Represents: Artists/Bands

Genres: All types of music

Contact: Marney Hansen

Management company based in Studio City, California.

Music + Art Management

222 Broadway Street
Asheville, NC 28801
Email: steve@musicandart.net
Website: http://musicandart.net
Website: https://www.facebook.com/Music-and-Art-Management-163558147005567/

Represents: Artists/Bands

Genres: Electronic; World; Experimental; Rock; Jazz

Contact: Steve Cohen, President

Full service management and production company specialising in the careers of performing and recording artists. Based in Asheville, North Carolina.

Music City Artists

7104 Peach Ct.
Brentwood, TN 37027
Fax: +1 (615) 266-6223
Email: cray@musiccityartists.com
Website: http://musiccityartists.com
Website: https://www.facebook.com/MusicCityArtists/

Represents: Artists/Bands

Genres: All types of music

Contact: Charles Ray, President / Agent

Full service booking agency representing nationally known artists for performing arts centers, casinos, and corporate entertainment.

Music Inc.

468 N. Camden Drive
Beverly Hills, CA 90210
Email: vince@musicinc.org
Website: http://www.musicinc.org

Represents: Artists/Bands

Genres: Pop

Contact: Vincent Pileggi

Management company based in Beverly Hills, California. No longer accepting unsolicited material as at January 2018. Check website for current status.

Mustang Agency

6119 Greenville Ave, Ste 361
75206 Dallas, Texas
Email: booking@mustangagency.com
Website: https://www.facebook.com/MustangAgency

Represents: Artists/Bands

Genres: Alternative; Country; Classic Rock; Metal; Pop; Rock

Established in 2003 by two prominent Attorneys located in Dallas, Texas, the Agency was created from a need to book bands nationally, regionally and locally.

Myriad Artists

PO BOX 550
Carrboro, NC 27510
Fax: +1 (919) 869-2410
Email: trish@myriadartists.com
Email: bookings@myriadartists.com
Website: http://www.myriadartists.com
Website: https://www.facebook.com/myriadartists/

Represents: Artists/Bands

Genres: Blues; Folk; Jazz; Americana

Contact: Trish Galfano

Management company based in Carrboro, North Carolina.

Nancy Fly Agency

Email: piano@nflyagency.com
Website: http://www.nflyagency.com

Represents: Artists/Bands

Genres: Americana; Traditional; Roots Rock; Blues; World

Contact: Nancy Fly

Now in semi-retirement, continues to represent just two long-term clients. No new acts considered.

Nettwerk Management

3900 West Alameda Ave, Suite 850
Burbank, CA 91505

NEW YORK
33 Irving Place
New York, NY 10003

BOSTON
15 Richdale Ave., Unit 203
Cambridge, MA 02140
Fax: +1 (747) 477-1093
Email: info@nettwerk.com
Website: http://www.nettwerk.com

Represents: Artists/Bands; Film / TV Composers; Producers; Songwriters; Sound Engineers; Studio Technicians

Genres: Contemporary; Christian; Electronic; Folk; Indie; Latin; Pop; Punk; Rap; Rock; Hip-Hop; Dance; Singer-Songwriter; World

Media company with offices in New York, London, Vancouver, Boston, Nashville, and Germany. Also label and music publishing company.

New Heights Entertainment

PO Box 8489
Calabasas, CA 91372
Email: info@newheightsent.com
Website: http://www.newheightsent.com

Represents: Artists/Bands; Producers; Songwriters

Genres: All types of music

Contact: Alan Melina

Privately held personal management and consulting firm based in Calabasas, California, with its core business focusing on Music Producers, Songwriters, Record Label Management, Music Publishing, Brand Development and Strategic Guidance for Entertainment Content and IP Creators. No unsolicited materials.

Nightside Entertainment, Inc.

Email: alsalzillo@nightsideentertainment.com
Website: https://www.nightsideentertainment.com
Website: https://www.facebook.com/nightsideentertainment/

Represents: Artists/Bands

Genres: All types of music

Full service music booking agency.

Outrider Music, LLC

Email: anne@outridermusic.com
Website: http://www.outridermusic.com

Represents: Artists/Bands; Lyricists; Songwriters

Genres: Post Rock; Progressive Rock; Post Metal; Hard Rock; Heavy Rock; Melodic Hardcore; Rock; Punk; Pop Rock; Pop Punk; Electronic Rock; Atmospheric Rock; Alternative; Alternative Rock; Acoustic Rock; Instrumental; Indie; Hardcore; Indie Rock; Ambient; Ambient Rock; Emo; Post Emo

Contact: Anne McGinnis

I was born and raised in Charlottesville, and I became obsessed with music at an early age. I spent my early teenage years playing guitar in various pop-punk and alternative rock bands, but it soon became clear to me that I enjoyed the behind-the-scenes work just as much, if not more, than actually playing. After graduating from Charlottesville High School, I got my degree in Music Business from New York University. While at NYU, I spent two semesters interning for Warner Music Group and I had the opportunity to meet and learn from some incredible people. I realized that what I really wanted to do was to help upcoming artists navigate the early stages of their careers. Growing up in Charlottesville, I saw too many of our "hometown heroes" get signed to bad record deals and wash out, and I wanted to help prevent that. I started Outrider Music because I wanted to be an advocate for local bands, to help them navigate both the fun stuff (branding, marketing, touring, booking) and the not-so-fun stuff (contracts, PROs, insurance, taxes). I want to be a part of your team.

Ozark Talent

718 Schwarz Rd
Lawrence, KS 66049
Email: ozarktalent@gmail.com
Website: https://www.facebook.com/pages/Ozark-Talent/833757923407465

Represents: Artists/Bands

Genres: All types of music

Contact: Steve Ozark

Management company based in Lawrence, Kansas.

Pacific Talent

Email: andy@pacifictalent.com
Website: http://www.pacifictalent.com
Website: https://www.instagram.com/pacifictalentpdx/

Represents: Artists/Bands

Genres: All types of music

Contact: Andy Gilbert

Management company based in Oregon.

Paradigm Talent Agency

8942 Wilshire Boulevard
Beverly Hills, CA 90211
Fax: +1 (310) 288-2000
Website: https://www.paradigmagency.com

Represents: Artists/Bands

Genres: All types of music

Talent agency with offices in Los Angeles, New York, Monterey, Nashville, San Diego, Austin, London, Berkeley, Chicago, and Toronto.

Paradise Artists

108 E Matilija St.
Ojai, CA 93023

5 Penn Plaza #2382
New York, NY 10001
Email: info@paradiseartists.com
Email: howie@paradiseartists.com
Website: http://www.paradiseartists.com

Represents: Artists/Bands

Genres: Rock; Rock and Roll; Pop

Contact: Howie Silverman; Bill Monot

Management company with offices in New York and California.

Persistent Management

PO Box 88456
Los Angeles, CA 90009
Email: pm@persistentmanagement.com
Website: http://www.persistentmanagement.com
Website: https://soundcloud.com/persistentmanagement

Represents: Artists/Bands

Genres: All types of music

Contact: Eric Knight

Management company based in Los Angeles. Submit your details through online Artist Submissions form, including links to music online. No postal submissions or phone calls.

Piedmont Talent

Email: info@piedmonttalent.com
Website: http://piedmonttalent.com
Website: https://www.facebook.com/PiedmontTalent/?ref=br_rs

Represents: Artists/Bands

Genres: Blues; Roots; Soul

Talent agency with offices in Los Angeles, New York, and Palm Beach, Florida.

PRA [Patrick Rains & Associates]

1255 Fifth Avenue, Suite 7K
New York, NY 10029
Fax: +1 (212) 860-5556
Email: pra@prarecords.com
Website: http://www.prarecords.com
Website: https://twitter.com/prarecords

Represents: Artists/Bands

Genres: Jazz; Pop; Rock

Contact: Patrick Rains; Stephanie Pappas

Management company based in New York. No unsolicited material.

Pretty Lights

Email: contact@prettylightsmusic.com
Website: http://prettylightsmusic.com
Website: https://soundcloud.com/prettylights

Represents: Artists/Bands

Genres: All types of music

Submit demos using online form, available via website.

Prodigal Son Entertainment

Brentwood, TN
Email: prodigalsonent@gmail.com
Website: http://www.prodigalson-entertainment.com
Website: https://www.facebook.com/ScottWilliamsPSE
Website: http://www.myspace.com/prodigalsonentertainment

Represents: Artists/Bands

Genres: Alternative; Country; Christian; Instrumental; Rock; Hard Rock

Contact: Scott Williams

Artist management and career consultancy services.

Progressive Global Agency (PGA)

PO Box 50294
Nashville, TN 37205
Fax: +1 (615) 354-9101
Email: info@pgamusic.com
Website: http://www.pgamusic.com

Represents: Artists/Bands

Genres: Pop; Rock; World

Contact: Buck Williams

Management company based in Nashville, Tennessee.

Pyramid Entertainment Group

377 Rector Place
, Suite 21A
New York, NY 10280
Fax: +1 (212) 242-6932
Email: smichaels@pyramid-ent.com
Website: https://pyramid-ent.com

Represents: Artists/Bands

Genres: Gospel; Jazz; Funk; Hip-Hop; R&B; Urban

Contact: Sal Michaels

Management company based in New York.

Q Prime Management, Inc.

729 Seventh Avenue, 16th Floor
New York, NY 10019

NASHVILLE OFFICE:
131 South 11th Sreet
Nashville, TN 37206
Fax: +1 (212) 302-9589
Email: newyork@qprime.com
Email: nashville@qprime.com
Website: http://www.qprime.com

Represents: Artists/Bands; Producers

Genres: Blues; Folk; Metal; Pop; Rock; Alternative; Singer-Songwriter

Contact: Randi Seplow

Management company with offices in New York, Los Angeles, Nashville and London. Not accepting unsolicited materials or demos as at February 2018.

Rainmaker Artists

PO Box 342229
Austin, TX 78734
Fax: +1 (512) 843-7500

Email: paul@rainmakerartists.com
Website: http://www.rainmakerartists.com
Website: https://www.facebook.com/rainmaker.artists

Represents: Artists/Bands

Genres: Pop; Rock

Management company based in Austin, Texas. Accepts unsolicited material.

Red Entertainment Agency

505 8th Avenue Suite 1004
New York, NY 10018
Fax: +1 (212) 563-9393
Email: info@redentertainment.com
Email: carloskeyes@redentertainment.com
Website: http://www.redentertainment.com
Website: https://www.facebook.com/RedEntertainmentAgencyGroup

Represents: Artists/Bands

Genres: Funk; Jazz; Gospel; Latin; Hip-Hop; Pop; Rock; R&B; Urban

Contact: Carlos Keyes

Since its founding in 2002, has established itself as a leading entertainment talent agency, guiding the careers of an elite roster of musical artists. Under the leadership of agency President, has carved out a distinctive niche in the entertainment landscape and earned a reputation for putting artists' interests above all else. With a select group of professional agents working side by side, the agency credo is one of team work and availability that translates into successful relationships for all clients.

The select yet diverse client list allows it to effectively compete with other large agencies while guaranteeing personalized attention to every client. With offices in New York City, provides representation to clients across its music, motion picture, television and personal appearances worldwide.

Red Light Management (RLM)

Charlottesville:
PO Box 1467
Charlottesville, VA 22902

New York:
10 East 40th Street, 22nd Floor
New York, NY 10005

Nashville:
1101 McGavock Street, Suite 300
Nashville, TN 37203

Los Angeles:
8439 Sunset Boulevard, 2nd Floor
Los Angeles, CA 90069

Atlanta:
1825 Lockeway Drive, Suite 204
Alpharetta, GA 30004

Seattle:
159 Western Avenue West, Suite 485
Seattle WA 98119
Email: info@redlightmanagement.com
Website: http://www.redlightmanagement.com
Website: http://twitter.com/redlightmgmt

Represents: Artists/Bands; Film / TV Composers; Songwriters; Studio Musicians

Genres: Blues; Christian; Country; Dance; Electronic; Hardcore; Indie; Latin; Metal; Pop; Rap; Hip-Hop; Rock; Singer-Songwriter; World

Management company with offices in Charlottesville, New York, Nashville, Los Angeles, London, Bristol, Atlanta, and Seattle.

Red Star Artist Management

Los Angeles
Email: MC@RedStarArtists.com
Email: SkaT@RedStarArtists.com
Website: http://www.redstarartists.com

Represents: Artists/Bands

Genres: Alternative Rock

Management company based in Los Angeles, providing an experienced management team to beginning artists, independently distributed artists, and established artists.

Regime Seventy-Two

Malibu, CA
Email: info@regimeinc.com
Website: http://www.regime72.com

Represents: Artists/Bands

Genres: All types of music

Management company based in Malibu, California, that is home to a wide variety of artists including musicians and actors.

Richard Varrasso Management

PO Box 387
Fremont, CA 94537-0387
Email: richard@varrasso.com
Website: http://www.varrasso.com
Website: https://www.facebook.com/richardvarrasso
Website: https://myspace.com/richardvarrasso

Represents: Artists/Bands; Comedians; DJs; Other Entertainers; Producers; Songwriters; Studio Musicians

Genres: All types of music

Contact: Richard Varrasso

Management company based in Fremont, California. Old school turned digital business leader with a proven track record of driving results. Skilled in the development and launch of new ventures. Highly regarded for ability to problem-solve and execute in complex, fast-moving environments, consistently exceeding operating plans.

Riot Artists

Email: staff@riotartists.com
Website: http://www.riotartists.com
Website: https://www.facebook.com/RiotArtists

Represents: Artists/Bands

Genres: World; Traditional; Contemporary

Management company specialising in World music reflecting traditional culture, and incorporating contemporary sounds to varying degrees. Books artists from around the world, with an emphasis on Canada, the US, Mexico, Brazil, and Europe.

Ron Rainey Management Inc.

8500 Wilshire Boulevard, Suite 525
Beverly Hills, CA 90211
Fax: +1 (310) 557-8421
Email: rrmgmt@aol.com
Website: http://www.ronrainey.com

Represents: Artists/Bands

Genres: Contemporary; Blues; Pop; Country; Rock

Contact: Ron Rainey; Greg Lewerke

Management company based in Beverly Hills, California.

RPM Music Productions

420 West 14th Street, Suite 6NW
New York, NY 10014
Email: info@rpm-productions.com
Website: http://rpm-productions.com

Represents: Artists/Bands

Genres: Jazz; Pop

Contact: Danny Bennett

Management company based in New York.

Russell Carter Artist Management

567 Ralph McGill Boulevard, NE
Atlanta, GA 30312
Fax: +1 (404) 377-5131
Email: russell.rcam@gmail.com
Website: https://www.facebook.com/pages/Russell-Carter-Artist-Management/174050332290?pnref=about.overview
Website: https://twitter.com/RCAM_mgnt
Website: https://myspace.com/rcam

Represents: Artists/Bands

Genres: Contemporary; Alternative; Americana; Blues; Folk; Indie; Jazz; Singer-Songwriter; Pop; Rock

Contact: Russell Carter

Management company based in Atlanta, Georgia.

Selak Entertainment, Inc.

466 Foothill Blvd. #184
La Canada, CA 91011
Fax: +1 (626)584-8122
Email: steve@selakentertainment.com
Website: https://selakentertainment.com

Represents: Artists/Bands; Comedians; Tribute Acts

Genres: All types of music

Management company based in La Canada, California. Not accepting any original material.

Semaphore Mgmt & Consulting

109 Franklin Street
Brooklyn, NY 11222
Email: taylor@semaphoremgmt.com
Website: https://www.semaphoremgmt.com

Represents: Artists/Bands

Genres: Alternative Atmospheric Avant-Garde Electronic Experimental Glam Industrial Heavy Hard Kraut Leftfield New Wave Non-Commercial Post Psychedelic Thrash Underground

Contact: Taylor Brode

Full scale artist management and consulting agency. We offer a la carte consulting and retainer services to bands and labels alike.

Sharpe Entertainment Services, Inc.

683 Palmera Avenue
Pacific Palisades, CA 90272
Fax: +1 (310) 230-2109
Email: frances@ses-la.com
Website: http://www.ses-la.com/SES

Represents: Artists/Bands; Film / TV Composers; Producers; Songwriters; Supervisors

Genres: Contemporary; Indie; Pop; Rock; Alternative; Singer-Songwriter

Contact: Wil Sharpe

Management company based in Pacific Palisades, California. Not accepting unsolicited material as at March 2018.

Siren Music Company

PO Box 12110
Portland, OR 97212-0110
Fax: +1 (503) 238-4771
Email: december@sirenmusiccompany.com
Website: http://www.sirenmusiccompany.com

Represents: Artists/Bands

Genres: Americana; Roots; Folk; Country; Alternative; Pop; Regional; Singer-Songwriter; Blues

Management company based in Portland, Oregon. Not accepting submissions as a March 2018 due to workload. Check website for current status.

SKH Music

540 President Street
Brooklyn, NY 11215
Email: skaras@skhmusic.com
Email: khagan@skhmusic.com
Website: http://www.skhmusic.com
Website: https://twitter.com/skhmusic

Represents: Artists/Bands; Lyricists; Producers

Genres: All types of music

Contact: Steve Karas; Keith Hagan

Management company formed in June 2009, based in Brooklyn, New York.

SMC Artists

1525 Aviation Boulevard, Suite 1000
Redondo Beach, CA 90278-2805
Email: ovavrin@smcartists.com
Website: https://www.smcartists.com

Represents: Film / TV Composers; Songwriters

Genres: All types of music

Management company representing film and TV composers and songwriters.

So What Media & Management

890 West End Avenue, #1A
New York, NY 10025
Fax: +1 (212) 877-9735
Email: sowhatasst@me.com

Represents: Artists/Bands

Genres: Pop; Rock

Contact: Lisa Barbaris

Management company representing musical artists in the areas of pop and rock.

Sorkin Productions

3742 Jasmine Avenue # 201
Los Angeles, CA 90034
Fax: +1 (310) 559-5581
Email: donsorkin@aol.com

Represents: Artists/Bands

Genres: Dance; Pop; R&B; Rock

Contact: Don Sorkin

Management company incorporated in California in 2000, currently based in Los Angeles.

Soundtrack Music Associates (SMA)

4133 Redwood Avenue, Suite 3030
Los Angeles, CA 90066
Email: INFO@SOUNDTRK.com
Website: http://soundtrk.com

Represents: Film / TV Composers; Supervisors

Genres: Soundtracks

Contact: John Tempereau; Koyo Sonae; Isabel Pappani

Represents award-winning composers, music supervisors and music editors for film, television and all media.

Sparks Entertainment Management Co.

PO Box 82510
Tampa, FL 33682
Email: sparksentertainment78@gmail.com
Website: http://bsparksent.com
Website: http://www.facebook.com/BSparksEntertainment
Website: http://www.myspace.com/ballnfresh

Represents: Artists/Bands

Genres: All types of music

Contact: Brian Sparks

Management company based in Tampa, Florida.

Spectrum Talent Agency

Email: chris@spectrumtalentagency.com
Email: jan@spectrumtalentagency.com
Website: http://spectrumtalentagency.com

Represents: Artists/Bands

Genres: Dance; Hip-Hop; Pop; R&B; House

Full service global booking agency.

Starkravin' Management

McLane & Wong
11135 Weddington Street, Suite #424
North Hollywood, CA 91601
Fax: +1 (818) 587-6802
Email: bcmclane@aol.com
Website: http://www.benmclane.com

Represents: Artists/Bands; Producers; Songwriters

Genres: Pop; R&B; Rock

Contact: Ben McLane

Management and entertainment law company based in North Hollywood. Provides personal management and legal services.

Sterling Artist Management

11054 Ventura Boulevard, #285
Studio City, California 91604
Fax: +1 (818) 907-5558
Email: mark@sterlingartist.com
Website: http://www.sterlingartist.com

Represents: Artists/Bands; Producers; Songwriters; Studio Musicians

Genres: All types of music, except: Ambient Black Metal Black Origin Blue Beat Break

Beat C-DUB Chill Classical Club Dance Dancehall Deep Funk Disco Doom Drum and Bass Dub Dubstep Emo Glitch Gothic Grime Grind Hardcore Hi-NRG Hip-Hop House IDM Jungle Lounge Melodicore Metal Mystical New Age Noise Core Ragga Rap Reggaeton Remix Trance Techno Synthpop Surf Spoken Word Skool Ska Shoegaze

Contact: Mark Sterling

Do not send demos without first making a written enquiry. Represents singer-songwriters, blues and jazz artists. If you do not fall into one of these categories, please don't consider contacting us.

Steve Stewart Entertainment

12400 Ventura Boulevard #900
Studio City, CA 91604
Email: stevestewart@stevestewart.com
Website: http://www.stevestewart.com

Represents: Artists/Bands; Film / TV Composers; Producers

Genres: Pop; Rock; Alternative; Hardcore

Contact: Steve Stewart

Management company based in Studio City, California. Boasts more than 20 years of experience and sales of more than 25 million records worldwide.

Steven Scharf Entertainment (SSE)

126 East 38th Street
New York, NY 10016
Fax: +1 (212) 725-9681
Email: SSCHARF@carlinamerica.com
Website: http://www.stevenscharf.com

Represents: Artists/Bands; Film / TV Composers; Producers; Songwriters; Supervisors

Genres: Alternative; Americana; Blues; Folk; Indie; Jazz; Metal; Pop; Rap; Hip-Hop; Rock; Roots; Singer-Songwriter; World; Soundtracks

Contact: Steven Scharf

Management company based in New York.

Stiefel Entertainment

21731 Ventura Boulevard, Suite 300
Woodland Hills, CA 91364
Fax: +1 (310) 271-5175
Email: contact@StiefelEnt.com
Website: http://www.stiefelent.com
Website: https://www.linkedin.com/company/stiefel-entertainment

Represents: Artists/Bands

Genres: Contemporary; Dance; Indie; Pop; Rock; Singer-Songwriter

Contact: Arnold Stiefel

Management company based in West Hollywood, California.

Street Smart Management

Los Angeles, CA
Email: sara@streetsmartmanagement.com
Website: https://www.facebook.com/streetsmartmanagement

Represents: Artists/Bands

Genres: Indie; Rock; Metal; Pop

Management company based in Los Angeles, California.

TAC Music Management

9971 E. Ida Place
Greenwood Village, CO 80111
Email: traceyann75@hotmail.com
Email: tachirhart75@gmail.com
Website: http://tacmusicmanagement.com

Represents: Artists/Bands; Songwriters; Studio Musicians; Tribute Acts

Genres: Acoustic; Classic; Hard; Traditional; Regional; Soulful; Heavy; Funky; Commercial; Alternative; Americana; Blues; Country; Folk; Fusion; Funk; Guitar based; Indie; Jazz; Metal; R&B; Rock; Rock and Roll; Roots; Rhythm and Blues; Singer-Songwriter; Rockabilly

Contact: Tracey Chirhart

Services include artist management, booking, promotion and marketing to both local and national artists. Genres include blues, rock, Americana, bluegrass, folk, country, and tributes.

Take Out Management

1129 Maricopa Hwy
Ojai, CA 93023
Email: AlexTakeOutManagement@gmail.com
Email: info@howiewood.com
Website: http://howiewood.com/take-out-management
Website: http://www.facebook.com/hrpcollege
Website: http://www.myspace.com/howardrosen

Represents: Artists/Bands; Producers

Genres: All types of music

Contact: Howard Rosen; Scotty G.; Samantha Schipman; Alex Louton

Management company based in Ojai, California. Submit music using form on website.

Ten Entertainment, Inc.

1449 Alteras Circle
Nashville, TN 37211
Fax: +1 (866) 230-3942
Email: INFO@tenentertainment.com
Email: shannon@tenentertainment.com
Website: http://www.tenentertainment.com

Represents: Artists/Bands

Genres: All types of music

Management company based in Nashville, Tennessee. Send query by email with links to your music online. No submissions by post.

Tenth Street Entertainment

700 San Vicente Blvd., #G410
West Hollywood, CA 90069

38 West 21st Street, Suite 300
New York, NY 10010
Email: info@10thst.com
Website: http://www.10thst.com

Represents: Artists/Bands

Genres: All types of music

International company with offices in LA, London, and New York.

That's Entertainment International Inc. (TEI Entertainment)

3820 E. La Palma Ave
Anaheim, CA 92807
Fax: +1 (714) 693-7963
Email: jmcentee@teientertainment.com
Website: http://www.teientertainment.com

Represents: Artists/Bands

Genres: All types of music

Contact: John D. McEntee, President

Celebrity Entertainment Resource Company with offices in Anaheim and Sacramento, California, and Las Vegas, Nevada.

Third Coast Talent

PO Box 334
Kingston Springs, TN 37082
Fax: +1 (615) 685-3332
Email: carrie@thirdcoasttalent.com
Website: https://www.thirdcoasttalent.com

Represents: Artists/Bands

Genres: Country

Contact: Carrie Moore-Reed

Management company based in Kingston Springs, Tennessee.

Threee

918 North Western Avenue,Suite A
Los Angeles, CA 90029
Fax: +1 (213) 381-5115
Email: info@threee.com
Website: http://www.threee.com

Represents: Film / TV Composers; Producers; Songwriters

Genres: All types of music

Contact: Erik Eger; Paul Adams

Management company based in Los Angeles, California, representing producers, mixers, songwriters, and composers.

Thunderbird Management

133 Industrial Park Road
Larose, LA 70373

Email: thunderbird@viscom.net
Website: http://www.thethunderbirdmanagementgroup.com/

Represents: Artists/Bands

Genres: All types of music

Contact: Rueben Williams; Adam Ross

Personal management and artist development company based in Larose, Louisiana.

TKO Artist Management

2303 21st Avenue South, 3rd Floor
Nashville, TN 37212
Fax: +1 (615) 292-3328
Email: receptionist@tkoartistmanagement.com
Website: http://www.tkoartistmanagement.com
Website: https://www.facebook.com/TKOArtistMgmt/

Represents: Artists/Bands

Genres: Country

Management company based in Nashville Tennessee.

Tom Callahan & Associates (TCA)

1200 Yarmouth Ave Suite 232
Boulder, CO 80304
Email: info@tomcallahan.com
Website: http://www.tomcallahan.com
Website: https://www.facebook.com/tom.callahan.378

Represents: Artists/Bands

Genres: All types of music

Full service music consulting company based in Boulder, Colorado, offering record promotion, publicity, internet marketing, production, and more.

Tony Margherita Management

Email: info@tmmchi.com
Website: http://tmmchi.com
Website: https://www.facebook.com/tmmchimgmt

Represents: Artists/Bands

Genres: Jazz; Rock

Contact: Tony Margherita; Brandy Breaux-Simkins; Deb Bernardini

Management company specialising in the exclusive worldwide representation of recording artists.

Tower Management Group

106 Shirley Drive
Hendersonville, TN 37075
Email: EdRussell@castlerecords.com
Website: http://www.castlerecords.com

Represents: Artists/Bands

Genres: Country; Rock; Blues

Management company based in Hendersonville, Tennessee. Send demo by post with code from website on front of package. No MP3 submissions by email.

True Talent Management

9663 Santa Monica Boulevard, Suite 320, Dept. HMI
Beverly Hills, CA 90210
Email: submissions@truetalentmgmt.com
Email: webinfo@truetalentmgmt.com
Website: http://www.truetalentmgmt.com

Represents: Artists/Bands; Producers; Songwriters; Supervisors

Genres: All types of music

Contact: Jennifer Yeko

Before sending material send query by email information on where your band is located, the type of music you play, how many CDs have you released, how many CDs have you sold, how often you play out, average draw of your shows, names & ages of members, website address, plus any other pertinent information.

Tunstall Management

1420 Willowbrooke Cir
Franklin, TN 37069
Fax: +1 (615) 376-9892
Email: tunstallmgnt@comcast.net

Represents: Artists/Bands

Genres: Alternative; Rock; Urban; R&B

Management company based in Franklin, Tennessee.

Tuscan Sun Music

Nashville, TN
Email: mgmt@angelica.org
Website: http://www.tuscansunmusic.com
Website: http://www.angelica.org

Represents: Artists/Bands

Genres: Ambient; New Age; Pop

Management company based in Nashville, Tennessee.

Two Chord Touring

Fax: +1 (512) 416-7531
Email: davis@atomicmusicgroup.com
Email: davismclarty@gmail.com
Website: https://www.twochordtouring.com
Website: https://www.facebook.com/Two-Chord-Touring-138801512850466/

Represents: Artists/Bands

Genres: Country; Folk; Rockabilly

Contact: Davis McLarty; Todd Gardner; Lacey Johnson

Management company focusing on booking live events.

Uncle Booking

5438 Winding Way Drive
Houston, TX 77091
Email: erik@unclebooking.com
Website: http://www.unclebooking.com

Represents: Artists/Bands

Genres: All types of music

Booking agency based in Texas.

Union Entertainment Group

Email: info@ueginc.com
Email: bryan@ueginc.com
Website: http://www.ueginc.com

Represents: Artists/Bands

Genres: Rock; Alternative; Blues; Country; Pop; Rap; Hip-Hop

Contact: Bryan Coleman

Music management company. Not accepting submissions as at July, 2018.

United Talent Agency

9336 Civic Center Drive
Beverly Hills, CA 90210
Fax: +1 (310) 385-1220

Represents: Artists/Bands

Genres: All types of music

International talent agency with offices in the US, UK, and Sweden.

Universal Attractions Agency

NEW YORK
15 West 36th Street, 8th Floor
New York, NY 10018

LOS ANGELES
22025 Ventura Boulevard, #305
Los Angeles, CA 91364

Fax: +1 (212) 333-4508 / +1 (646) 304-5178
Email: info@universalattractions.com
Website: http://universalattractions.com
Website: https://www.facebook.com/UAAtalent/

Represents: Artists/Bands

Genres: All types of music

Talent agency with offices in New York and Los Angeles.

Variety Artists International

1924 Spring Street
Paso Robles, CA 93446
Fax: +1 (805) 545-5559
Email: Bob@varietyart.com
Email: John@varietyart.com
Website: http://www.varietyart.com

Represents: Artists/Bands

Genres: Folk; Jazz; Pop; Rap; Rock

Management company providing tour booking services.

Vector Management

PO Box 120479
Nashville, TN 37212

276 Fifth Avenue, Suite 604
New York, NY 10001

LOS ANGELES
9350 Civic Center Drive
Beverly Hills, CA 90210
Email: info@vectormgmt.com
Website: http://www.vectormgmt.com

Represents: Artists/Bands; Songwriters

Genres: Contemporary; Alternative; Americana; Country; Folk; Gospel; Metal; Pop; Rock; Singer-Songwriter

Management company with offices in Nashville, New York, Los Angeles, and London.

Velvet Hammer Music & Management Group

9911 W Pico Blvd # 350W
Los Angeles, CA 90035
Email: sendusyourmusic@velvethammer.net
Email: info@velvethammer.net
Website: http://www.velvethammer.net
Website: https://www.facebook.com/velvethammermusicandmanagementgroup
Website: http://myspace.com/velvethammermusic

Represents: Artists/Bands

Genres: All types of music

Contact: David Benveniste (Beno); Mark Wakefield; Jimmy Throgmorton; Ravand Rustin; Bryn Bennett; Taylor Brooks; Hailey Johnson; Alyssa Lesto; Samantha Waterman; Susan Silver; Samantha Surtida

Prides itself on identifying quality talent. Submit demos by email – all demos listened to.

Walker Entertainment Group

PO Box 7926
Houston, TX 77270
Email: info@walkerentertainmentgroup.com
Website: http://www.walkerentertainmentgroup.com
Website: https://www.facebook.com/walkerentertainmentgrouptx/

Represents: Artists/Bands

Genres: All types of music

Global provider of event management, production, and entertainment services.

Wayward Goose Entertainment Group LLC

Lakewood Ranch, FL
Email: info@wwgentertainment.com
Website: https://wwgentertainment.com

Represents: Artists/Bands

Genres: Jazz

Management company with offices in Florida and the Netherlands.

Wolfson Entertainment, Inc.

2659 Townsgate Road, Suite 119
Westlake Village, CA 91361
Fax: +1 (805) 494-1122
Email: info@wolfsonent.com
Website: http://wolfsonent.com
Website: https://www.facebook.com/Wolfsonent

Represents: Artists/Bands

Genres: All types of music

Contact: Jonathan Wolfson; Dillon Barbosa; Christian Brown; Sammy Wolfson

Management company based in Westlake Village, California.

Worldsound, LLC

17837 1st Ave South
Seattle, WA 98148
Email: Warren@WorldSound.com
Email: Alex@WorldSound.com
Website: http://www.worldsound.com
Website: https://www.facebook.com/worldsoundllc

Represents: Artists/Bands

Genres: Celtic; Folk; Pop; Rock; World; Rock and Roll

Contact: Warren Wyatt; Alex Barragan; Morgan Eattock

Management company founded in Southern California in 1992, now based in Seattle, Washington.

UK Managers

For the most up-to-date listings of these and hundreds of other managers, visit https://www.musicsocket.com/managers

*To claim your **free** access to the site, please see the back of this book.*

0114 Records

Sheffield
Email: 0114records.submissions@gmail.com
Website: http://0114records.com

Represents: Artists/Bands

Genres: Alternative; Folk; Garage; Indie; Rock; Punk; Hard Rock; Reggae; Singer-Songwriter; Ska

Independent record label and artist management company based in Sheffield. Send query by email with links to music online. Must be over 18, live in the UK, and play original music.

360 Artist Development

42 Western Avenue
Birstall
WF17 0PF
Email: info@360artistdevelopment.com
Email: matthew@360artistdevelopment.com
Website: http://www.360artistdevelopment.com
Website: https://www.facebook.com/360artistdevelopment

Represents: Artists/Bands

Genres: All types of music

Management / consultancy company based in Wakefield.

A&R Factory

Email: info@anrfactory.com
Website: http://www.anrfactory.com
Website: https://www.facebook.com/anrfactory

Represents: Artists/Bands

Genres: All types of music

Management company based in London. Send demos through online submission form on website.

ADSRecords

Email: music@adsrecords.co.uk
Email: podcast@adsrecords.co.uk
Website: https://www.adsrecords.co.uk
Website: https://soundcloud.com/adsrecordsuk

Represents: Artists/Bands

Genres: Acoustic; Alternative; Indie; Pop; Singer-Songwriter

Contact: Alex Dale-Staples

Artist management and composition services. To be considered for Artist Management send query by email, with "Artist Management" in the subject line, links to your music, and a 50-word description.

AEC Music Management

Email: adrian@aecmusicmanagement.com
Website: http://www.aecmusicmanagement.com
Website: https://facebook.com/aecmusicmanagement

Represents: Artists/Bands

Genres: Singer-Songwriter; Pop; Rock; Folk

Contact: Adrian

Artist management, A&R consultancy and live showcase events. Send query by email with MP3 attachments or links to music online.

AirMTM

Shepherds Building West
Rockley Road
Shepherds Bush
London
W14 0DA
Email: info@airmtm.com
Website: http://www.airmtm.com
Website: http://www.myspace.com/airmtm

Represents: Artists/Bands

Genres: All types of music

Send query by email with details of your act and links to your music online.

Amour:Music

Email: info@amourmusic.co.uk
Website: https://amourmusic.co.uk
Website: https://soundcloud.com/amourmusicuk

Represents: Artists/Bands

Genres: Contemporary; Singer-Songwriter

Contact: James Brister

Send query by email with links to streaming music online. No attachments or download links.

Aneko Music

Bournemouth / London
Email: ed@anekomusic.com
Website: http://anekomusic.com
Website: https://www.facebook.com/AnekoMusic

Represents: Artists/Bands

Genres: All types of music

Contact: Ed Hill

A Bournemouth and London based artist management company, record label and radio promotions agency. Send query by email with links to music online. Response not guaranteed unless interested.

Anger Management

4-7 Forewoods Common
Holt
Wiltshire
BA14 6PJ
Email: george@anger-management.co
Website: https://www.anger-management.co
Website: https://www.facebook.com/AngerManagement100

Represents: Artists/Bands

Genres: All types of music

Provides artist and tour management services.

Anglo Management

Unit 435, The Metal Box Factory
30 Great Guildford Street
London
SE1 0HS
Email: info@anglomanagement.co.uk
Website: http://www.anglomanagement.co.uk

Represents: Artists/Bands

Genres: All types of music

Management company based in London. Send demo by post or by email.

The Animal Farm

4th Floor, Block A
The Biscuit Factory
100 Clements Road
London
SE16 4DG
Email: info@theanimalfarm.co.uk
Website: http://www.theanimalfarm.co.uk

Website: https://www.facebook.com/theanimalfarmmusic

Represents: Artists/Bands

Genres: All types of music

Send query by email giving link to Facebook or other website where you can be seen and your music heard. Include reason for approach. No MP3 attachments by email. Do not expect feedback.

ASM Talent

4th Floor, 63/66 Hatton Garden
London
EC1N 8LE
Email: albert@missioncontrol.net
Email: albert@asmtalent.co.uk
Website: https://asmanagement.co.uk

Represents: Artists/Bands

Genres: All types of music

Contact: David Samuel; Jason Samuel; Albert Samuel

Management company with music and TV and press departments. Clients have appeared on numerous high profile TV entertainment shows. Send query by email with links to music online.

Associated London Management

London
Email: martin@associatedlondonmanagement.com
Email: jason@associatedlondonmanagement.com
Website: http://www.associatedlondonmanagement.com
Website: https://facebook.com/ALMgmt

Represents: Artists/Bands

Genres: Alternative

Management company based in London. Send demos as MP3 attachments by email.

Atum Management Ltd

Email: info@atummanagement.com
Website: http://www.atummanagement.com
Website: https://soundcloud.com/atummanagement

Represents: Artists/Bands

Genres: All types of music

Management company based in London. Send demos by email.

Audio Bay Management

Bristol
Email: jon@audiobaymanagement.com
Website: http://audiobaymanagement.com

Represents: Artists/Bands

Genres: Acoustic; Classical; Electronic; Folk; Indie; Pop

Music company offering management, sync and licensing, and consultancy. Send query by email with links to music online.

Autonomy Music Group

6a Tileyard Studios
London
N7 9AH
Email: hi@autonomymusicgroup.com
Website: http://autonomymusicgroup.com
Website: http://autonomymusicgroup.com

Represents: Artists/Bands; DJs; Producers

Genres: All types of music

Provides bespoke artist and campaign services to artists, bands, producers, record labels and DJs. Send query via online form on website.

Avenoir

40 Hawkes Way
Maidstone
Kent
ME15 9ZL
Email: enquiries@avenoirrecords.com
Website: https://avenoirrecords.com
Website: https://twitter.com/AvenoirOfficial

Represents: Artists/Bands

Genres: All types of music

Artist management and consultancy firm based in Maidstone, Kent. Send query via form on website.

B&H Management

PO Box 1162
Bovingdon
Hertfordshire
HP1 9DE
Email: simon@bandhmanagement.demon.co.uk
Website: http://www.sessionmusicians.co.uk

Represents: Artists/Bands

Genres: Commercial; Pop; Urban

Contact: Simon Harrison

Seeks pop and urban material with commercial potential. Send query by email with CV, MP3, and link to your website.

B.H. Hopper Management Ltd.

Shepherds Building – Unit G7
Rockley Road
London
W14 0DA
Email: hopper@hopper-management.com
Website: http://www.hoppermanagement.com

Represents: Artists/Bands

Genres: Jazz

Management company based in London handling Jazz artists only. Send demo by post.

Bandzmedia

Email: info@bandzmedia.com
Website: http://www.bandzmedia.com
Website: https://www.facebook.com/Bandzmedia

Represents: Artists/Bands

Genres: Acoustic; Pop; Rock; Soul; R&B

Contact: Jude Bumby

Management company based in York. Send introductory email with brief bio and link to your music online in first instance. No MP3s. No hip hop/rap/garage, thrash/death metal, or techno.

Bear Music Management

Hampshire
Email: info@bearmusicmanagement.co.uk
Website: https://www.bearmusicmanagement.co.uk
Website: https://www.facebook.com/bearmusicmanagementuk/

Represents: Artists/Bands

Genres: Indie; Pop; Rock

Management company based in Hampshire. Send query by email or through contact form on website with bio and links to music online.

Bernie Nelson Artist Management

Email: bernnelson@yahoo.com
Website: https://www.twitter.com/iambernienelson
Website: https://www.instagram.com/bernie85/

Represents: Artists/Bands

Genres: Folk; Indie; Singer-Songwriter

Send query by email with links to music online.

Big Bear Music

PO BOX 944
EDGBASTON
BIRMINGHAM
B16 8UT
Email: admin@bigbearmusic.com
Website: http://www.bigbearmusic.com
Website: http://www.birminghamjazzfestival.com

Represents: Artists/Bands

Genres: Blues; Jazz; Swing

Contact: Jim Simpson

Represents and tours jazz, blue and swing attractions of the highest quality, mostly those signed to the Record label. We also oranise events and jazz festivals, including a midlands jazz festival established in 1985. Send query by email with MP3s, links, bio and photo.

Big Dipper Productions Ltd

41 Finsbury Park Road
London
N4 2JY
Email: contact@wearebigdipper.com
Website: http://www.wearebigdipper.com

Represents: Artists/Bands

Genres: Indie; Pop; Rock

Management company based in London. Send query by email with links to music online.

Big Hug Management

Email: jeff@bighugmanagement.com
Website: http://www.bighugmanagement.com
Website: https://www.facebook.com/bighugmanagement

Represents: Artists/Bands

Genres: All types of music

Contact: Jeff Powell

Send query by email with links to music online.

Big Life Management

67-69 Chalton Street
London
NW1 1HY
Email: reception@biglifemanagement.com
Website: http://www.biglifemanagement.com

Represents: Artists/Bands; Producers

Genres: All types of music

Management company based in London, representing bands, solo artists, and producers. Send query by email with links to music online.

BiGiAM Promotions & Management

Brighton
Email: info@bigiam.co.uk
Website: http://bigiam.co.uk
Website: http://www.facebook.com/bigiammusic

Represents: Artists/Bands

Genres: All types of music

Contact: Alison Hildyard; Mark Ede; Roderick Udo

We promote, advise and manage businesses, events and personal creativity linked to music and the arts. Our portfolio is relatively wide and relatively varied; we play a significant role in the development, project management, marketing/promotions and sponsorship of a number of Brighton area based events.

If you think we can help your company/band/event etc, please approach us for a no obligation chat; we may well be less expensive than you think. Our aim is to provide unrivalled value and excellence in everything we do.

Black Bleach Records

Manchester
Email: blackbleachrecords@gmail.com
Website: http://blackbleachrecords.com
Website: https://www.facebook.com/blackbleachrecords

Represents: Artists/Bands

Genres: Alternative; Electronic; Garage; Indie; Pop; Post Punk; Psychedelic Rock; Punk; Punk Rock; Shoegaze

Record label based in Manchester. Send query by email with links to music online.

Black Fox Management

1 Blythe Road
London
W14 0HG
Email: generalenquiries@blackfoxmanagement.com
Website: http://blackfoxmanagement.com
Website: https://twitter.com/pollyrocker5

Represents: Artists/Bands

Genres: All types of music

Contact: Polly Comber; Josh Smith

Management company based in London. Send demos by email.

BORDR

One Central Square
Cardiff
Email: bordrmanagement@gmail.com
Website: https://www.bordrmanagement.com
Website: https://www.facebook.com/bordrmanagement/

Represents: Artists/Bands

Genres: All types of music

Management company based in Cardiff. Send query by email with MP3s or links to music online.

BUT! Management

BUT! Music Group
Walsingham Cottage
7 Sussex Square
Brighton
BN2 1FJ
Email: jamesie@butgroup.com
Email: sue@butgroup.com
Website: http://www.butgroup.com
Website: https://www.facebook.com/The-BUT-Music-Group-1596947130561446/

Represents: Artists/Bands; Producers; Songwriters

Genres: Alternative; Pop; Rock; Singer-Songwriter

Contact: Allan James; Sue Flood

Management, label, and publishing company based in Brighton. Founded to promote and develop new UK talent both domestically and internationally. Has a policy of listening to and providing feedback on anything received. Send demos by post.

Chicken Grease Presents

Brighton
Email: lawrence@chickengreasepresents.com
Website: https://www.chickengreasepresents.com

Represents: Artists/Bands

Genres: Jazz; Hip-Hop; Soul

Artist development agency based in Brighton. Send query by email with links to music online or MP3 attachments.

Closer Artists Management & Publishing

Matrix Complex
91 Peterborough Road
London
SW6 3BU
Email: info@closerartists.com
Website: http://www.closerartists.com
Website: https://soundcloud.com/closer-artists

Represents: Artists/Bands

Genres: All types of music

Contact: Paul McDonald; Ryan Lofthouse

Management and publishing company based in London. Send demos through Soundcloud.

CMP Entertainment

Anchor Courtyard
Atlantic Pavilion
Albert Dock
Liverpool
L3 4AS
Email: info@cmpentertainment.com
Website: http://www.cmpentertainment.com
Website: https://www.facebook.com/CMPEntertainment

Represents: Artists/Bands; Tribute Acts

Genres: All types of music

Contact: Chas Cole; Rob Stringer

Management company based in Liverpool. Will consider all types of music, but works mainly with pop acts. Send demos by post.

Consolidated Artists

PO Box 87
Tarporley
CW6 9FN
Fax: +44 (0) 1829 730499
Email: alecconsol@aol.com
Email: ross@consolidatedartists.co.uk
Website: http://www.consolidatedartists.co.uk

Represents: Artists/Bands

Genres: Pop; Rock

Contact: Alec Leslie

Management company based in Tarporley. Send query by email with links to music online.

Covert Talent Management

Email: covertdemos@gmail.com
Email: simon@coverttalent.com
Website: http://www.coverttalent.com
Website: https://twitter.com/coverttalent

Represents: Artists/Bands; Producers; Songwriters

Genres: All types of music

Contact: Simon King

Career management company, focused on creative, strategic, and brand development. Send demos by email.

Create Management

Email: kyd@createmanagement.com
Email: info@createmanagement.com
Website: http://www.createmanagement.com
Website: http://www.thecreategroup.co.uk

Represents: Artists/Bands; Producers

Genres: Commercial; Pop; Singer-Songwriter

Record label based in Godalming, Surrey. Send soundcloud links or MP3s by email.

Creating Monsters

Email: matthew@creatingmonsters.com
Email: T@creatingmonsters.com
Website: http://www.creatingmonsters.com
Website: https://soundcloud.com/creating-monsters-ltd

Represents: Artists/Bands

Genres: All types of music

Contact: Matthew Haynes

Music production, management and artist development label. Send query by email with soundcloud links.

Crockford Management

Email: info@crockfordmanagement.com
Website: http://www.crockfordmanagement.com
Website: https://www.facebook.com/crockfordmgmt/

Represents: Artists/Bands

Genres: All types of music

Contact: Paul Crockford

Manager with over 35 years of experience. His clients have sold over 250 million albums worldwide. Send submissions by email.

Culture City

17 Mann Island
Liverpool
Email: info@culturecity.co.uk
Website: https://www.culturecity.co.uk
Website: https://www.facebook.com/CultureCityTV/

Represents: Artists/Bands

Genres: All types of music

Artist management company based in Liverpool. Send query by email with details of your act and links to music online.

Defenders Ent

Industrial Estate
3A Juno Way, London
SE14 5RW
Email: music@defendersent.com
Email: info@defendersent.com
Website: https://www.defendersent.com

Represents: Artists/Bands

Genres: Dance; Reggae; R&B; Rap

Send demos by email only with links to music online (no MP3 attachments).

Deltasonic Records

Liverpool
Email: annheston@live.com
Website: http://deltasonicrecords.co.uk
Website: https://soundcloud.com/deltasonic-records

Represents: Artists/Bands

Genres: All types of music

Management company based in Liverpool. Send query via online form on website, with soundcloud links.

Deluxxe Management

Email: info@deluxxe.co.uk
Website: http://www.deluxxe.co.uk
Website: https://twitter.com/Delilah8888
Website: http://www.myspace.com/deluxxemanagement

Represents: Artists/Bands

Genres: All types of music

Contact: Diane Wagg

Love to hear new music and listen to all submissions, but no posted demos or emailed MP3s. Send links to website or webpage where you have three or four tracks to listen to, and info about you and your live work. Response not guaranteed if not interested.

Denizen Artist Management

Antenna
Beck Street
Nottingham
NG1 1EQ
Email: kristi@denizen.uk.com
Website: http://denizen.uk.com
Website: https://www.twitter.com/denizenartists

Represents: Artists/Bands

Genres: All types of music

Artist management arm of a music company based in Nottingham, also running label and publishing services. Send demo by email as MP3 up to 10MB maximum with short bio and links to any online content.

Disaster Artist Management

Walthamstow
London
Email: nick@disasterartistmanagement.co.uk
Email: john.talbot@disasterartists.co.uk
Website: https://www.disasterartists.co.uk
Website: https://twitter.com/disasterarts

Represents: Artists/Bands

Genres: Indie; Pop; Rock

Management company based in Walthamstow, London. Send submissions by email.

Dissention Records + Artist Management

Wye Valley Barn
Brockweir Common
Chepstow
NP16 7NU
Email: matthew@dissentionrecords.com
Email: dissentionrecords@gmail.com
Website: https://www.dissentionrecords.com

Represents: Artists/Bands; Film / TV Composers; Other Entertainers

Genres: Alternative; Punk

Contact: Matthew Harris

Record label and artist management company originally founded in the States but now based in the UK. Send query by email with files or links to music online.

East City

London
Email: demo@eastcitymanagement.com
Website: https://twitter.com/artistmanager
Website: https://www.linkedin.com/in/taverner

Represents: Artists/Bands

Genres: Alternative; Dance; Indie

Manager based in London. Send query by email with links to streaming music online.

Electric Pineapple Music

Tileyard Studios
Tileyard Road
Kings Cross
London
N7 9AH
Email: info@electricpineapplemusic.co.uk
Website: http://www.electricpineapplemusic.co.uk
Website: https://www.facebook.com/ElectricPineappleClub

Represents: Artists/Bands

Genres: All types of music

Management company based in London. Describes itself as "management with morals". Send query by email with links to your music online.

Elephant Management

Manchester
Email: elephantmgmt@outlook.com
Website: https://elephantmanagement.site123.me
Website: https://www.facebook.com/elephantmanagement/

Represents: Artists/Bands

Genres: Alternative; Psychedelic Rock; Shoegaze

Music management and promotion company based in Manchester. Send query by email with links to music online.

Empire Artist Management

60 Chamberlayne Road
London
NW10 3JH
Fax: +44 (0) 20 8968 5999
Email: info@empire-management.co.uk
Website: http://www.empire-management.co.uk

Represents: Artists/Bands; Producers; Songwriters

Genres: All types of music

Contact: Neale Easterby; Richard Ramsey

Management company based in London, representing well-known artists, as well as producers and writers. Send email with links to music online.

End of the Trail Creative

Email: kelly@endofthetrailcreative.co.uk
Website: https://www.endofthetrailcreative.co.uk

Represents: Artists/Bands

Genres: All types of music

Management company and record label.

Enso Music Management

Email: rachaelh@ensomgmt.com
Email: elliott@ensomgmt.com
Website: http://ensomgmt.com
Website: https://www.facebook.com/ensomanagement/

Represents: Artists/Bands

Genres: Metal

Southwest based band management, booking and PR company. Specialises in Metal. Send query by email with links to music online.

Epic Venom

Email: sarah@epicVenom.com
Website: http://www.epicvenom.com
Website: https://www.facebook.com/EpicVenom/

Represents: Artists/Bands

Genres: Rock

Contact: Sarah Furbey

Rock band management including PR, bookings, travel management, event scheduling, and financial record keeping. Submit demos by email.

F&G Management

Unit D
63 Salusbury Road
London
NW6 6NJ
Email: gavino@fgmusica.com
Website: http://www.fgmusica.com
Website: https://www.facebook.com/fgdjtrade

Represents: Artists/Bands; DJs

Genres: Alternative; Dance; Electronic; Experimental; House; Techno

Contact: Gavino Prunas

Started as a DJ booking agency in the late eighties. Interested in music which is eclectic, different, or quirky. Send demo by email.

Factory Music Management & Agency Ltd

216 Cheriton High Street
Folkestone
Kent
CT19 4HS
Email: Sharon@factorymusic.co.uk
Email: andy@factorymusic.co.uk
Website: http://www.factorymusic.co.uk
Website: https://www.facebook.com/factorymusicagency

Represents: Artists/Bands

Genres: Metal; Thrash; Rock

Contact: Sharon Richardson; Andy Richardson; Fergal Holmes

Management company based in Folkestone, Kent, specialising in metal and rock. Send query by email with links to online EPK, Youtube, or dropbox. Do not send large files by email. Also accepts submissions on CD by post.

Fat Penguin Management

Leamington Spa
Warwickshire
Midlands
Email: chris@fatpenguinmanagement.co.uk
Website: http://fatpenguinmanagement.co.uk
Website: https://www.facebook.com/fatpenguinmgt

Represents: Artists/Bands; Producers

Genres: Acoustic; Alternative; Folk; Indie; Rock; Singer-Songwriter; Acoustic Alternative Americana

Contact: Chris Rogers

Already working with a number of notable artists and producers.

We offer three different levels of services to artists, music businesses and music producers alike. Ranging from basic music consultancy and booking support all the way up to the full treatment with full music management services.

Fave Sounds

Email: hello@favesounds.com
Website: https://www.favesounds.com
Website: https://www.facebook.com/favesounds/

Represents: Artists/Bands

Genres: All types of music

Send submissions via contact form on website.

Feed Your Head

Email: fyhpresents@gmail.com
Website: http://www.fyhpresents.com

Represents: Artists/Bands

Genres: Alternative; Electronic; Dance; Indie

Send query by email with links to 2 or 3 tracks online.

Ferocious Talent

Email: crociousmaura@gmail.com
Email: ferociousjonny1@gmail.com
Website: http://www.ferocioustalent.com

Represents: Artists/Bands

Genres: All types of music

Artist service company offering artist management, music consultancy, music business development, agency and rights management, label services, and in-house production. Send query by email with links to music online. No file attachments.

Finger Lickin' Management

6 Windmill Street
London
W1T 2JB
Email: info@fingerlickin.co.uk
Email: amie@fingerlickin.co.uk
Website: http://www.fingerlickinmanagement.co.uk
Website: https://soundcloud.com/fingerlickinmanagement
Website: http://www.myspace.com/FingerLickinRecords

Represents: Artists/Bands

Genres: Dance; Electronic; Hip-Hop; Break Beat

Management company based in London. Send query by email with links to music online.

Flat50

Stratford
London
Email: paul@flat50.co.uk
Email: info@flat50.co.uk
Website: http://www.flat50.co.uk
Website: https://twitter.com/Flat50_Music

Represents: Artists/Bands

Genres: Alternative; Blues; Folk; Rock; Indie; Singer-Songwriter

Artist representation, promotion, and management company based in London. Send demos or queries by email.

Flow State Music

2 Commercial Street
Edinburgh
EH6 6JA
Email: kyle@flowstatemusic.co.uk
Website: https://flowstatemusic.co.uk
Website: https://www.facebook.com/flowstateedinburgh/

Represents: Artists/Bands; DJs

Genres: Alternative Dance; Electronic

Music company based in Edinburgh, offering Event Production; Artist & Tour Management; Live Music Promotion; Music Programming; Digital Communications (Social Media / Direct Marketing). Send query by email with links to music online.

Formidable Music Management

Email: carl@formidable-mgmt.com
Email: c.marcantonio@hotmail.com
Website: https://soundcloud.com/formidable-management
Website: https://twitter.com/carlmarcantonio

Represents: Artists/Bands

Genres: All types of music

Contact: Carl Marcantonio

Send demos by email.

Freaks R Us

Email: freaks@freaksrus.net
Website: http://www.freaksrus.net
Website: https://www.facebook.com/freakartists

Represents: Artists/Bands

Genres: Alternative; Electronic; Experimental; Post Punk

Record label and management company. Send query by email with MP3 attachments or links to music online.

Freedom Management

Unit 2, King Street Cloisters
Clifton Walk
London
W6 0GY
Email: freedom@frdm.co.uk
Website: http://www.frdm.co.uk

Represents: Artists/Bands; Producers; Songwriters

Genres: Indie; Pop; Commercial

Management company based in London. Send demos by post.

Friends Vs Music Ltd

London
Email: pip@friendsvsmusic.com
Website: https://www.friendsvsmusic.com
Website: https://twitter.com/pipvsrecords

Represents: Artists/Bands; Producers

Genres: All types of music

Artist and producer management company and music consultancy based in London. Approach via form on website.

Front Room Songs

Email: katie@frontroomsongs.com
Website: https://frontroomsongs.com
Website: https://twitter.com/Frontroomsongs

Represents: Artists/Bands

Genres: Folk; Pop; Roots; World

Provides artist and project management for a growing roster of emerging artists spanning the folk / roots / world and pop genres. Send query through online contact form with links to music online.

Fruition Music

Email: rod@fruitionmusic.co.uk
Website: http://www.fruitionmusic.co.uk

Represents: Artists/Bands

Genres: Dance; Indie

Send query by email with MP3s or links to music online.

Future Songs

Email: michael@futuresongs.co.uk
Website: http://futuresongs.co.uk
Website: http://futuresongs.co.uk

Represents: Artists/Bands; Producers; Songwriters

Genres: Pop; R&B; Singer-Songwriter

Independent music company specialising in management and publishing. Send demos by email as MP3s or soundcloud links.

Golden Arm

Unit 18, Walters Workshops
249 Kensal Road
London
Email: info@goldenarm.me
Website: http://www.goldenarm.me

Represents: Artists/Bands

Genres: Alternative; Indie; Pop; Rock

Management company based in London. Send query by email with links to music online.

Goo Music Management Ltd

Email: contact@goomusic.net
Email: ben@goomusic.net
Website: http://www.goomusic.net
Website: https://www.facebook.com/goomusic

Represents: Artists/Bands

Genres: Alternative; Indie; Rock

Contact: Ben Kirby

Send query by email, giving links to music online on websites or MySpace etc. No postal submissions.

GR Management

974 Pollokshaws Road
Glasgow
G41 2HA
Email: info@grmanagement.co.uk

Represents: Artists/Bands

Genres: Commercial; Mainstream

Contact: Rab Andrew

Will consider anything with commercial appeal. Send demo with one-page bio and photo by post.

Grapevine Music Agency

April Cottage
Downend Terrace
Puriton
Somerset
TA6 4TJ
Fax: +44 (0) 7713 161669
Email: info@grapevinemusicagency.co.uk
Website: http://www.grapevinemusicagency.co.uk

Represents: Artists/Bands

Genres: Americana; Blues; Country; Folk; Roots

Contact: Bob & Claire

Record label based in Puriton, Somerset. Not accepting new acts as at February 2017. Check website for current status.

Grizzly Management

70 Chiswick High Road
London
Email: info@grizzlymanagement.com
Email: andy@grizzlymanagement.com
Website: http://grizzlymanagement.com
Website: https://www.facebook.com/grizzlymanagement

Represents: Artists/Bands

Genres: All types of music

Contact: Andrew Viitalahde-Pountain

Artist management company based in London. Send query by email with links to music online.

Guild Productions

Liverpool
Email: guildproductions@hotmail.com
Website: http://guildproductions.webs.com
Website: https://www.facebook.com/guildproductions

Represents: Artists/Bands

Genres: All types of music

A team of Engineers/Producers, Artist Managers and Songwriters, based in Liverpool. Offers artist management and other services for which artists are charged.

Guvnor Management

Email: info@guvnormanagement.co.uk
Website: https://www.guvnormanagement.co.uk
Website: https://www.facebook.com/GuvnorManagement/?ref=settings

Represents: Artists/Bands; Comedians; Other Entertainers; Tribute Acts

Genres: Pop; Rock

Management company based in Swansea, Wales. Send query by email with links to music online.

Hand in Hive Independent Records & Management

London
Email: contact@handinhive.com
Email: tristan@handinhive.com
Website: http://www.handinhive.com
Website: https://soundcloud.com/hand-in-hive

Represents: Artists/Bands

Genres: Indie

Independent record label and artist management company based in London. Send query by email with links to music online.

Hannah Management

Matix Studio
91 Peterborough Road
Fulham
London
SW6 3BU
Email: info@hannahmanagement.co.uk
Website: http://www.hannahmanagement.co.uk
Website: https://soundcloud.com/hannahmanagement
Website: https://myspace.com/barberahannah

Represents: Artists/Bands; Producers

Genres: All types of music

Contact: A&R

A London based artist and producer management company.

The founder has been successfully managing artists and working in music publishing since 1978. The management team manage record producers as well as up and coming bands.

They have purposely kept their roster small with the intention of working with the best talent and helping them develop all aspects of their career.

Happy House Management & Marketing Services

Email: happyhousemanagement@gmail.com
Website: http://happyhousemanagement.weebly.com
Website: https://www.facebook.com/happyhousemgmt

Represents: Artists/Bands

Genres: All types of music

Contact: Danny Watson

Management, marketing and product management company. Send query by email with links to music online.

Heard and Seen

Greens Court
West Street
Midhurst
West Sussex
GU29 9NQ
Email: enquiries@heardandseen.com
Website: http://www.heardandseen.com
Website: https://www.facebook.com/Heard-and-Seen-Ltd-197097010394361/

Represents: Artists/Bands

Genres: All types of music

Offers a range of services to artists, including management. See website for full details. Prefers to receive demos on CD by post. Include bio and photo.

Heist or Hit

12 Hilton Street
Manchester
M1 1JF
Email: mgmt@heistorhit.com
Email: team@heistorhit.com
Website: http://www.heistorhit.com
Website: https://www.facebook.com/heistorhitrecords

Represents: Artists/Bands

Genres: Acoustic; Alternative; Indie

Management company based in Manchester. Send postcard with URL (such as a private Soundcloud playlist), an email address, and a few words on the back.

Holier than Thou (HTT) Music

91 Masons Road
Stratford Upon Avon
Warwickshire
CV37 9NE
Email: David@httmusic.co.uk
Website: http://www.holierthanthou.co.uk
Website: http://www.httmusic.co.uk
Website: http://www.myspace.com/holierthanthourecords

Represents: Artists/Bands; Tribute Acts

Genres: Rock; Metal; Electronic; Alternative; Melodic Metal; Progressive Metal; Gothic Metal; Melodic Thrash

Contact: David Begg

Offers music management, digital distribution, new release promotions, and music publishing admin. Handles Rock, Metal, and sub-genres including Electronic Crossovers. No CDs or MP3 attachments. Send query by email with links to music online.

Holy-Toto

103 Gaunt Street
London
SE1 6DP
Email: josh@holy-toto.com
Website: https://holy-toto.com

Represents: Artists/Bands

Genres: Dance; Electronic; Hip-Hop; Pop; R&B

Management company based in London. Send query by email with links to music online.

Hot Gem

Glasgow
Email: demos@hotgem.co.uk
Email: clair@hotgem.co.uk
Website: http://www.hotgem.co.uk
Website: https://soundcloud.com/hotgemtunes

Represents: Artists/Bands

Genres: Ambient; Dance; Electronic; Experimental; Pop

Musician management and label based in Glasgow. Accepts demos, but must have difference / unique sound. No indie guitar bands. Send demos by email as MP3 attachments, or via soundcloud.

Hot Vox

London
Email: info@hotvox.co.uk
Email: sam@hotvox.co.uk
Website: https://hotvox.co.uk
Website: https://www.facebook.com/hotvox

Represents: Artists/Bands

Genres: All types of music

Music management, promotion and production company based in London, helping the aspirations of both new and established artists. Send query using form on website.

House of Us

Email: us@houseofus.co.uk
Website: http://www.houseofus.co.uk

Represents: Artists/Bands

Genres: Dance; House; Indie; Pop

Music management collective. Send query by email with links to music online.

HQ Familia

38 Charles Street
Leicester
Email: yasin@hqrecording.co.uk
Email: yasinelashrafi1980@live.co.uk
Website: http://www.hqrecording.co.uk/hq-familia/
Website: http://soundcloud.com/hqrecording

Represents: Artists/Bands

Genres: Electronic; Urban

Collective of like minded artists with associated record label and recording studio. Submit demos by post or by email.

ie:music

111 Frithville Gardens
London
W12 7JQ
Email: info@iemusic.co.uk
Website: http://www.iemusic.co.uk
Website: https://www.facebook.com/iemusic-150700438296856

Represents: Artists/Bands

Genres: All types of music

Submit demos by post, or send web links by email. Include contact details with valid email address.

Ignition Management

54 Linhope Street
London
NW1 6HL
Fax: +44 (0) 20 7258 0962
Email: chris@ignition.co.uk
Website: http://www.ignition.co.uk

Represents: Artists/Bands

Genres: Alternative; Indie; Pop; Rock

Contact: Marcus Russell, Managing Director

Management company based in London. Not accepting unsolicited demos as at March 2018. Check website for current status.

Incendia Music

4th Floor
Park House
22 Park Street
Croydon
CR0 1YE
Email: Lulu@incendia-management.co.uk
Email: info@incendia-management.co.uk
Website: http://incendia-management.co.uk
Website: https://soundcloud.com/incendia-music-management

Represents: Artists/Bands; Songwriters

Genres: Metal; Rock; Progressive

Contact: Lulu Davis

Artist Management, Publicity, and Consultancy services for Rock, Prog and Metal bands and artists.

Indevine

Email: sean@indevine.com
Website: http://www.indevine.com

Represents: Artists/Bands

Genres: All types of music

Manager of a songwriter and several bands. Send query by email with links to music online.

Insomnia Music UK

Email: info@insomniamusic.co.uk
Website: http://insomniamusic.co.uk
Website: https://www.facebook.com/InsomniaMusicUK/

Represents: Artists/Bands

Genres: Commercial; Pop

Music management company specialising in pop and commercial. Query by email in first instance.

Interlude Artists

London Borough of Wandsworth
London
SW12
Email: demos@interludeartists.co.uk
Email: ryan.walter@interludeartists.co.uk
Website: http://interludeartists.co.uk
Website: http://facebook.com/interludeartists

Represents: Artists/Bands; Songwriters

Genres: All types of music

Contact: Ryan Walter

A music and artist development agency based in London, established in 2010. Send query by email with links to music online.

Intertalent Rights Group

Intertalent House
46 Charlotte Street
London
W1T 2GS
Email: info@intertalentgroup.com
Website: https://intertalentgroup.com

Represents: Artists/Bands

Genres: Classical; Pop

Accepts contact by post with CV and SAE, but prefers contact by email with links to music online.

Intune Addicts

PO Box 121
Hove
East Sussex
BN3 4YY
Email: info@intuneaddicts.com
Website: http://intuneaddicts.com
Website: https://www.facebook.com/intuneaddicts

Represents: Artists/Bands

Genres: All types of music

Contact: Bob James; Mark Smutz Smith; Graham Peacock; Holly Glanvill

Management company based in Hove. Send query by email, describing achievements to date.

Involved Management

London
Email: info@involvedmanagement.com
Website: http://www.involvedmanagement.com

Represents: Artists/Bands

Genres: Chill; Electronic; House; Trance; Progressive House

Management company with offices in London and Los Angeles.

Island Music Management

Email: info@islandmusicmanagement.com
Website: https://www.islandmusicmanagement.com
Website: https://twitter.com/silkroybooth

Represents: Artists/Bands

Genres: Commercial; Indie

Contact: Andy Booth

Management company based on the Isle of Wight. Send query by email with links to music online.

JA Artist Management

Email: info@jaartistmanagement.com
Website: https://www.jaartistmanagement.com
Website: https://www.facebook.com/JAArtistManagement

Represents: Artists/Bands

Genres: All types of music

Artist Management for South Coast UK bands and solo artists. Send query by email with links to music and other relevant material online.

James Joseph Music Management

85 Cicada Road
London
SW18 2PA

Email: jj3@jamesjoseph.co.uk
Website: http://www.jamesjoseph.co.uk

Represents: Artists/Bands

Genres: All types of music

Contact: James Joseph

Management company with offices in London, UK, and Los Angeles, California. Send demo by post.

JBLS Management

Unit 13, The Tay Building
2A Wrentham Avenue
London
NW10 3HA
Email: louise@jblsmanagement.com
Email: jo@jblsmanagement.com
Website: http://www.jblsmanagement.com
Website: https://www.facebook.com/JBLSManagement/

Represents: Artists/Bands; Producers; Songwriters

Genres: Electronic; Alternative; Pop; Singer-Songwriter

Contact: Louise Smith

London management company representing artists, producers, remixers, mixers, and writers.

JD & Co.

Email: jdandco@mail.com
Website: http://www.jdandcomusic.com
Website: https://soundcloud.com/jdandcomusic

Represents: Artists/Bands

Genres: All types of music

Manages artists, brands and creative concepts, implementing them to ensure that they can maximise all revenues and opportunities through touring, production and promotion. Send query by email with links to music online.

John Waller Management

The Old Truman Brewery
91 Brick Lane
London
E1 6QL
Email: john@johnwaller.net
Website: https://www.facebook.com/john.waller.777
Website: https://twitter.com/AAAJayboy
Website: https://myspace.com/johnwallermanagement

Represents: Artists/Bands

Genres: All types of music

Contact: John Waller

Management company based in London. Takes on fee-paying clients only, so you must have proper funding to take an album project to market. If so, send demo by email.

Jost Music

Email: info@jostmusic.co.uk
Website: https://www.jostmusic.co.uk
Website: https://soundcloud.com/user-883894064

Represents: Artists/Bands

Genres: All types of music

Record label providing various services, including management. Send query by email with links to music online.

Jude Street Management

Email: info@judestreet.com
Email: paul@judest.com
Website: http://judestreet.com
Website: https://soundcloud.com/grandpastan

Represents: Artists/Bands; Film / TV Composers; Producers

Genres: Alternative; Pop; Indie; Classical

Contact: Paul Devaney; Jeff Fernandez

Music services and management company based in East London and established in 2005. Provides professional representation for bands, artists, producers and composers/arrangers in the fields of Alt/Pop/Indie, Classical, Games, Film and TV. Send query by email with links to music online.

Karma Artists Music LLP

Unit 31, Tileyard Studios
Tileyard Road
Kings Cross
London
N7 9AH
Email: info@karmaartists.co.uk
Website: http://www.karmaartists.co.uk
Website: https://www.facebook.com/karmaartistsuk

Represents: Artists/Bands; Producers; Songwriters

Genres: All types of music

Contact: Jordan Jay; Ross Gautreau

Multi-faceted entertainment company based in London, representing a roster with combined sales of over 100 million units. Send query by email with soundcloud links to your three best songs.

Key Music Management

1E Basil Chambers
65 High Street
Manchester
M4 1FS
Email: contact@keymusicmanagement.com
Website: http://www.keymusicmanagement.com
Website: https://www.facebook.com/keymusicmanagement

Represents: Artists/Bands

Genres: Alternative

Contact: Richard Jones; Adam Daly; Ryan Terpstra

Management company based in Manchester. Send query by email, including details of your act and links to your music online.

KRMB Management & Consultancy

Metropolis Studios
70 Chiswick High Road
London
W4 1SY
Email: kreynolds@krmbmanagement.com
Email: krmb@mac.com
Website: http://www.krmbmanagement.com
Website: https://www.facebook.com/krmbmanagement

Represents: Artists/Bands

Genres: All types of music

Contact: Kevin Reynolds

Management and consultancy company offering artist development, creative direction, talent management, corporate entertainment, and consultancy.

Laissez Faire Club

Email: jeremy@laissezfaireclub.com

Represents: Artists/Bands

Genres: All types of music

Contact: Jeremy Lloyd

Originally a live promotions company, now focuses solely on artist management.

Landstar Management

7a Chapel Street
Lancaster
Lancashire
LA1 1NZ
Fax: +44 (0) 1524 843499
Email: turnbuis@hotmail.com
Website: http://www.myspace.com/landstarmanagement

Represents: Artists/Bands; Film / TV Composers; Producers; Sound Engineers

Genres: Heavy Metal; Thrash; Indie; New Age; Electronic; Rock; Alternative Atmospheric Celtic Electronic Experimental Hard Heavy Industrial; Ambient Garage Gothic Guitar based Indie Metal Mystical New Age Punk Rock World

Contact: Stuart Turnbull; Sylvia Thomas

State that they have no preferrence on bands or styles, but specifically mention the genres above. Send query by email giving details of your act and your music, or send demo by post.

Line-Up pmc

10 Matthew Close
Newcastle upon Tyne

NE6 1XD
Fax: +44 (0) 191 275 9745
Email: chrismurtagh@line-up.co.uk
Website: http://www.line-up.co.uk

Represents: Artists/Bands

Genres: World

Contact: Chris Murtagh

Promotions and marketing consultancy company with over 25 years of experience specialising in live arts performance, ethnic and World Music. May not necessarily offer representation, but may pass your demo on to relevant contacts if potential is seen.

Liquid Management

139 Southerland Avenue, 1st Floor
Maida Vale
London
W9 1ES
Email: steve@Liquidmanagement.net
Website: http://www.liquidmanagement.net
Website: https://www.facebook.com/Liquid-Management-90757576588/

Represents: Artists/Bands; DJs; Producers

Genres: All types of music

Contact: Steve Dix

Management company with 20 years of managing artists through all levels of the music industry. Send query by email in first instance, with links to music, bio, and photos.

Listen to This Management

Email: grant@lttmusicmanagement.com
Email: charl@lttmusicmanagement.com
Website: https://lttmusicmanagement.com
Website: https://www.facebook.com/listentothisuk

Represents: Artists/Bands

Genres: Alternative; Alternative Country; Rock; Indie

Contact: Grant Tilbury; Charlotte Final

Artist and tour management company. Send query by email with links to music online.

Little White Bear Music

London
Email: james@littlewhitebearmusic.com
Website: https://twitter.com/mrjamesmatthews

Represents: Artists/Bands

Genres: Pop; R&B; Rock; Singer-Songwriter; Soul

Contact: James Matthews

Artist management based in London.

Lo-Five

3/2 The Printworks
14 Norval Street
Glasgow
G11 7RX
Email: robin@robinmorton.com
Website: http://www.robinmorton.com
Website: http://soundcloud.com/lo-five/

Represents: Artists/Bands

Genres: Acoustic; Alternative Country; Indie; Modern Folk

Contact: Robin Morton

Management company based in Glasgow.

LSH Management

146 Seven Sisters Road
London
N7 7PL
Email: info@lshmanagement.com
Website: https://www.lshmanagement.com
Website: https://soundcloud.com/lshmanagement

Represents: Artists/Bands

Genres: Indie; Jazz; Pop

Management company based in London. Send query by email with links to music online, and bio. No attachments or postal submissions.

Lyricom

Email: james@lyricom.co.uk
Website: https://lyricom.co.uk

Represents: Artists/Bands

Genres: Indie; Singer-Songwriter; Urban

Management company representing singer songwriters, solo artists, and bands. Currently expanding its roster. Send query by email with Soundcloud or YouTube links to a maximum of two songs.

M24 Management

Email: m24managementagency@gmail.com
Website: https://www.facebook.com/M24ManagementAgency

Represents: DJs

Genres: House

Management company representing House DJs.

Machine Management

Studio 16
London Fields Studios
11-17 Exmouth Place
London
E8 3RW
Email: Info@machinemanagement.co.uk
Website: http://www.machinemanagement.co.uk

Represents: Artists/Bands

Genres: All types of music

Management company based in London. Send demo by email.

MaDa Music Entertainment

London
Email: Adam@Madamusic.com
Website: http://www.madamusic.com
Website: https://soundcloud.com/mada-music

Represents: Artists/Bands; Producers

Genres: All types of music

London based multi divisional entertainment company specialising in Artist and Producer Management, Events, PR and Consultancy. Particularly interested in pop, indie, and rock, but will consider most genres. Send query by email with bio and links to music online.

Madrigal Music artist management

Guy Hall
Awre
Gloucestershire
GL14 1EL
Email: artists@madrigalmusic.co.uk
Email: nickf@madrigalmusic.co.uk
Website: http://www.madrigalmusic.co.uk
Website: https://www.facebook.com/madrigalmusic

Represents: Artists/Bands

Genres: Indie; Rock; Singer-Songwriter

Contact: Nick Ford

Send demo by post, preferably quality finished masters. Include SAE if return required. No MP3 submissions by email. No hip-hop or manufactured pop.

Major Labl

Website: https://www.majorlabl.com
Website: https://www.facebook.com/MajorLabl/

Represents: Artists/Bands

Genres: All types of music

Offers marketing and management services for unsigned and independent artists.

Map Music Ltd

46 Grafton Road
London
NW5 3DU
Email: info@mapmusic.net
Email: LaToyah@mapmusic.net
Website: http://www.mapmusic.net
Website: https://www.facebook.com/mapstudiocafe

Represents: Artists/Bands

Genres: All types of music

Management company based in London. Send CD by post.

Mat Ong Management

Il Palazzo
7 Water St

Liverpool
L2 0RD
Email: info@matongmanagement.co.uk
Website: http://www.matongmanagement.co.uk

Represents: Artists/Bands; DJs

Genres: Folk; Pop

Contact: Mat Ong

Handles UK and international bands and DJs. Send demo by post only.

Math Mgmt

Email: info@mathmgmt.com
Website: http://www.mathmgmt.com
Website: https://soundcloud.com/mathmgmt

Represents: Artists/Bands

Genres: Acoustic; Alternative; Indie

Management company based in Manchester. Send query by email with links to music online.

Maven Phoenix

Email: hello@mavenphoenix.com
Website: https://www.facebook.com/mavenphoenix
Website: http://www.soundcloud.com/maven_phoenix

Represents: Artists/Bands

Genres: Alternative; Electronic; Grime; Rap; Urban

A European entertainment entity with a global outlook on how tech, digital and social impact on Music. Works across Switzerland, France, Germany, and UK, focusing on future development and management of today's up and coming artists. Specialises in Business management, Legal Advice, Artist management, Consultancy and Bookings.

MBM (Music Business Management Ltd)

Labrican
Healey Dell Nature Reserve
Rochdale
OL12 6BG
Email: info@mbmcorporate.co.uk
Email: phil@mbmcorporate.co.uk
Website: https://www.mbmcorporate.co.uk
Website: https://www.facebook.com/MBMCorporate

Represents: Artists/Bands; DJs; Tribute Acts

Genres: All types of music

Contact: Phil Barrett

Entertainment consultancy and artiste management. Specialises in Tributes and Tribite shows. Make approach using form on website.

Me&You Music

Email: meandyoumusic@yahoo.co.uk
Website: https://www.facebook.com/meandyoumusic1

Represents: Artists/Bands

Genres: All types of music

Record label / promotions / online PR / artist management. Send query by email with links to music online.

Memphia Music Management

Bristol
Email: jp@memphia.com
Website: https://www.memphia.com
Website: https://www.facebook.com/MemphiaMM/

Represents: Artists/Bands

Genres: All types of music

Management company based in Bristol. Query by email or by phone.

Metal Music Bookings

London
Fax: +44 (0) 20 7084 0323
Email: contact@metalmusicbookings.com
Email: denise@metalmusicbookings.com
Website: http://www.metalmusicbookings.com
Website: https://www.facebook.com/MetalMusicBookings

Represents: Artists/Bands

Genres: Alternative; Metal; Rock

Contact: Denise Dale

Independent Booking Agency based in London, specialising in representing artists in the Heavy Metal and Rock genres, but willing to consider other genres. Send query by email with bio and links to music online.

MHM Music

Email: hq@mhmmusic.com
Website: http://www.mhmmusic.com
Website: https://www.facebook.com/mhmmusichq/

Represents: Artists/Bands

Genres: All types of music

Record label, publishing, distribution and management. Send query by email with links to music online.

Mill Lane Artist Management

Email: marcus@milllaneartistmanagement.co.uk
Website: http://www.milllaneartistmanagement.co.uk

Represents: Artists/Bands

Genres: Blues; Jazz; Funk; Hip-Hop; Soul; R&B; Rap; Grime

Contact: Marcus Summerfield

Artist Management business based in Stockton-On-Tees, looking after talented musicians with the focus of advancing their careers in the industry. Send query by email with links to music online.

Miller Music Management

Fax: +44 (0) 20 8964 4965
Email: info@m-music-m.com
Website: http://www.m-music-m.com

Represents: Artists/Bands

Genres: Indie; Rock; Singer-Songwriter

Contact: Carrie Hustler

Management company with offices in London and Los Angeles. Send demo by email with bio and Soundcloud link.

Modest! Management

The Matrix Complex
91 Peterborough Road
London
SW6 3BU
Email: info@modestmanagement.com
Email: lisa@modestmanagement.com
Website: http://www.modestmanagement.com
Website: https://www.facebook.com/modestmanagement

Represents: Artists/Bands

Genres: Pop

Contact: Richard Griffiths; Harry Magee

Management company based in London, handling several X-Factor winners/finalists. Send demos by email.

Moksha Management

PO Box 102
London
E15 2HH
Fax: +44 (0) 20 8519 6834
Email: recordings@moksha.co.uk
Email: info@moksha.co.uk
Website: http://www.moksha.co.uk
Website: https://twitter.com/mokshamgt

Represents: Artists/Bands

Genres: Alternative Electronic Fusion; Contemporary; Dance

Demos preferred as streaming weblinks.

Mother Artist Management

Email: mark@motherartistmanagement.com
Email: lucy@motherartistmanagement.com
Website: http://www.motherartistmanagement.com
Website: https://www.facebook.com/motherartistmanagement/

Represents: Artists/Bands

Genres: All types of music

Send query by email with bio and links to music online.

Musicarchy Media

3 Gower Street
1 Floor
London
Email: info@musicarchymedia.com
Website: https://www.musicarchymedia.com

Represents: Artists/Bands

Genres: Alternative; Gothic; Indie; Metal; Rock; Hard; Heavy

Contact: Kiara

Rock and Metal management and record label based in London since 2014. Founded by chart topping vocalist.

musicmedia

788-790 Finchley Road
London
NW11 7TJ
Email: info@musicmediaartists.com
Website: http://www.musicmediaevents.com
Website: https://www.facebook.com/pages/musicmedia-events/110527535666030

Represents: Artists/Bands

Genres: Pop; Acoustic; Alternative; Folk

Management company with parent company registered offices in London. Send links to your music online in first instance.

Nettwerk Management UK

15 Adeline Place, Ground Floor
London
WC1B 3AJ
Fax: +44 (0) 20 7456 9501
Email: info@nettwerk.com
Website: http://www.nettwerk.com
Website: https://www.facebook.com/nettwerkmusicgroup

Represents: Artists/Bands

Genres: All types of music

Management company headquartered in Vancouver, with offices in London, Hamburg, LA, New York, and Boston. Send query by email with links to streaming music online.

New Level Music Management

Oxford
Email: newlevelmgmt@gmail.com
Website: https://www.facebook.com/NewLevelMgmt
Website: https://twitter.com/NewLevelMgmt

Represents: Artists/Bands

Genres: All types of music

Music management based in Oxford, with contacts with UK and international record labels, publishers, promoters, and booking agents. Provides artist management, tour booking / management, professional guidance, PR, release campaigns, and contract negotiation, but does not accept unsolicited artists.

NewLevel Management

Oxford
Email: newlevelmgmt@gmail.com
Website: https://www.facebook.com/NewLevelMgmt
Website: https://twitter.com/NewLevelMgmt

Represents: Artists/Bands

Genres: All types of music

Contact: Paul Eynstone

Music management company based in Oxford. Offers artist management, tour booking, professional guidance, tour management, PR, label mailouts, release campaign co-ordination, and contract negotiation. Send query by email with links to music online, or contact via Facebook.

Nightswimming Management

London
Email: info@nightswimming-management.com
Email: lucy@nightswimming-management.com
Website: http://www.nightswimming-management.com
Website: https://soundcloud.com/nightswimming-mgmt

Represents: Artists/Bands

Genres: All types of music

Management company based in London. Send demos by email.

No Half Measures Ltd

1st Floor
5 Eagle Street
Glasgow
G4 9XA
Email: info@nohalfmeasures.com
Website: http://nohalfmeasures.com
Website: https://www.facebook.com/nohalfmeasures

Represents: Artists/Bands

Genres: All types of music

Based in Glasgow, Scotland, working in the areas of artist management; intellectual property & rights management; music publishing; recording, manufacturing, distribution, marketing & promotion; live performance, presentation & touring; event management and logistics; sponsorship & branding; merchandise; and more. Send demo by post, or by email as links or MP3s.

Northern Music Co. Ltd

5A Victoria Road
Saltaire
Shipley
West Yorkshire
BD18 3LA
Fax: +44 (0) 1274 593546
Email: demos@northernmusic.co.uk
Email: info@northernmusic.co.uk
Website: http://www.northernmusic.co.uk
Website: https://www.facebook.com/NMCLtd

Represents: Artists/Bands

Genres: Metal; Rock

Contact: Andy Farrow

Send query by email with your band/act's name in the subject line, with details on what you are looking for; links to stream your music; a brief bio of your band/act; links to your website / social media / videos; and any details of existing industry partners / releases / live dates, etc.

Off the Chart Promotions

17 Spitfire Road
Upper Cambourne
Cambridgeshire
CB23 6FL
Email: tim@offthechart.co.uk
Website: http://www.offthechart.co.uk
Website: https://www.facebook.com/offthechartpromotions

Represents: Artists/Bands

Genres: Folk; Pop; Rock; Indie; Singer-Songwriter

Management company based in Cambridge. Works with artists from the East of England and London. Send demos by email with links to music online at soundcloud, mixcloud, or dropbox.

Oh Mercy Artist Management

PO Box 1103
Chislehurst
BR7 9BA
Email: info@ohmercymanagement.com
Website: http://www.ohmercymanagement.com
Website: https://www.facebook.com/Ohmercymanagement

Represents: Artists/Bands; Producers

Genres: Indie; Pop

Management company based in Chislehurst. Send demos by post, or send MP3s or links by email.

Once Upon A Time Management Ltd

3rd Floor, 118-120 Great Titchfield Street
London
W1W 6SS
Email: info@onceuponatimemusic.co.uk
Website: http://www.onceuponatimemusic.co.uk
Website: https://soundcloud.com/onceuponatimemusic
Website: https://myspace.com/onceuponatimemusicuk

Represents: Artists/Bands

Genres: All types of music

Contact: Francisco Garcia; Roland Hill

Management, record label, and publishing company. Founded in 2009 by two professionals with nearly 25 years of music industry between them, including A&R; management; marketing; publishing; and promotions. Send query by email with links to streaming music online.

OnDaBeat Talent Management

West London Art Factory
153 Dukes Road
London
W3 0SL
Email: mgmt@odbentltd.com
Website: https://ondabeat.co.uk
Website: https://soundcloud.com/ondabeatmgmt

Represents: Artists/Bands

Genres: Drum and Bass; Electronic; House; Hip-Hop; Rap; Techno

Management company and record studios based in London. Send query by email with links to music online.

One Fifteen

A&R
One Fifteen
1 Globe House
Middle Lane Mews
London
N8 8PN
Fax: +44 (0) 20 8442 7561
Email: demos@onefifteen.com
Email: enquiries@onefifteen.com
Website: http://www.onefifteen.com

Represents: Artists/Bands

Genres: All types of music

Contact: Tom O'Rourke

If submitting by email prefers links to your SoundCloud, YouTube or Facebook page. If you insist on sending MP3s, send no more than two. Include short bio, photo, social media links, and upcoming gig listings. CDs cannot be returned. Aims to listen to everything, but response not guaranteed if not interested.

141a Management

Email: admin@art19.co.uk
Website: https://www.141amanagement.co.uk
Website: https://www.facebook.com/141amanagementcompany/?fref=ts

Represents: Artists/Bands

Genres: All types of music

Music management company representing artists from all music genres. Send query by email with links to music online. No MP3 attachments.

140dB Management Limited

London
Email: info@140db.co.uk
Website: http://www.140db.co.uk
Website: https://www.facebook.com/140dBManagement/

Represents: Artists/Bands; Producers

Genres: All types of music

Contact: Ros Earls

Management company based in London. Represents artists and producers. Send query by email with links to music online.

Park Records

PO Box 651
Oxford
OX2 9RB
Fax: +44 (0) 1865 204556
Email: parkoffice@parkrecords.com
Website: http://www.parkrecords.com
Website: https://www.facebook.com/Park-Records-154023671336938/

Represents: Artists/Bands

Genres: Folk; Singer-Songwriter; Roots; Acoustic; Folk Rock

Music company based in Oxford, including record label and management and PR services. Send demo with photo by email. Particularly interested in hearing from female singer-songwriters.

Perfect Havoc Ltd

Flat 7
46 De Beauvoir Crescent
London
N1 5RY
Email: info@perfecthavoc.com
Website: https://perfecthavoc.com
Website: https://soundcloud.com/perfecthavocmusic

Represents: Artists/Bands

Genres: Dance; Disco; House

London-based music entertainment management, record label, club night and blog. Send query by email with soundcloud links.

Perry Road Records

75 Perry Road
Buckden
Cambridgeshire
PE19 5XG
Email: enquiries@perryroadrecords.co.uk
Website: https://www.perryroadrecords.co.uk
Website: https://www.facebook.com/pages/Perry-Road-Records/140101102757735

Represents: Artists/Bands

Genres: Country; Blues; Indie; Rock

Contact: Gilly Lee

Independent record label and artist management based in Buckden, Cambridge. Send demo by post or send links to music online by email.

Pieces of 8 Music

London
Email: info@piecesof8music.com
Website: http://piecesof8music.com
Website: https://www.facebook.com/Piecesof8Music

Represents: Artists/Bands; Producers; Songwriters; Sound Engineers

Genres: All types of music

Contact: James Morgan; Thea Lillepalu

Boutique management company set up to representing artists, producers, engineers, mixers and songwriters on a professional level. Send query by email with links to music online. No attachments.

Pillar Artists

Newcastle upon Tyne
Email: pillar.artists@gmail.com
Website: https://www.musicglue.com/pillar-artists
Website: https://facebook.com/PillarArtists

Represents: Artists/Bands

Genres: Acoustic; Alternative; Guitar based; Indie

Management agency based in Newcastle Upon Tyne. Also involved with independent gig promotion, PR, and booking. Send query by email with bio and links to music online.

Plus Music

Hoxton
London
Email: info@plusmusic.co.uk
Website: http://www.plusmusic.co.uk

Represents: Artists/Bands

Genres: Funk; Pop; R&B; Soul

Contact: Desmond Chisholm

Looking for male or female singers aged 16-23. Send MP3 with recent photo(s) and social media links by email. See website for full details.

PMS Music Management

122 London Road
Rayleigh
Essex
SS6 9BN
Fax: +44 (0) 1268 784807
Email: pmsmusicmgt@yahoo.co.uk
Website: http://pmsmusicmanagement.weebly.com

Represents: Artists/Bands; Tribute Acts

Genres: All types of music

Contact: Peter Scott

Send demo by post or email. MP3 preferred but not essential. Currently managing

Indie/pop/rock but open to all genres. 'If I like it, I can represent it!' Welcomes all submissions in the form of CD, MP3 or video on DVD together with a biography and links to your Website, Myspace and any other relevant links. Particularly keen to work with unsigned bands.

Pond Life Songs

London
Email: info@pondlifesongs.com
Website: http://www.pondlifesongs.com
Website: https://soundcloud.com/pondlifesongs

Represents: Artists/Bands

Genres: All types of music

Contact: Keith Aspden

Record label based in London, specialising in artist development and management. Send demos by email. Responds to all submissions.

Possessive Management

Email: contact@possessivemanagement.com
Email: amanda@possessivemanagement.com
Website: https://www.facebook.com/PossessiveManagement
Website: https://twitter.com/PossessiveMgmt

Represents: Artists/Bands

Genres: Metal; Punk; Rock; Progressive; Thrash; Hardcore

Management company specialising in rock, metal and hardcore bands. Send query by email with links to music online.

Primitive Management

The Lexington
96-98 Pentonville Road
London
N1 9JB
Email: claire@primitivemanagement.com
Website: http://primitivemanagement.com

Represents: Artists/Bands; Producers

Genres: Alternative; Pop; Rock

Contact: Claire Southwick

Management company based in London, representing artists and producers.

Prolifica Management

London
Email: info@prolifica.co.uk
Email: colin@prolifica.co.uk
Website: http://www.prolificamanagement.co.uk
Website: https://www.facebook.com/prolificamanagement/

Represents: Artists/Bands

Genres: All types of music

Contact: Colin Schaverien; Stefano Anselmetti

London-based Music Management and Production Company. Send demo by email.

Psycho Management Company

Sollys Mill
Mill Lane
Godalming
Surrey
GU7 1EY

LONDON OFFICE:
111 Clarance Road
Wimbledon
London
SW19 8QB
Fax: +44 (0) 1483 419504
Email: info@psycho.co.uk
Email: patrick@psycho.co.uk
Website: http://www.psycho.co.uk

Represents: Artists/Bands; Comedians; DJs; Other Entertainers; Tribute Acts

Genres: All types of music

Contact: Patrick Haveron

Management company based in Godalming, Surrey. Represents circus acts, entertainment acts, lookalikes, music acts, name acts, and tribute acts. Query in first instance by phone or email. Send demo upon request.

Push Music Management

London
Email: info@pushmusicmanagement.com
Website: http://www.pushmusicmanagement.com
Website: https://twitter.com/pushmusicmgmt
Website: http://www.myspace.com/pushmusicmanagement

Represents: Artists/Bands

Genres: All types of music

Management company based in London. Send email with links to your music online.

QV

London
Email: info@qveenmanagement.com
Website: https://www.qveenmanagement.com
Website: https://twitter.com/teamqveen

Represents: Artists/Bands

Genres: Commercial; Electronic; Urban

Bespoke music management company based in London. Hands on, caring, and female focused. Send query by email with short bio and links to music online.

Qveen Management

Way Out Studios
London
E14 7DE
Email: qv@qveenmanagement.com
Website: https://www.qveenmanagement.com

Represents: Artists/Bands

Genres: Commercial; Electronic; Urban

Female-led management company based in London. Send query by email with bio and links to music online.

Radius Music Ltd

Email: info@radiusmusic.co.uk
Website: http://www.radiusmusic.co.uk

Represents: Artists/Bands; Producers; Songwriters

Genres: All types of music

Management company based in London. Send links to SoundCloud / Bandcamp etc. by email or via form on website. Due to time constraints, unable to reply to everyone.

Raw Power Management

Bridle House
36 Bridle Lane
London
W1F 9BZ
Fax: +44 (0) 845 331 3500
Email: info@rawpowermanagement.com
Website: http://www.rawpowermanagement.com
Website: http://www.facebook.com/rawpowermanagement
Website: http://www.myspace.com/rawpowermanagement

Represents: Artists/Bands

Genres: Punk Rock; Alternative; Metal; Rock

Punk rock management company based in London. Send demos as MP3s or links to music online by email.

Real Media Music

Email: info@realmediamusic.co.uk
Website: http://www.realmediamusic.co.uk
Website: https://www.facebook.com/RealMediaMusic

Represents: Artists/Bands

Genres: All types of music

International artist booking and management. Send query by email with links to music online. No submissions by post. Response only if interested.

Rebel Rebel

Email: info@rebelrebelartists.co.uk
Website: https://www.facebook.com/rebelrebelartists
Website: https://twitter.com/rebelrebelarti

Represents: Artists/Bands

Genres: Alternative; Electronic; Indie; Pop

Bespoke artist management / PR / bookings / consultancy. Send query by email with links to streaming music. No attachments.

Reckless Yes

Email: pete@recklessyes.com
Email: sarah@recklessyes.com
Website: http://recklessyes.com
Website: https://www.facebook.com/RecklessYes/

Represents: Artists/Bands

Genres: Acoustic; Alternative; Guitar based; Indie

Contact: Pete; Sarah

Independent record label, management and live music agency. See website for demo submission guidelines.

Red Afternoon Management

Email: submissions@redafternoonmanagement.co.uk
Email: info@redafternoonmanagement.co.uk
Website: https://www.redafternoonmanagement.co.uk
Website: https://www.facebook.com/Red-Afternoon-Management

Represents: Artists/Bands

Genres: All types of music

Contact: Lewis Forrest

Management company founded in 2016, set up to champion up and coming bands and artists. Services include: Artist Management, Booking, Promotion, and Consulting. Willing to consider all music types, but background is in rock, indie, and punk. Send submissions by email or through online form on website.

Red Grape Music

82 Chestnut Grove
New Malden
Surrey
KT3 3JS
Email: info@redgrapemusic.com
Website: https://www.redgrapemusic.com

Represents: Artists/Bands

Genres: Acoustic; Folk; Pop; Singer-Songwriter

Management company and record label based in New Malden, Surrey. Not accepting submissions as at January 2019. Check website for current status.

RGM Production

Email: info@ryangloveronline.com
Website: http://ryangloveronline.com
Website: https://www.facebook.com/RGMproductionLtd/

Represents: Artists/Bands

Genres: Pop; R&B; Soul

A Dorset and Hampshire based music production, management and artist development company. Send query by email with Soundcloud or Youtube links.

Rhythmic Records Management and Production

Email: info@rhythmic-records.co.uk
Website: https://www.rhythmic-records.co.uk
Website: https://www.facebook.com/RhythmicRecordsUK/?ref=bookmarks

Represents: Artists/Bands

Genres: Dance; Hip-Hop; House; Pop

Independent record label and management company based in London. Submit query with links to music online through form on website or by email.

Right Chord Music

Email: Mark@rightchordmusic.com
Website: http://www.rightchordmusic.co.uk
Website: https://soundcloud.com/right-chord-music
Website: http://www.facebook.com/rightchordmusic

Represents: Artists/Bands

Genres: Acoustic; Folk; Pop; Rock; Alternative; Indie

Contact: Mark Knight

Management company based in London. Provides traditional management services plus "pay-as-you-go" services and training workshops and mentoring

RM2 Music

Email: info@rm2music.co.uk
Website: http://rm2music.co.uk
Website: https://www.facebook.com/RM2Music

Represents: Artists/Bands

Genres: Reggae; R&B; Soul

Contact: Diane Dunkley

Management company based just outside London, covering the United Kingdom and Europe. Send query by email with links to your music online.

ROAR Global Ltd

ROAR House
46 Charlotte Street
London
W1T 2GS
Email: info@roarglobal.com
Website: http://www.roarglobal.com

Represents: Artists/Bands

Genres: Alternative Rock; Pop; Urban; Guitar based

Contact: Jonathan Shalit

Career management company, based in London, representing talent in music and a range of other areas. Send 3-track demo by post, with bio and photo.

Rock Hippie Management & Music

Email: info@rockhippiemanagement.com
Email: rebecca@rockhippiemanagement.com
Website: https://www.facebook.com/rockhippiem/
Website: https://twitter.com/RockHippieM

Represents: Artists/Bands; Comedians; DJs; Songwriters; Tribute Acts

Genres: All types of music

Contact: Rebecca

Management company based in London. For management enquiries send email with subject "[management] + your name or the name of your band" with link to your music and short bio. Include details of what you expect from a manager, in more detail than simply "I/We want a record deal". No MP3 attachments.

Rollover Productions

29 Beethoven Street
London
W10 4LG
Fax: +44 (0) 8717 142605
Email: a-r@rollover.co.uk
Email: music.studios@rollover.co.uk
Website: http://www.rollover.co.uk
Website: https://www.facebook.com/RolloverMusicLondon
Website: http://www.myspace.com/rollovermusic

Represents: Artists/Bands

Genres: All types of music

Contact: Phillip Jacobs

Query by telephone. Send demo upon invitation only. Do not send demos by email.

Rollover

29 Beethoven Street
London
W10 4LG
Fax: +44 (0) 20 8968 1047
Website: http://www.rollover.co.uk

Represents: Artists/Bands

Genres: All types of music

Management company based in London. Contact by phone in first instance, then submit demo by post upon request.

Rough Diamond

London
Website: https://www.roughdiamondmusic.org
Website: https://twitter.com/roughdiamondldn

Represents: Artists/Bands

Genres: All types of music

Artist development and production company based in London.

Roundface Music Management

Dunfermline
Scotland
Email: george@roundfacemusic.com
Website: http://www.roundfacemusic.com
Website: https://www.facebook.com/RFmusicmanagement/

Represents: Artists/Bands

Genres: All types of music

Contact: George Murray

Offers Music Management and Consultancy to Artists based in Dunfermline, Scotland. Send query by email with MP3 attachments or links to music online.

Running Media Group Ltd

14 Victoria Road
Douglas
Isle of Man
IM2 4ER
Email: management@runningmedia.com
Email: info@runningmedia.com
Website: http://www.runningmedia.com

Represents: Artists/Bands

Genres: Singer-Songwriter

Contact: Dave Armstrong

Send demo by post. Will listen to all demos submitted, but response only if interested.

S&B Creative

Email: info@snbcreative.com
Website: http://www.snbcreative.com

Represents: Artists/Bands; Film / TV Composers; Producers; Songwriters

Genres: All types of music

Talent management, record label, brand consultancy, and scors for film and TV. Send query by email with links to music online.

Salvation Records

Email: info@salvationrecords.co.uk
Website: https://www.facebook.com/thesoundofsalvationrecords
Website: https://soundcloud.com/salvationrecords

Represents: Artists/Bands

Genres: Electronic; Garage; Psychedelic Rock; Punk

Contact: Anthony Nyland

Record label and artist management.

Saviour Management

London
Email: james@svrmgmt.com
Email: angelo@svrmgmt.com
Website: http://saviourmgmt.tumblr.com
Website: https://www.facebook.com/saviourmanagement

Represents: Artists/Bands

Genres: Alternative; Metal; Pop Punk

Contact: James Illsley; Angelo Pandolfi

Management company based in London. Send query by email with bio and links to social media and music online.

Scope Music Management

Email: info@scopemusicmanagement.com
Website: http://www.scopemusicmanagement.com
Website: https://www.facebook.com/ScopeMusicMgmt/

Represents: Artists/Bands

Genres: All types of music

Management company founded in 2012, boasting an eclectic roster of artists and bands. Send query by email with SoundCloud or YouTube links.

Seditious Records

Email: info@seditiousrecords.com
Website: http://www.seditiousrecords.com
Website: https://www.facebook.com/seditiousrecords

Represents: Artists/Bands

Genres: Heavy Metal

Management company specialising in finding and developing new heavy metal talent. Send query by email with links to music online.

SEG Music UK

3rd Floor
85a Great Portland Street
London
W1W 7JR
Email: music@seginternational.com
Website: http://www.seginternational.com
Website: http://twitter.com/SEG_Music

Represents: Artists/Bands; Producers; Sound Engineers

Genres: All types of music

Music company based in London. Send demos as MP3 attachments by email.

Serious

51 Kingsway Place
Sans Walk
Clerkenwell
London
EC1R 0LU
Fax: +44 (0) 20 7324 1881
Website: http://www.serious.org.uk
Website: http://www.facebook.com/seriouslivemusic

Represents: Artists/Bands

Genres: Jazz; World; Contemporary

Management company based in London producing jazz, international, and contemporary music, and offering management, music publishing and the production of concerts, tours and special events. Send query via form on website, including links to music online.

74 Promotions

94 Centurion Road
Brighton
BN1 3LN
Email: andy@74promotions.com
Website: http://www.74promotions.com
Website: https://www.facebook.com/74-Promotions-181204548583646/

Represents: Artists/Bands

Genres: All types of music

Contact: Andy Hollis

Management company based in Brighton. Send demo by email or by post.

SGM Music Group Ltd

Base Studios
Unit 14
Rufford Road Trading Estate
Stourbridge
West Midlands
DY9 7ND
Email: info@sgmmusicgroup.com
Website: http://www.scottgarrettmanagement.com
Website: https://www.facebook.com/scottgarrettmusicmanagement

Represents: Artists/Bands

Genres: Pop; Rock

Contact: Scott Garrett

Management company based in Stourbridge, West Midlands. Send demos by post or send query by email with links to music online.

SGO Ltd

PO Box 2015
Salisbury
SP2 7WU
Fax: +44 (0) 1747 870678
Email: sgomusic@sgomusic.com
Website: http://www.sgomusic.com
Website: http://www.facebook.com/SGOMusic

Represents: Artists/Bands

Genres: All types of music

Contact: Stuart Ongley

Management company based in Salisbury. Send query in first instance. No unsolicited demos.

Shaw Thing Management

20 Coverdale Road
London
N11 3FG
Email: charlie@shawthingmanagement.com
Email: hills@shawthingmanagement.com

Website: http://www.shawthingmanagement.com

Represents: Artists/Bands

Genres: Pop

Contact: Charlie Owen

Send demo as MP3 file by email, including any additional information, such as photos etc.

Sidewinder Management Ltd

Email: sdw@sidewindermgmt.com
Website: http://www.sidewindermgmt.com

Represents: Artists/Bands

Genres: All types of music

Contact: Simon Watson

Management company based in Brighton and Hove. Send query by email with links to music online. No MP3 attachments.

Solar Management

Unit 10 Union Wharf
23 Wenlock Road
London
N1 7SB
Email: info@solarmanagement.co.uk
Website: http://www.solarmanagement.co.uk
Website: http://soundcloud.com/solarmanagement
Website: http://www.myspace.com/solarmanagement

Represents: Artists/Bands; Producers

Genres: All types of music

Contact: Carol Crabtree

Eexperience in producer and artist development, recording, touring, budgeting and all producer and artist contracts. Send email with links to music online. No MP3 attachments.

Sound Consultancy

Resound Media
Kingsley House
Church Lane
Shurdington
Cheltenham
GL51 4TQ
Email: hey@soundconsultancy.co.uk
Website: http://www.soundconsultancy.co.uk
Website: https://www.facebook.com/soundconsultancy

Represents: Artists/Bands

Genres: All types of music

Cheltenham music company offering artist development, mentoring, and promotion packages. Considers all genres, but mainly acoustic, rock, and folk. Send MP3s by email.

The Soundcheck Group

29 Wardour Street
London
W1D 6PS
Email: daniel@thesoundcheckgroup.com
Website: http://www.thesoundcheckgroup.com
Website: https://www.facebook.com/thesoundcheckgroup1

Represents: Artists/Bands

Genres: All types of music

Contact: Daniel Hinchliffe

Management company based in London. Send query by email with links to music online.

Stoa Sounds

Email: james@stoasounds.co.uk
Website: http://www.stoasounds.co.uk

Represents: Artists/Bands; Producers; Songwriters

Genres: Indie; Pop; Singer-Songwriter

London-based management company and record label established in 2014. Send query by email with link to music online.

Storm5 Management

Resound Media
Brincliffe House
59 Wostenholm Road
Sheffield
S7 1LE
Email: info@storm5management.com

Website: http://www.storm5management.com
Website: https://www.facebook.com/storm5management/

Represents: Artists/Bands

Genres: All types of music

Management company based in Sheffield. Send query by email with links to music online.

Sugar House Music

Email: info@sugarhousemusic.co.uk
Website: http://www.sugarhousemusic.co.uk
Website: http://www.soundcloud.com/sugarhousemusic
Website: http://www.myspace.com/sugarhousemusicuk

Represents: Artists/Bands

Genres: Indie; New Wave; Pop; Rock

Contact: Lee McCarthy; Ady Hall

Send email with links to music online (soundcloud / myspace etc. only – no MP3 attachments).

SugarNova

St John St
London
Email: info@SugarNova.com
Website: http://sugarnova.com
Website: https://www.facebook.com/SugarNovaGroup

Represents: Artists/Bands

Genres: Hip-Hop; Indie; Jazz; Pop; R&B; Urban

Management company dealing mainly with musicians, but also actors, models, fashion designers and athletes. Send demo by email, including three tracks, photo, and links to social networking sites.

Tap Music

Email: info@tapmgmt.com
Website: https://tap-music.com
Website: https://www.facebook.com/tapmusicofficial/

Represents: Artists/Bands

Genres: All types of music

Music management company with offices in London, Berlin and LA. Make initial contact by email.

Tape

London
Email: info@taperec.com
Website: http://www.taperec.com
Website: https://www.facebook.com/TAPEWORLD

Represents: Artists/Bands

Genres: All types of music, except: Metal; Techno

Management company with offices in London and Barcelona. Send demos by email as MP3 attachments.

Tara Newman Artist Management

Thurrock
RM18 7RP
Email: TNArtistManagement@hotmail.com
Website: https://www.musicglue.com/tnartistmanagement/
Website: https://www.facebook.com/TNArtistManagement

Represents: Artists/Bands

Genres: Indie; Pop; Rock

Send query by email with demo as MP3 attachment.

Third Bar Artist Development

C/O Oh yeah Music Centre
15-21 Gordon Street
Belfast
BT1 2GH
Email: candice@thirdbar.co.uk
Email: thirdbarsubmissions@gmail.com
Website: http://thirdbar.co.uk
Website: https://www.facebook.com/thirdbar

Represents: Artists/Bands

Genres: All types of music

Contact: Davy Matchett

Artist development business based in Belfast. Send music via online file transfer system (see website).

Third Rock Music

Email: info@thirdrockmusic.co.uk
Website: http://www.thirdrockmusic.co.uk
Website: https://soundcloud.com/third-rock-recordings

Represents: Artists/Bands

Genres: All types of music

Management and publishing company. Send query with MP3s by email.

This Is Music Ltd

Studio 2
Excel Building
6-16 Arbutus Street
Haggerston
London
E8 4DT
Email: simon@thisismusicltd.com
Website: http://thisismusicltd.com
Website: https://www.soundcloud.com/this-is-music

Represents: Artists/Bands; Producers

Genres: Electronic; Underground; Indie; Pop

Contact: Simon Gold

Music company based in London and Los Angeles. Provides management and label services for artists and producers.

Tileyard Music

15 Tileyard Studios
Tileyard Road
Kings Cross
London
N7 9AH
Email: Jason@tileyardmusic.co.uk
Email: info@tileyardmusic.co.uk
Website: http://www.tileyard.co.uk/music

Represents: Artists/Bands

Genres: Dance; Hip-Hop; Folk; Pop; Rock; Urban

Boutique management and publishing company, formed in October 2012. Send query by email with soundcloud links.

Tilt Shift Music

Email: tiltshiftmusic@yahoo.co.uk
Website: https://www.facebook.com/TiltShiftMusic
Website: https://twitter.com/@tiltshiftmusic

Represents: Artists/Bands

Genres: All types of music

Management company open to all types of music, but particularly interested in Electronic and Pop. Send demos by email.

Tone Management

22 The Close
Saxton
Leeds
West Yorkshire
LS9 8HW
Email: hello@tonemgmt.com
Website: http://tonemgmt.com
Website: https://www.facebook.com/ToneMGMT

Represents: Artists/Bands

Genres: Metal; Rock; Pop; Post Rock; Hardcore; Punk

Contact: Tom Bellhouse; Tom Ghannad; Tony Boden; Kim Kelly; Sofi Nowell

Management company with offices in Leeds, London, Bristol, and New York. Send query by email with links to streaming music online. No attachments.

Toonteen Industries: Management & Promotions

Email: demos@toonteen.co.uk
Email: joe@toonteen.co.uk
Website: https://www.toonteen.co.uk
Website: https://www.myspace.com/toonteenindustries

Represents: Artists/Bands

Genres: Acoustic Alternative Heavy Progressive Ambient Emo Hardcore Indie Metal Pop Punk Rock

Contact: Joe Weaver

Management company based in Bury St Edmunds. Promotes shows with various bands in venues all over East Anglia, but mainly focued within Bury St Edmunds. Also manages bands and solo artists. Send query by email with links to music online. No attachments.

TRYB Management

Email: alex@trybmanagement.com
Website: https://www.trybmanagement.com
Website: https://twitter.com/trybmanagement

Represents: Artists/Bands

Genres: Pop

Music management company, based in Bristol. Currently managing new pop artist LENN.

Feel free to get in touch!

UAC Management

Email: hristo@uacmanagement.co.uk
Email: thrasher@uacmanagement.co.uk
Website: http://www.uacmanagement.co.uk
Website: https://www.facebook.com/uacmanagement/?fref=nf

Represents: Artists/Bands

Genres: All types of music

Contact: Hristo Penchev; Kevin Thrasher

Full service management company based in the UK. Make initial contact by email.

United Stage International Ltd

Apartment 1
160 New Kings Road
London
SW6 4LZ
Email: valerie@unitedstage.co.uk
Email: info@unitedstage.co.uk
Website: https://www.unitedstage.co.uk
Website: https://www.facebook.com/UnitedStageInternational

Represents: Artists/Bands

Genres: Electronic; Indie; Rock

International office of Scandinavia's largest booking agency. Send query by email with bio and links to music online.

Universal Talent Group

71-75 Shelton Street
Covent Garden
London
WC2H 9JQ
Email: info@universaltalentgroup.co.uk
Website: http://www.universaltalentgroup.co.uk

Represents: Artists/Bands

Genres: Pop

Management company based in London. Send submissions through online form on website.

Various Artists Management

37 Lonsdale Road
London
NW6 6RA
Email: info@variousartistsmanagement.com
Website: http://variousartistsmanagement.com
Website: https://www.facebook.com/variousartistsmanagement

Represents: Artists/Bands; Producers

Genres: All types of music

Management company with offices in London and Los Angeles.

Verdigris Management

London
Email: info@verdigrismanagement.com
Website: http://www.verdigrismanagement.com

Represents: Artists/Bands

Genres: All types of music

Contact: Sam

Management company based in London. Send demos by email.

Viral Music

Brunswick Mill
Manchester
M40 7EZ
Email: info@viralmusicuk.com
Website: https://www.viralmusicuk.com
Website: https://www.facebook.com/ViralMusicUK/

Represents: Artists/Bands; DJs

Genres: Dance; House; Commercial

Management company providing conservatoire-trained, professionally-accomplished musicians to the nightlife entertainment industry, as well as for a wide range of other events, including weddings and private/corporate functions. Send query by email or through contact form on website, with links to music online.

The Volume Group

Email: jay@thevolumegroup.com
Website: http://www.thevolumegroup.com
Website: https://www.facebook.com/thevolumegroup

Represents: Artists/Bands

Genres: All types of music

Management company with a combined 35 years of music industry experience. Send query by email with links to music online.

The Weird and the Wonderful

London
Email: info@theweirdandthewonderful.com
Website: http://theweirdandthewonderfulofficial.tumblr.com
Website: https://www.facebook.com/theweirdandthewonderfulofficial

Represents: Artists/Bands

Genres: Electronic; Folk; House; Techno; Urban

A multi-discipline music and arts talent consultancy and management company with offices in London/Berlin/LA.

Wildlife Entertainment Ltd

Unit F, 21 Heathmans Road
Hammersmith And Fulham
London
SW6 4TJ
Email: info@wildlife-entertainment.com
Website: http://www.wildlife-entertainment.com

Represents: Artists/Bands

Genres: Indie; Rock; R&B

Contact: Ian McAndrew

Management company based in South West London. Send query by email and follow up with demo upon request.

Woosh Entertainments Ltd

108 Biggar Road
Edinburgh
EH10 7DU
Email: hello@woosh.tv
Email: keith@woosh.tv
Website: http://www.woosh.tv
Website: https://www.facebook.com/wooshevents

Represents: Artists/Bands; DJs

Genres: Acoustic; Folk; Indie; Pop; Rock; Singer-Songwriter

Contact: Keith Easton

Management company based in Edinburgh. Send query by email with links to music online.

XIX Entertainment Ltd

UNIT 5B
The Albion Riverside
London
SW11 4AX
Email: info@xixentertainment.com
Website: http://www.xixentertainment.com

Represents: Artists/Bands

Genres: All types of music

Management company responsible for such shows as American Idol and Little Britain USA. Has offices in London, Los Angeles, New York, Paris, and Nashville. Send demos by post or email.

XVII Music Group

Brighton
Email: info@xviimusic.com
Website: https://xviimusic.com
Website: https://soundcloud.com/xviimusicgroup

Represents: Artists/Bands

Genres: All types of music

Artists development and record label based in Brighton. Send demos by email.

Yellowbrick Music

5-7 Vernon Yard
London
W11 2DX
Email: info@yellowbrickmusic.com
Email: meredith@yellowbrickmusic.com
Website: https://yellowbrickmusic.com
Website: https://twitter.com/YellBrickMusic

Represents: Artists/Bands

Genres: All types of music

Label service company based in London, offering artists a creative range of support and tools. Send query by email with links to streaming music online, or send submissions by post. No download links.

Young Guns

2 Princes Street
Mayfair
London
W1B 2LB
Email: hello@younggunsgroup.com
Email: enquiries@younggunsuk.com
Website: http://younggunsgroup.com
Website: https://www.facebook.com/YoungGunsLtd

Represents: Artists/Bands; Producers; Studio Musicians

Genres: Classical; Jazz; Pop; Fusion

Contact: Dominic and Alexander Lyon

Management company based in London. Send two contrasting tracks as MP3s by email.

Canadian Managers

For the most up-to-date listings of these and hundreds of other managers, visit https://www.musicsocket.com/managers

*To claim your **free** access to the site, please see the back of this book.*

Bedlam Music Management

290 Gerrard St East
Toronto, ON M5A 2G4

LOS ANGELES
4525 Russell Ave #1
Los Angeles CA 90027

NASHVILLE
1300 Clinton St, Suite 205
Nashville, TN 37203
Email: info@bedlammusicmgt.com
Website: http://www.bedlammusicmgt.com

Represents: Artists/Bands

Genres: All types of music

A full service artist management company based in Toronto, Canada, with offices in Los Angeles and Nashville.

Panacea Entertainment

2nd Floor, 9868a 33 Avenue
Edmonton, AB T6N 1C6

US OFFICE:
13587 Andalusia Drive East
Santa Rosa Valley, CA 93012
Fax: +1 (780) 490-5255
Email: info@panacea-ent.com
Website: http://panaceaentertainment.com

Represents: Artists/Bands; Film / TV Composers; Producers; Songwriters

Genres: All types of music

Contact: Eric Gardner

Management company based in Edmonton, Alberta. Not accepting submissions as at February 2018.

Managers Index

This section lists managers by their genres, with directions to the section of the book where the full listing can be found.

You can create your own customised lists of managers using different combinations of these subject areas, plus over a dozen other criteria, instantly online at https://www.musicsocket.com.

*To claim your **free** access to the site, please see the back of this book.*

All types of music

360 Artist Development (*UK*)
A&R Factory (*UK*)
Abba-Tude Entertainment (*US*)
ACA Music & Entertainment (*US*)
Aesthetic V (*US*)
AirMTM (*UK*)
AMW Group Inc. (*US*)
Aneko Music (*UK*)
Anger Management (*UK*)
Anglo Management (*UK*)
The Animal Farm (*UK*)
APA (Agency for the Performing Arts) (*US*)
ASM Talent (*UK*)
Atum Management Ltd (*UK*)
Autonomy Music Group (*UK*)
Avenoir (*UK*)
Azoff Music Management (*US*)
Backstage Entertainment (*US*)
Bandguru Management (*US*)
Bedlam Music Management (*Can*)
Big Hug Management (*UK*)
Big Life Management (*UK*)
Big Noise (*US*)
BiGiAM Promotions & Management (*UK*)
Black Fox Management (*UK*)
BORDR (*UK*)
Brent Music Management (*US*)
Celebrity Enterprises (CE) Inc. (*US*)
Circle Talent Agency (*US*)
Class Act Productions/Management (*US*)
Closer Artists Management & Publishing (*UK*)
CMP Entertainment (*UK*)
Covert Talent Management (*UK*)
Creating Monsters (*UK*)
Creative Artists Agency (CAA) (*US*)
Crockford Management (*UK*)
Crush Music Media Management (*US*)
Culture City (*UK*)
Deltasonic Records (*UK*)
Deluxxe Management (*UK*)
Denizen Artist Management (*UK*)
The Derek Power Company & Kahn Power Pictures (*US*)
East Coast Entertainment (ECE) (*US*)
Electric Pineapple Music (*UK*)
Empire Artist Management (*UK*)
End of the Trail Creative (*UK*)
Fave Sounds (*UK*)
Ferocious Talent (*UK*)
Formidable Music Management (*UK*)
Friends Vs Music Ltd (*UK*)
Gary Stamler Management (*US*)
The Gorfaine/Schwartz Agency, Inc. (*US*)
Grizzly Management (*UK*)
Guild Productions (*UK*)

Hannah Management (*UK*)
Happy House Management & Marketing Services (*UK*)
Heard and Seen (*UK*)
Heart & Soul Artist Management (*US*)
HGRS Artist Management (*US*)
Hot Vox (*UK*)
Howard Rosen Promotion, Inc. (*US*)
ie:music (*UK*)
Indevine (*UK*)
Interlude Artists (*UK*)
International Creative Management (ICM) Partners (*US*)
Intune Addicts (*UK*)
Invasion Group, Ltd (*US*)
JA Artist Management (*UK*)
James Joseph Music Management (*UK*)
Jampol Artist Management (*US*)
JD & Co. (*UK*)
John Waller Management (*UK*)
Jost Music (*UK*)
Karma Artists Music LLP (*UK*)
KBH Entertainment (*US*)
KRMB Management & Consultancy (*UK*)
Laissez Faire Club (*UK*)
Liquid Management (*UK*)
Machine Management (*UK*)
MaDa Music Entertainment (*UK*)
Major Labl (*UK*)
Map Music Ltd (*UK*)
MBM (Music Business Management Ltd) (*UK*)
Me&You Music (*UK*)
MEGA Music Management (*US*)
Memphia Music Management (*UK*)
The MGMT Company (*US*)
MHM Music (*UK*)
Michael Kline Artists (*US*)
Million Dollar Artists (*US*)
Mother Artist Management (*UK*)
MSH Management (*US*)
Music City Artists (*US*)
Nettwerk Management UK (*UK*)
New Heights Entertainment (*US*)
New Level Music Management (*UK*)
NewLevel Management (*UK*)
Nightside Entertainment, Inc. (*US*)
Nightswimming Management (*UK*)
No Half Measures Ltd (*UK*)
Once Upon A Time Management Ltd (*UK*)
One Fifteen (*UK*)
141a Management (*UK*)
140dB Management Limited (*UK*)
Ozark Talent (*US*)
Pacific Talent (*US*)
Panacea Entertainment (*Can*)
Paradigm Talent Agency (*US*)
Persistent Management (*US*)
Pieces of 8 Music (*UK*)
PMS Music Management (*UK*)
Pond Life Songs (*UK*)
Pretty Lights (*US*)
Prolifica Management (*UK*)
Psycho Management Company (*UK*)
Push Music Management (*UK*)
Radius Music Ltd (*UK*)
Real Media Music (*UK*)
Red Afternoon Management (*UK*)
Regime Seventy-Two (*US*)
Richard Varrasso Management (*US*)
Rock Hippie Management & Music (*UK*)
Rollover Productions (*UK*)
Rollover (*UK*)
Rough Diamond (*UK*)
Roundface Music Management (*UK*)
S&B Creative (*UK*)
Scope Music Management (*UK*)
SEG Music UK (*UK*)
Selak Entertainment, Inc. (*US*)
74 Promotions (*UK*)
SGO Ltd (*UK*)
Sidewinder Management Ltd (*UK*)
SKH Music (*US*)
SMC Artists (*US*)
Solar Management (*UK*)
Sound Consultancy (*UK*)
The Soundcheck Group (*UK*)
Sparks Entertainment Management Co. (*US*)
Sterling Artist Management (*US*)
Storm5 Management (*UK*)
Take Out Management (*US*)
Tap Music (*UK*)
Tape (*UK*)
Ten Entertainment, Inc. (*US*)
Tenth Street Entertainment (*US*)
That's Entertainment International Inc. (TEI Entertainment) (*US*)
Third Bar Artist Development (*UK*)
Third Rock Music (*UK*)
Threee (*US*)
Thunderbird Management (*US*)
Tilt Shift Music (*UK*)
Tom Callahan & Associates (TCA) (*US*)
True Talent Management (*US*)
UAC Management (*UK*)
Uncle Booking (*US*)
United Talent Agency (*US*)
Universal Attractions Agency (*US*)

Various Artists Management (*UK*)
Velvet Hammer Music & Management Group (*US*)
Verdigris Management (*UK*)
The Volume Group (*UK*)
Walker Entertainment Group (*US*)
Wolfson Entertainment, Inc. (*US*)
XIX Entertainment Ltd (*UK*)
XVII Music Group (*UK*)
Yellowbrick Music (*UK*)

Acoustic

ADSRecords (*UK*)
Audio Bay Management (*UK*)
Bandzmedia (*UK*)
Fat City Artists (*US*)
Fat Penguin Management (*UK*)
Heist or Hit (*UK*)
Hello! Booking, Inc. (*US*)
Kari Estrin Management & Consulting (*US*)
Lo-Five (*UK*)
Math Mgmt (*UK*)
musicmedia (*UK*)
Outrider Music, LLC (*US*)
Park Records (*UK*)
Pillar Artists (*UK*)
Reckless Yes (*UK*)
Red Grape Music (*UK*)
Right Chord Music (*UK*)
TAC Music Management (*US*)
Toonteen Industries: Management & Promotions (*UK*)
Woosh Entertainments Ltd (*UK*)

Alternative

0114 Records (*UK*)
ADSRecords (*UK*)
Advanced Alternative Media (AAM) (*US*)
Artist in Mind (*US*)
Associated London Management (*UK*)
Big Hassle Management (*US*)
Bitchin' Entertainment (*US*)
Black Bleach Records (*UK*)
Burgess World Co. (*US*)
BUT! Management (*UK*)
Deep South Artist Management (*US*)
Dissention Records + Artist Management (*UK*)
East City (*UK*)
Elephant Management (*UK*)
F&G Management (*UK*)
Fat Penguin Management (*UK*)
Feed Your Head (*UK*)
5B Artist Management (*US*)
Flat50 (*UK*)
Flow State Music (*UK*)
Freaks R Us (*UK*)
Golden Arm (*UK*)
Goo Music Management Ltd (*UK*)
Halfpipe Entertainment (*US*)
Heist or Hit (*UK*)
Holier than Thou (HTT) Music (*UK*)
Ignition Management (*UK*)
Impact Artist Management (*US*)
JBLS Management (*UK*)
Jude Street Management (*UK*)
Key Music Management (*UK*)
Kuper Personal Management (*US*)
Landstar Management (*UK*)
Listen to This Management (*UK*)
Lo-Five (*UK*)
Loggins Promotion (*US*)
Lookout Management (*US*)
M. Hitchcock Management (*US*)
Math Mgmt (*UK*)
Maven Phoenix (*UK*)
Metal Music Bookings (*UK*)
MOB Agency (*US*)
Moksha Management (*UK*)
Monqui Presents (*US*)
Musicarchy Media (*UK*)
musicmedia (*UK*)
Mustang Agency (*US*)
Outrider Music, LLC (*US*)
Pillar Artists (*UK*)
Primitive Management (*UK*)
Prodigal Son Entertainment (*US*)
Q Prime Management, Inc. (*US*)
Raw Power Management (*UK*)
Rebel Rebel (*UK*)
Reckless Yes (*UK*)
Red Star Artist Management (*US*)
Right Chord Music (*UK*)
ROAR Global Ltd (*UK*)
Russell Carter Artist Management (*US*)
Saviour Management (*UK*)
Semaphore Mgmt & Consulting (*US*)
Sharpe Entertainment Services, Inc. (*US*)
Siren Music Company (*US*)
Steve Stewart Entertainment (*US*)
Steven Scharf Entertainment (SSE) (*US*)
TAC Music Management (*US*)
Toonteen Industries: Management & Promotions (*UK*)
Tunstall Management (*US*)
Union Entertainment Group (*US*)
Vector Management (*US*)

Ambient

Angelica Arts & Entertainment (*US*)
Bitchin' Entertainment (*US*)
Hot Gem (*UK*)

Landstar Management (*UK*)
Outrider Music, LLC (*US*)
Toonteen Industries: Management & Promotions (*UK*)
Tuscan Sun Music (*US*)

Americana

Artist in Mind (*US*)
Bitchin' Entertainment (*US*)
Brilliant Productions (*US*)
Deep South Artist Management (*US*)
Fat Penguin Management (*UK*)
Grapevine Music Agency (*UK*)
Kari Estrin Management & Consulting (*US*)
KCA Artists (*US*)
Kuper Personal Management (*US*)
Loggins Promotion (*US*)
Mike's Artist Management (*US*)
Myriad Artists (*US*)
Nancy Fly Agency (*US*)
Russell Carter Artist Management (*US*)
Siren Music Company (*US*)
Steven Scharf Entertainment (SSE) (*US*)
TAC Music Management (*US*)
Vector Management (*US*)

Atmospheric

Landstar Management (*UK*)
Outrider Music, LLC (*US*)
Semaphore Mgmt & Consulting (*US*)

Avant-Garde

Semaphore Mgmt & Consulting (*US*)

Blues

Act 1 Entertainment (*US*)
Artist Representation and Management (ARM) Entertainment (*US*)
Big Bear Music (*UK*)
Bitchin' Entertainment (*US*)
Brilliant Productions (*US*)
Burgess World Co. (*US*)
Cantaloupe Music Productions, Inc. (*US*)
Collin Artists (*US*)
Columbia Artists Management Inc. (CAMI) (*US*)
Concerted Efforts (*US*)
Emcee Artist Management (*US*)
Fat City Artists (*US*)
Flat50 (*UK*)
Fleming Artists (*US*)
Grapevine Music Agency (*UK*)
Harmony Artists (*US*)
Impact Artist Management (*US*)
KCA Artists (*US*)
The Kurland Agency (*US*)
Len Weisman, Personal Manager (*US*)
Mill Lane Artist Management (*UK*)
Myriad Artists (*US*)
Nancy Fly Agency (*US*)
Perry Road Records (*UK*)
Piedmont Talent (*US*)
Q Prime Management, Inc. (*US*)
Red Light Management (RLM) (*US*)
Ron Rainey Management Inc. (*US*)
Russell Carter Artist Management (*US*)
Siren Music Company (*US*)
Steven Scharf Entertainment (SSE) (*US*)
TAC Music Management (*US*)
Tower Management Group (*US*)
Union Entertainment Group (*US*)

Break Beat

Finger Lickin' Management (*UK*)

Celtic

Columbia Artists Management Inc. (CAMI) (*US*)
Fat City Artists (*US*)
Landstar Management (*UK*)
Worldsound, LLC (*US*)

Chill

Involved Management (*UK*)

Christian

25 Artist Agency (*US*)
The Brokaw Company (*US*)
Deep South Artist Management (*US*)
Jeff Roberts & Associates (*US*)
Nettwerk Management (*US*)
Prodigal Son Entertainment (*US*)
Red Light Management (RLM) (*US*)

Classic

Act 1 Entertainment (*US*)
American Artists Corporation (*US*)
Arslanian & Associates, Inc. (*US*)
Artist Representation and Management (ARM) Entertainment (*US*)
Big Beat Productions, Inc. (*US*)
Bill Hollingshead Productions, Inc. Talent Agency (*US*)
Entertainment Services International (*US*)
Mustang Agency (*US*)
TAC Music Management (*US*)

Classical

Audio Bay Management (*UK*)
BBA Management & Booking (*US*)
Bitchin' Entertainment (*US*)
Columbia Artists Management Inc. (CAMI) (*US*)
Dawn Elder Management (*US*)
Intertalent Rights Group (*UK*)
Jude Street Management (*UK*)
Young Guns (*UK*)

Club

Empire Artist Management (*US*)

Commercial
B&H Management (*UK*)
Create Management (*UK*)
Freedom Management (*UK*)
GR Management (*UK*)
Insomnia Music UK (*UK*)
Island Music Management (*UK*)
QV (*UK*)
Qveen Management (*UK*)
TAC Music Management (*US*)
Viral Music (*UK*)
Contemporary
Amour:Music (*UK*)
Artist in Mind (*US*)
Big Beat Productions, Inc. (*US*)
Black Dot Management (*US*)
Booking Entertainment (*US*)
Chapman & Co. Management (*US*)
Collin Artists (*US*)
Columbia Artists Management Inc. (CAMI) (*US*)
Fleming Artists (*US*)
Impact Artist Management (*US*)
Kragen & Company (*US*)
M. Hitchcock Management (*US*)
Michael Hausman Artist Management Inc. (*US*)
MM Music Agency (*US*)
Moksha Management (*UK*)
Nettwerk Management (*US*)
Riot Artists (*US*)
Ron Rainey Management Inc. (*US*)
Russell Carter Artist Management (*US*)
Serious (*UK*)
Sharpe Entertainment Services, Inc. (*US*)
Stiefel Entertainment (*US*)
Vector Management (*US*)
Country
Act 1 Entertainment (*US*)
American Artists Corporation (*US*)
American Artists Entertainment Group (*US*)
Artist Representation and Management (ARM) Entertainment (*US*)
Big Beat Productions, Inc. (*US*)
Bitchin' Entertainment (*US*)
Brick Wall Management (*US*)
The Brokaw Company (*US*)
Buddy Lee Attractions, Inc. (*US*)
Bulletproof Artist Management (*US*)
Case Entertainment Group Inc. (*US*)
Circle City Records USA (*US*)
Columbia Artists Management Inc. (CAMI) (*US*)
Deep South Artist Management (*US*)
Fat City Artists (*US*)
Grapevine Music Agency (*UK*)
Hello! Booking, Inc. (*US*)
Impact Artist Management (*US*)
Kragen & Company (*US*)
Listen to This Management (*UK*)
Lo-Five (*UK*)
Loggins Promotion (*US*)
Lupo Entertainment (*US*)
M. Hitchcock Management (*US*)
Maine Road Management (*US*)
Major Bob Music, Inc. (*US*)
Mascioli Entertainment (*US*)
McGhee Entertainment (*US*)
Michael Anthony's Electric Events (*US*)
Monqui Presents (*US*)
Mustang Agency (*US*)
Perry Road Records (*UK*)
Prodigal Son Entertainment (*US*)
Red Light Management (RLM) (*US*)
Ron Rainey Management Inc. (*US*)
Siren Music Company (*US*)
TAC Music Management (*US*)
Third Coast Talent (*US*)
TKO Artist Management (*US*)
Tower Management Group (*US*)
Two Chord Touring (*US*)
Union Entertainment Group (*US*)
Vector Management (*US*)
Dance
Celebrity Talent Agency Inc. (*US*)
Defenders Ent (*UK*)
East City (*UK*)
F&G Management (*UK*)
Feed Your Head (*UK*)
Finger Lickin' Management (*UK*)
Flow State Music (*UK*)
Fruition Music (*UK*)
Holy-Toto (*UK*)
Hot Gem (*UK*)
House of Us (*UK*)
Loggins Promotion (*US*)
Moksha Management (*UK*)
Nettwerk Management (*US*)
Perfect Havoc Ltd (*UK*)
Red Light Management (RLM) (*US*)
Rhythmic Records Management and Production (*UK*)
Sorkin Productions (*US*)
Spectrum Talent Agency (*US*)
Stiefel Entertainment (*US*)
Tileyard Music (*UK*)
Viral Music (*UK*)
Disco
Big Beat Productions, Inc. (*US*)

Perfect Havoc Ltd (*UK*)
Drum and Bass
OnDaBeat Talent Management (*UK*)
Electronic
Audio Bay Management (*UK*)
Bitchin' Entertainment (*US*)
Black Bleach Records (*UK*)
Empire Artist Management (*US*)
F&G Management (*UK*)
Feed Your Head (*UK*)
Finger Lickin' Management (*UK*)
Flow State Music (*UK*)
Freaks R Us (*UK*)
Halfpipe Entertainment (*US*)
Holier than Thou (HTT) Music (*UK*)
Holy-Toto (*UK*)
Hot Gem (*UK*)
HQ Familia (*UK*)
Involved Management (*UK*)
JBLS Management (*UK*)
Landstar Management (*UK*)
Maven Phoenix (*UK*)
Moksha Management (*UK*)
Music + Art Management (*US*)
Nettwerk Management (*US*)
OnDaBeat Talent Management (*UK*)
Outrider Music, LLC (*US*)
QV (*UK*)
Qveen Management (*UK*)
Rebel Rebel (*UK*)
Red Light Management (RLM) (*US*)
Salvation Records (*UK*)
Semaphore Mgmt & Consulting (*US*)
This Is Music Ltd (*UK*)
United Stage International Ltd (*UK*)
The Weird and the Wonderful (*UK*)
Emo
Outrider Music, LLC (*US*)
Toonteen Industries: Management & Promotions (*UK*)
Experimental
Bitchin' Entertainment (*US*)
F&G Management (*UK*)
Freaks R Us (*UK*)
Hot Gem (*UK*)
Landstar Management (*UK*)
Music + Art Management (*US*)
Semaphore Mgmt & Consulting (*US*)
Folk
0114 Records (*UK*)
AEC Music Management (*UK*)
Artist in Mind (*US*)
Audio Bay Management (*UK*)
Bernie Nelson Artist Management (*UK*)
Bitchin' Entertainment (*US*)
Bulletproof Artist Management (*US*)
Case Entertainment Group Inc. (*US*)
Columbia Artists Management Inc. (CAMI) (*US*)
Concerted Efforts (*US*)
DCA Productions (*US*)
Fat City Artists (*US*)
Fat Penguin Management (*UK*)
Flat50 (*UK*)
Fleming Artists (*US*)
Front Room Songs (*UK*)
Grapevine Music Agency (*UK*)
Hello! Booking, Inc. (*US*)
Impact Artist Management (*US*)
Kari Estrin Management & Consulting (*US*)
KCA Artists (*US*)
Kuper Personal Management (*US*)
Lo-Five (*UK*)
M. Hitchcock Management (*US*)
Maine Road Management (*US*)
Mat Ong Management (*UK*)
musicmedia (*UK*)
Myriad Artists (*US*)
Nettwerk Management (*US*)
Off the Chart Promotions (*UK*)
Park Records (*UK*)
Q Prime Management, Inc. (*US*)
Red Grape Music (*UK*)
Right Chord Music (*UK*)
Russell Carter Artist Management (*US*)
Siren Music Company (*US*)
Steven Scharf Entertainment (SSE) (*US*)
TAC Music Management (*US*)
Tileyard Music (*UK*)
Two Chord Touring (*US*)
Variety Artists International (*US*)
Vector Management (*US*)
The Weird and the Wonderful (*UK*)
Woosh Entertainments Ltd (*UK*)
Worldsound, LLC (*US*)
Funk
Bitchin' Entertainment (*US*)
Fat City Artists (*US*)
Mill Lane Artist Management (*UK*)
Plus Music (*UK*)
Pyramid Entertainment Group (*US*)
Red Entertainment Agency (*US*)
TAC Music Management (*US*)
Funky
TAC Music Management (*US*)
Fusion
Moksha Management (*UK*)
TAC Music Management (*US*)
Young Guns (*UK*)

Garage
0114 Records (*UK*)
Black Bleach Records (*UK*)
Landstar Management (*UK*)
Salvation Records (*UK*)
Glam
Semaphore Mgmt & Consulting (*US*)
Gospel
Celebrity Talent Agency Inc. (*US*)
Circle City Records USA (*US*)
Concerted Efforts (*US*)
Fat City Artists (*US*)
Fresh Flava Entertainment (*US*)
KCA Artists (*US*)
Len Weisman, Personal Manager (*US*)
Pyramid Entertainment Group (*US*)
Red Entertainment Agency (*US*)
Vector Management (*US*)
Gothic
Bitchin' Entertainment (*US*)
Holier than Thou (HTT) Music (*UK*)
Landstar Management (*UK*)
Musicarchy Media (*UK*)
Grime
Maven Phoenix (*UK*)
Mill Lane Artist Management (*UK*)
Guitar based
Landstar Management (*UK*)
Pillar Artists (*UK*)
Reckless Yes (*UK*)
ROAR Global Ltd (*UK*)
TAC Music Management (*US*)
Hard
0114 Records (*UK*)
Landstar Management (*UK*)
Musicarchy Media (*UK*)
Outrider Music, LLC (*US*)
Prodigal Son Entertainment (*US*)
Semaphore Mgmt & Consulting (*US*)
TAC Music Management (*US*)
Hardcore
Outrider Music, LLC (*US*)
Possessive Management (*UK*)
Red Light Management (RLM) (*US*)
Steve Stewart Entertainment (*US*)
Tone Management (*UK*)
Toonteen Industries: Management & Promotions (*UK*)
Heavy
Landstar Management (*UK*)
Musicarchy Media (*UK*)
Outrider Music, LLC (*US*)
Seditious Records (*UK*)
Semaphore Mgmt & Consulting (*US*)
TAC Music Management (*US*)
Toonteen Industries: Management & Promotions (*UK*)
Hip-Hop
Bitchin' Entertainment (*US*)
The Brokaw Company (*US*)
Celebrity Talent Agency Inc. (*US*)
Chicken Grease Presents (*UK*)
DAS Communications Ltd (*US*)
Finger Lickin' Management (*UK*)
First Access Entertainment (*US*)
Fresh Flava Entertainment (*US*)
Halfpipe Entertainment (*US*)
Hello! Booking, Inc. (*US*)
Holy-Toto (*UK*)
Len Weisman, Personal Manager (*US*)
Lippman Entertainment (*US*)
Loggins Promotion (*US*)
Lupo Entertainment (*US*)
Mauldin Brand Agency (*US*)
Mill Lane Artist Management (*UK*)
Nettwerk Management (*US*)
OnDaBeat Talent Management (*UK*)
Pyramid Entertainment Group (*US*)
Red Entertainment Agency (*US*)
Red Light Management (RLM) (*US*)
Rhythmic Records Management and Production (*UK*)
Spectrum Talent Agency (*US*)
Steven Scharf Entertainment (SSE) (*US*)
SugarNova (*UK*)
Tileyard Music (*UK*)
Union Entertainment Group (*US*)
House
Bitchin' Entertainment (*US*)
F&G Management (*UK*)
House of Us (*UK*)
Involved Management (*UK*)
M24 Management (*UK*)
OnDaBeat Talent Management (*UK*)
Perfect Havoc Ltd (*UK*)
Rhythmic Records Management and Production (*UK*)
Spectrum Talent Agency (*US*)
Viral Music (*UK*)
The Weird and the Wonderful (*UK*)
House
Bitchin' Entertainment (*US*)
F&G Management (*UK*)
House of Us (*UK*)
Involved Management (*UK*)
M24 Management (*UK*)
OnDaBeat Talent Management (*UK*)
Perfect Havoc Ltd (*UK*)
Rhythmic Records Management and Production (*UK*)

Spectrum Talent Agency (*US*)
Viral Music (*UK*)
The Weird and the Wonderful (*UK*)

Indie

0114 Records (*UK*)
ADSRecords (*UK*)
Advanced Alternative Media (AAM) (*US*)
Artist in Mind (*US*)
Audio Bay Management (*UK*)
Bear Music Management (*UK*)
Bernie Nelson Artist Management (*UK*)
Big Dipper Productions Ltd (*UK*)
Big Hassle Management (*US*)
Black Bleach Records (*UK*)
Columbia Artists Management Inc. (CAMI) (*US*)
Disaster Artist Management (*UK*)
East City (*UK*)
Fat Penguin Management (*UK*)
Feed Your Head (*UK*)
Flat50 (*UK*)
Freedom Management (*UK*)
Fruition Music (*UK*)
Golden Arm (*UK*)
Goo Music Management Ltd (*UK*)
Halfpipe Entertainment (*US*)
Hand in Hive Independent Records & Management (*UK*)
Heist or Hit (*UK*)
Hello! Booking, Inc. (*US*)
House of Us (*UK*)
Ignition Management (*UK*)
Impact Artist Management (*US*)
In De Goot Entertainment (*US*)
Island Music Management (*UK*)
Jude Street Management (*UK*)
Landstar Management (*UK*)
Listen to This Management (*UK*)
Lo-Five (*UK*)
LSH Management (*UK*)
Lyricom (*UK*)
Madrigal Music artist management (*UK*)
Maine Road Management (*US*)
Math Mgmt (*UK*)
Miller Music Management (*UK*)
Monqui Presents (*US*)
Musicarchy Media (*UK*)
Nettwerk Management (*US*)
Off the Chart Promotions (*UK*)
Oh Mercy Artist Management (*UK*)
Outrider Music, LLC (*US*)
Perry Road Records (*UK*)
Pillar Artists (*UK*)
Rebel Rebel (*UK*)
Reckless Yes (*UK*)
Red Light Management (RLM) (*US*)
Right Chord Music (*UK*)
Russell Carter Artist Management (*US*)
Sharpe Entertainment Services, Inc. (*US*)
Steven Scharf Entertainment (SSE) (*US*)
Stiefel Entertainment (*US*)
Stoa Sounds (*UK*)
Street Smart Management (*US*)
Sugar House Music (*UK*)
SugarNova (*UK*)
TAC Music Management (*US*)
Tara Newman Artist Management (*UK*)
This Is Music Ltd (*UK*)
Toonteen Industries: Management & Promotions (*UK*)
United Stage International Ltd (*UK*)
Wildlife Entertainment Ltd (*UK*)
Woosh Entertainments Ltd (*UK*)

Industrial

Landstar Management (*UK*)
Semaphore Mgmt & Consulting (*US*)

Instrumental

Bitchin' Entertainment (*US*)
Collin Artists (*US*)
Columbia Artists Management Inc. (CAMI) (*US*)
Outrider Music, LLC (*US*)
Prodigal Son Entertainment (*US*)

Jazz

Act 1 Entertainment (*US*)
B.H. Hopper Management Ltd. (*UK*)
BBA Management & Booking (*US*)
Big Bear Music (*UK*)
Big Beat Productions, Inc. (*US*)
Bitchin' Entertainment (*US*)
Black Dot Management (*US*)
Booking Entertainment (*US*)
Burgess World Co. (*US*)
Cantaloupe Music Productions, Inc. (*US*)
Celebrity Talent Agency Inc. (*US*)
Chapman & Co. Management (*US*)
Chicken Grease Presents (*UK*)
Collin Artists (*US*)
Columbia Artists Management Inc. (CAMI) (*US*)
Concerted Efforts (*US*)
Dawn Elder Management (*US*)
Emcee Artist Management (*US*)
Entourage Talent Associates, Ltd (*US*)
Fat City Artists (*US*)
Fresh Flava Entertainment (*US*)
Halfpipe Entertainment (*US*)
Harmony Artists (*US*)
Hello! Booking, Inc. (*US*)
Impact Artist Management (*US*)

Ina Dittke & Associates (*US*)
The Kurland Agency (*US*)
Loggins Promotion (*US*)
LSH Management (*UK*)
Maine Road Management (*US*)
The Management Ark, Inc. (*US*)
Mars Jazz (*US*)
Mascioli Entertainment (*US*)
Mill Lane Artist Management (*UK*)
MM Music Agency (*US*)
Music + Art Management (*US*)
Myriad Artists (*US*)
PRA [Patrick Rains & Associates] (*US*)
Pyramid Entertainment Group (*US*)
Red Entertainment Agency (*US*)
RPM Music Productions (*US*)
Russell Carter Artist Management (*US*)
Serious (*UK*)
Steven Scharf Entertainment (SSE) (*US*)
SugarNova (*UK*)
TAC Music Management (*US*)
Tony Margherita Management (*US*)
Variety Artists International (*US*)
Wayward Goose Entertainment Group LLC (*US*)
Young Guns (*UK*)

Kraut

Semaphore Mgmt & Consulting (*US*)

Latin

BBA Management & Booking (*US*)
Cantaloupe Music Productions, Inc. (*US*)
Celebrity Talent Agency Inc. (*US*)
Collin Artists (*US*)
Columbia Artists Management Inc. (CAMI) (*US*)
Harmony Artists (*US*)
Impact Artist Management (*US*)
Ina Dittke & Associates (*US*)
Nettwerk Management (*US*)
Red Entertainment Agency (*US*)
Red Light Management (RLM) (*US*)

Leftfield

Semaphore Mgmt & Consulting (*US*)

Lounge

Angelica Arts & Entertainment (*US*)
Halfpipe Entertainment (*US*)

Mainstream

GR Management (*UK*)

Melodic

Holier than Thou (HTT) Music (*UK*)
Outrider Music, LLC (*US*)

Metal

Artist Representation and Management (ARM) Entertainment (*US*)
Bitchin' Entertainment (*US*)
Enso Music Management (*UK*)
Factory Music Management & Agency Ltd (*UK*)
5B Artist Management (*US*)
Holier than Thou (HTT) Music (*UK*)
In De Goot Entertainment (*US*)
Incendia Music (*UK*)
Landstar Management (*UK*)
McGhee Entertainment (*US*)
Metal Music Bookings (*UK*)
Musicarchy Media (*UK*)
Mustang Agency (*US*)
Northern Music Co. Ltd (*UK*)
Outrider Music, LLC (*US*)
Possessive Management (*UK*)
Q Prime Management, Inc. (*US*)
Raw Power Management (*UK*)
Red Light Management (RLM) (*US*)
Saviour Management (*UK*)
Seditious Records (*UK*)
Steven Scharf Entertainment (SSE) (*US*)
Street Smart Management (*US*)
TAC Music Management (*US*)
Tone Management (*UK*)
Toonteen Industries: Management & Promotions (*UK*)
Vector Management (*US*)

Modern

Artist in Mind (*US*)
Lo-Five (*UK*)

Mystical

Landstar Management (*UK*)

New Age

Angelica Arts & Entertainment (*US*)
Landstar Management (*UK*)
Tuscan Sun Music (*US*)

New Wave

Semaphore Mgmt & Consulting (*US*)
Sugar House Music (*UK*)

Non-Commercial

Semaphore Mgmt & Consulting (*US*)

Pop

ADSRecords (*UK*)
Advanced Alternative Media (AAM) (*US*)
AEC Music Management (*UK*)
American Artists Entertainment Group (*US*)
Angelica Arts & Entertainment (*US*)
Artist in Mind (*US*)
Audio Bay Management (*UK*)
B&H Management (*UK*)
Bandzmedia (*UK*)
Bear Music Management (*UK*)
Big Dipper Productions Ltd (*UK*)
Big Hassle Management (*US*)

Bitchin' Entertainment (*US*)
Black Bleach Records (*UK*)
Booking Entertainment (*US*)
Brick Wall Management (*US*)
The Brokaw Company (*US*)
Buddy Lee Attractions, Inc. (*US*)
Bulletproof Artist Management (*US*)
BUT! Management (*UK*)
Case Entertainment Group Inc. (*US*)
Circle City Records USA (*US*)
Columbia Artists Management Inc. (CAMI) (*US*)
Consolidated Artists (*UK*)
Create Management (*UK*)
D. Bailey Management, Inc. (*US*)
DAS Communications Ltd (*US*)
Dawn Elder Management (*US*)
DCA Productions (*US*)
Deep South Artist Management (*US*)
Direct Management Group (DMG) (*US*)
Disaster Artist Management (*UK*)
East End Management (*US*)
Entourage Talent Associates, Ltd (*US*)
Fat City Artists (*US*)
First Access Entertainment (*US*)
Fleming Artists (*US*)
Freedom Management (*UK*)
Front Room Songs (*UK*)
Future Songs (*UK*)
Golden Arm (*UK*)
Guvnor Management (*UK*)
Halfpipe Entertainment (*US*)
Hello! Booking, Inc. (*US*)
Holy-Toto (*UK*)
Hot Gem (*UK*)
House of Us (*UK*)
Ignition Management (*UK*)
IMC Entertainment Group (*US*)
In De Goot Entertainment (*US*)
Insomnia Music UK (*UK*)
Intertalent Rights Group (*UK*)
Intrigue Music (*US*)
JBLS Management (*UK*)
Jude Street Management (*UK*)
KCA Artists (*US*)
Lippman Entertainment (*US*)
Little White Bear Music (*UK*)
Loggins Promotion (*US*)
LSH Management (*UK*)
Lupo Entertainment (*US*)
Major Bob Music, Inc. (*US*)
Mat Ong Management (*UK*)
Mauldin Brand Agency (*US*)
Michael Anthony's Electric Events (*US*)
Michael Hausman Artist Management Inc. (*US*)
Mike's Artist Management (*US*)
Modest! Management (*UK*)
Monqui Presents (*US*)
Music Inc. (*US*)
musicmedia (*UK*)
Mustang Agency (*US*)
Nettwerk Management (*US*)
Off the Chart Promotions (*UK*)
Oh Mercy Artist Management (*UK*)
Outrider Music, LLC (*US*)
Paradise Artists (*US*)
Plus Music (*UK*)
PRA [Patrick Rains & Associates] (*US*)
Primitive Management (*UK*)
Progressive Global Agency (PGA) (*US*)
Q Prime Management, Inc. (*US*)
Rainmaker Artists (*US*)
Rebel Rebel (*UK*)
Red Entertainment Agency (*US*)
Red Grape Music (*UK*)
Red Light Management (RLM) (*US*)
RGM Production (*UK*)
Rhythmic Records Management and Production (*UK*)
Right Chord Music (*UK*)
ROAR Global Ltd (*UK*)
Ron Rainey Management Inc. (*US*)
RPM Music Productions (*US*)
Russell Carter Artist Management (*US*)
Saviour Management (*UK*)
SGM Music Group Ltd (*UK*)
Sharpe Entertainment Services, Inc. (*US*)
Shaw Thing Management (*UK*)
Siren Music Company (*US*)
So What Media & Management (*US*)
Sorkin Productions (*US*)
Spectrum Talent Agency (*US*)
Starkravin' Management (*US*)
Steve Stewart Entertainment (*US*)
Steven Scharf Entertainment (SSE) (*US*)
Stiefel Entertainment (*US*)
Stoa Sounds (*UK*)
Street Smart Management (*US*)
Sugar House Music (*UK*)
SugarNova (*UK*)
Tara Newman Artist Management (*UK*)
This Is Music Ltd (*UK*)
Tileyard Music (*UK*)
Tone Management (*UK*)
Toonteen Industries: Management & Promotions (*UK*)
TRYB Management (*UK*)
Tuscan Sun Music (*US*)

Union Entertainment Group (*US*)
Universal Talent Group (*UK*)
Variety Artists International (*US*)
Vector Management (*US*)
Woosh Entertainments Ltd (*UK*)
Worldsound, LLC (*US*)
Young Guns (*UK*)

Post
Black Bleach Records (*UK*)
Freaks R Us (*UK*)
Outrider Music, LLC (*US*)
Semaphore Mgmt & Consulting (*US*)
Tone Management (*UK*)

Progressive
Holier than Thou (HTT) Music (*UK*)
Incendia Music (*UK*)
Involved Management (*UK*)
Outrider Music, LLC (*US*)
Possessive Management (*UK*)
Toonteen Industries: Management & Promotions (*UK*)

Psychedelic
Black Bleach Records (*UK*)
Elephant Management (*UK*)
Halfpipe Entertainment (*US*)
Salvation Records (*UK*)
Semaphore Mgmt & Consulting (*US*)

Punk
0114 Records (*UK*)
Bitchin' Entertainment (*US*)
Black Bleach Records (*UK*)
Dissention Records + Artist Management (*UK*)
Freaks R Us (*UK*)
Landstar Management (*UK*)
Nettwerk Management (*US*)
Outrider Music, LLC (*US*)
Possessive Management (*UK*)
Raw Power Management (*UK*)
Salvation Records (*UK*)
Saviour Management (*UK*)
Tone Management (*UK*)
Toonteen Industries: Management & Promotions (*UK*)

R&B
Act 1 Entertainment (*US*)
American Artists Corporation (*US*)
American Artists Entertainment Group (*US*)
Bandzmedia (*UK*)
Big Beat Productions, Inc. (*US*)
Bitchin' Entertainment (*US*)
Black Dot Management (*US*)
Booking Entertainment (*US*)
Case Entertainment Group Inc. (*US*)
Celebrity Talent Agency Inc. (*US*)
Collin Artists (*US*)
Columbia Artists Management Inc. (CAMI) (*US*)
D. Bailey Management, Inc. (*US*)
Defenders Ent (*UK*)
Fat City Artists (*US*)
First Access Entertainment (*US*)
Fresh Flava Entertainment (*US*)
Future Songs (*UK*)
Halfpipe Entertainment (*US*)
Holy-Toto (*UK*)
IMC Entertainment Group (*US*)
Impact Artist Management (*US*)
Len Weisman, Personal Manager (*US*)
Lippman Entertainment (*US*)
Little White Bear Music (*UK*)
Loggins Promotion (*US*)
Lupo Entertainment (*US*)
Major Bob Music, Inc. (*US*)
Mascioli Entertainment (*US*)
Mauldin Brand Agency (*US*)
Mill Lane Artist Management (*UK*)
Plus Music (*UK*)
Pyramid Entertainment Group (*US*)
Red Entertainment Agency (*US*)
RGM Production (*UK*)
RM2 Music (*UK*)
Sorkin Productions (*US*)
Spectrum Talent Agency (*US*)
Starkravin' Management (*US*)
SugarNova (*UK*)
TAC Music Management (*US*)
Tunstall Management (*US*)
Wildlife Entertainment Ltd (*UK*)

Rap
Bitchin' Entertainment (*US*)
Case Entertainment Group Inc. (*US*)
Defenders Ent (*UK*)
First Access Entertainment (*US*)
Len Weisman, Personal Manager (*US*)
Lippman Entertainment (*US*)
Loggins Promotion (*US*)
Mauldin Brand Agency (*US*)
Maven Phoenix (*UK*)
Mill Lane Artist Management (*UK*)
Nettwerk Management (*US*)
OnDaBeat Talent Management (*UK*)
Red Light Management (RLM) (*US*)
Steven Scharf Entertainment (SSE) (*US*)
Union Entertainment Group (*US*)
Variety Artists International (*US*)

Reggae
0114 Records (*UK*)
Act 1 Entertainment (*US*)

Celebrity Talent Agency Inc. (*US*)
Defenders Ent (*UK*)
Fat City Artists (*US*)
RM2 Music (*UK*)

Regional
Big Beat Productions, Inc. (*US*)
Brilliant Productions (*US*)
Cantaloupe Music Productions, Inc. (*US*)
MM Music Agency (*US*)
Siren Music Company (*US*)
TAC Music Management (*US*)

Remix
Halfpipe Entertainment (*US*)

Rhythm and Blues
TAC Music Management (*US*)

Rock and Roll
Fat City Artists (*US*)
Paradise Artists (*US*)
TAC Music Management (*US*)
Worldsound, LLC (*US*)

Rock
0114 Records (*UK*)
Act 1 Entertainment (*US*)
Advanced Alternative Media (AAM) (*US*)
AEC Music Management (*UK*)
American Artists Corporation (*US*)
American Artists Entertainment Group (*US*)
Arslanian & Associates, Inc. (*US*)
Artist in Mind (*US*)
Artist Representation and Management (ARM) Entertainment (*US*)
Bandzmedia (*UK*)
BBA Management & Booking (*US*)
Bear Music Management (*UK*)
Big Beat Productions, Inc. (*US*)
Big Dipper Productions Ltd (*UK*)
Big Hassle Management (*US*)
Bill Hollingshead Productions, Inc. Talent Agency (*US*)
Bitchin' Entertainment (*US*)
Black Bleach Records (*UK*)
Booking Entertainment (*US*)
Brick Wall Management (*US*)
The Brokaw Company (*US*)
Buddy Lee Attractions, Inc. (*US*)
Bulletproof Artist Management (*US*)
Burgess World Co. (*US*)
BUT! Management (*UK*)
Case Entertainment Group Inc. (*US*)
Concerted Efforts (*US*)
Consolidated Artists (*UK*)
D. Bailey Management, Inc. (*US*)
DAS Communications Ltd (*US*)
Dave Kaplan Management (*US*)
Dawn Elder Management (*US*)
DCA Productions (*US*)
Deep South Artist Management (*US*)
Disaster Artist Management (*UK*)
East End Management (*US*)
Elephant Management (*UK*)
Emcee Artist Management (*US*)
Entertainment Services International (*US*)
Entourage Talent Associates, Ltd (*US*)
Epic Venom (*UK*)
Factory Music Management & Agency Ltd (*UK*)
Fat Penguin Management (*UK*)
5B Artist Management (*US*)
Flat50 (*UK*)
Fleming Artists (*US*)
Fresh Flava Entertainment (*US*)
Golden Arm (*UK*)
Goo Music Management Ltd (*UK*)
Guvnor Management (*UK*)
Halfpipe Entertainment (*US*)
Hello! Booking, Inc. (*US*)
Holier than Thou (HTT) Music (*UK*)
Ignition Management (*UK*)
Impact Artist Management (*US*)
In De Goot Entertainment (*US*)
Incendia Music (*UK*)
Intrigue Music (*US*)
Kuper Personal Management (*US*)
Landstar Management (*UK*)
Lippman Entertainment (*US*)
Listen to This Management (*UK*)
Little White Bear Music (*UK*)
Loggins Promotion (*US*)
Lookout Management (*US*)
Lupo Entertainment (*US*)
M. Hitchcock Management (*US*)
Madrigal Music artist management (*UK*)
Maine Road Management (*US*)
Mascioli Entertainment (*US*)
McGhee Entertainment (*US*)
Metal Music Bookings (*UK*)
Michael Anthony's Electric Events (*US*)
Michael Hausman Artist Management Inc. (*US*)
Mike's Artist Management (*US*)
Miller Music Management (*UK*)
MOB Agency (*US*)
Monqui Presents (*US*)
Music + Art Management (*US*)
Musicarchy Media (*UK*)
Mustang Agency (*US*)
Nancy Fly Agency (*US*)
Nettwerk Management (*US*)
Northern Music Co. Ltd (*UK*)

Off the Chart Promotions (*UK*)
Outrider Music, LLC (*US*)
Paradise Artists (*US*)
Park Records (*UK*)
Perry Road Records (*UK*)
Possessive Management (*UK*)
PRA [Patrick Rains & Associates] (*US*)
Primitive Management (*UK*)
Prodigal Son Entertainment (*US*)
Progressive Global Agency (PGA) (*US*)
Q Prime Management, Inc. (*US*)
Rainmaker Artists (*US*)
Raw Power Management (*UK*)
Red Entertainment Agency (*US*)
Red Light Management (RLM) (*US*)
Red Star Artist Management (*US*)
Right Chord Music (*UK*)
ROAR Global Ltd (*UK*)
Ron Rainey Management Inc. (*US*)
Russell Carter Artist Management (*US*)
Salvation Records (*UK*)
SGM Music Group Ltd (*UK*)
Sharpe Entertainment Services, Inc. (*US*)
So What Media & Management (*US*)
Sorkin Productions (*US*)
Starkravin' Management (*US*)
Steve Stewart Entertainment (*US*)
Steven Scharf Entertainment (SSE) (*US*)
Stiefel Entertainment (*US*)
Street Smart Management (*US*)
Sugar House Music (*UK*)
TAC Music Management (*US*)
Tara Newman Artist Management (*UK*)
Tileyard Music (*UK*)
Tone Management (*UK*)
Tony Margherita Management (*US*)
Toonteen Industries: Management & Promotions (*UK*)
Tower Management Group (*US*)
Tunstall Management (*US*)
Union Entertainment Group (*US*)
United Stage International Ltd (*UK*)
Variety Artists International (*US*)
Vector Management (*US*)
Wildlife Entertainment Ltd (*UK*)
Woosh Entertainments Ltd (*UK*)
Worldsound, LLC (*US*)

Rockabilly
Act 1 Entertainment (*US*)
Fat City Artists (*US*)
Hello! Booking, Inc. (*US*)
TAC Music Management (*US*)
Two Chord Touring (*US*)

Roots
Act 1 Entertainment (*US*)
Brilliant Productions (*US*)
Dawn Elder Management (*US*)
Fleming Artists (*US*)
Front Room Songs (*UK*)
Grapevine Music Agency (*UK*)
Impact Artist Management (*US*)
Kari Estrin Management & Consulting (*US*)
KCA Artists (*US*)
Kuper Personal Management (*US*)
Nancy Fly Agency (*US*)
Park Records (*UK*)
Piedmont Talent (*US*)
Siren Music Company (*US*)
Steven Scharf Entertainment (SSE) (*US*)
TAC Music Management (*US*)

Shoegaze
Black Bleach Records (*UK*)
Elephant Management (*UK*)

Singer-Songwriter
0114 Records (*UK*)
ADSRecords (*UK*)
AEC Music Management (*UK*)
Amour:Music (*UK*)
Artist in Mind (*US*)
Bernie Nelson Artist Management (*UK*)
Bitchin' Entertainment (*US*)
Brick Wall Management (*US*)
Burgess World Co. (*US*)
BUT! Management (*UK*)
Concerted Efforts (*US*)
Create Management (*UK*)
Entourage Talent Associates, Ltd (*US*)
Fat Penguin Management (*UK*)
Flat50 (*UK*)
Future Songs (*UK*)
Impact Artist Management (*US*)
JBLS Management (*UK*)
KCA Artists (*US*)
Kragen & Company (*US*)
Lippman Entertainment (*US*)
Little White Bear Music (*UK*)
Lyricom (*UK*)
Madrigal Music artist management (*UK*)
McGhee Entertainment (*US*)
Michael Hausman Artist Management Inc. (*US*)
Miller Music Management (*UK*)
Nettwerk Management (*US*)
Off the Chart Promotions (*UK*)
Park Records (*UK*)
Q Prime Management, Inc. (*US*)
Red Grape Music (*UK*)
Red Light Management (RLM) (*US*)
Running Media Group Ltd (*UK*)

Russell Carter Artist Management (*US*)
Sharpe Entertainment Services, Inc. (*US*)
Siren Music Company (*US*)
Steven Scharf Entertainment (SSE) (*US*)
Stiefel Entertainment (*US*)
Stoa Sounds (*UK*)
TAC Music Management (*US*)
Vector Management (*US*)
Woosh Entertainments Ltd (*UK*)

Ska
0114 Records (*UK*)
Fat City Artists (*US*)

Soul
Act 1 Entertainment (*US*)
Bandzmedia (*UK*)
Chicken Grease Presents (*UK*)
Concerted Efforts (*US*)
Halfpipe Entertainment (*US*)
Len Weisman, Personal Manager (*US*)
Little White Bear Music (*UK*)
Major Bob Music, Inc. (*US*)
Mill Lane Artist Management (*UK*)
Piedmont Talent (*US*)
Plus Music (*UK*)
RGM Production (*UK*)
RM2 Music (*UK*)

Soulful
TAC Music Management (*US*)

Soundtracks
Kraft-Engel Management (*US*)
Soundtrack Music Associates (SMA) (*US*)
Steven Scharf Entertainment (SSE) (*US*)

Spoken Word
Bitchin' Entertainment (*US*)

Surf
Bill Hollingshead Productions, Inc. Talent Agency (*US*)
Halfpipe Entertainment (*US*)

Swing
Act 1 Entertainment (*US*)
American Artists Corporation (*US*)
Big Bear Music (*UK*)
Cantaloupe Music Productions, Inc. (*US*)
Collin Artists (*US*)
Fat City Artists (*US*)
Harmony Artists (*US*)
Mascioli Entertainment (*US*)

Techno
Bitchin' Entertainment (*US*)
Empire Artist Management (*US*)
F&G Management (*UK*)
OnDaBeat Talent Management (*UK*)
The Weird and the Wonderful (*UK*)

Thrash
Factory Music Management & Agency Ltd (*UK*)
Holier than Thou (HTT) Music (*UK*)
Landstar Management (*UK*)
Possessive Management (*UK*)
Semaphore Mgmt & Consulting (*US*)

Traditional
Dawn Elder Management (*US*)
Nancy Fly Agency (*US*)
Riot Artists (*US*)
TAC Music Management (*US*)

Trance
Bitchin' Entertainment (*US*)
Involved Management (*UK*)

Underground
In De Goot Entertainment (*US*)
Semaphore Mgmt & Consulting (*US*)
This Is Music Ltd (*UK*)

Urban
B&H Management (*UK*)
Bitchin' Entertainment (*US*)
Black Dot Management (*US*)
HQ Familia (*UK*)
Lippman Entertainment (*US*)
Loggins Promotion (*US*)
Lyricom (*UK*)
Maven Phoenix (*UK*)
Pyramid Entertainment Group (*US*)
QV (*UK*)
Qveen Management (*UK*)
Red Entertainment Agency (*US*)
ROAR Global Ltd (*UK*)
SugarNova (*UK*)
Tileyard Music (*UK*)
Tunstall Management (*US*)
The Weird and the Wonderful (*UK*)

World
Angelica Arts & Entertainment (*US*)
Bitchin' Entertainment (*US*)
Cantaloupe Music Productions, Inc. (*US*)
Collin Artists (*US*)
Columbia Artists Management Inc. (CAMI) (*US*)
Concerted Efforts (*US*)
Dawn Elder Management (*US*)
Fat City Artists (*US*)
Front Room Songs (*UK*)
Impact Artist Management (*US*)
Ina Dittke & Associates (*US*)
Landstar Management (*UK*)
Line-Up pmc (*UK*)
McGhee Entertainment (*US*)
Music + Art Management (*US*)
Nancy Fly Agency (*US*)

Nettwerk Management (*US*)
Progressive Global Agency (PGA) (*US*)
Red Light Management (RLM) (*US*)
Riot Artists (*US*)
Serious (*UK*)
Steven Scharf Entertainment (SSE) (*US*)
Worldsound, LLC (*US*)

Get Free Access to the MusicSocket Website

To claim your free access to the **MusicSocket** website simply go to https://www.musicsocket.com/subscribe and begin the subscription process as normal. When you are given the opportunity to enter a voucher / coupon enter the following code:

- MSC-JEM-459

You should then be able to take out a subscription for free, or a longer term subscription at a reduced price.

Please note that this code will only remain valid until the release of the next edition, and is only permitted for use in the creation of one account for the owner of this book.

If you need any assistance please email support@musicsocket.com.

If you have found this book useful, please consider leaving a review on the website where you bought it!

What you get

Once you have set up access to ths site you will be able to benefit from all the following features:

Databases

All our databases are updated almost every day, and include powerful search facilities to help you find exactly what you need. Searches that used to take you hours or even days in print books or on search engines can now be done in seconds, and produce more accurate and up-to-date information. You can try out any of our databases before you subscribe:

- Search **over 2,000 record labels**
- Search **over 1,300 managers**

PLUS advanced features to help you with your search:

- Save searches and save time – set up to 15 search parameters specific to your work, save them, and then access the search results with a single click whenever you log in. You can even save multiple different searches if you have different types of work you are looking to place.
- Add personal notes to listings, visible only to you and fully searchable – helping you to organise your actions.

- Set reminders on listings to notify you when to submit your work, when to follow up, when to expect a reply, or any other custom action.
- Track which listings you've viewed and when, to help you organise your search – any listings which have changed since you last viewed them will be highlighted for your attention!

Daily email updates

As a subscriber you will be able to take advantage of our email alert service, meaning you can specify your particular interests and we'll send you automatic email updates when we change or add a listing that matches them. So if you're interested in labels dealing in hard rock in the United States you can have us send you emails with the latest updates about them – keeping you up to date without even having to log in.

User feedback

Our databases all include a user feedback feature that allows our subscribers to leave feedback on each listing – giving you not only the chance to have your say about the markets you contact, but giving a unique artist's perspective on the listings.

Save on copyright protection fees

If you're sending your work away to record labels or managers, you should consider first protecting your copyright. As a subscriber to **MusicSocket** you can do this through our site and save 10% on the copyright registration fees normally payable for protecting your work internationally through the Intellectual Property Rights Office.

Terms and conditions

The promotional code contained in this publication may be used by the owner of the book only to create one subscription to MusicSocket at a reduced cost, or for free. It may not be used by or disseminated to third parties. Should the code be misused then the owner of the book will be liable for any costs incurred, including but not limited to payment in full at the standard rate for the subscription in question. The code may be used at any time until the end of the calendar year named in the title of the publication, after which time it will become invalid. The code may be redeemed against the creation of a new account only – it cannot be redeemed against the ongoing costs of keeping a subscription open. In order to create a subscription a method of payment must be provided, but there is no obligation to make any payment. Subscriptions may be cancelled at any time, and if an account is cancelled before any payment becomes due then no payment will be made. Once a subscription has been created, the normal schedule of payments will begin on a monthly, quarterly, or annual basis, unless a life Subscription is selected, or the subscription is cancelled prior to the first payment becoming due. Subscriptions may be cancelled at any time, but if they are left open beyond the date at which the first payment becomes due and is processed then payments will not be refundable.

www.ingramcontent.com/pod-product-compliance
Lightning Source LLC
LaVergne TN
LVHW010058110826
845155LV00028B/394

* 9 7 8 1 9 0 9 9 3 5 3 0 3 *